A

and

BEYOND

To Pearl,

Warm regards

Lisette

Books by Lisette Larkins

Difficult People: A Gateway to Enlightenment

Talking to Extraterrestrials:
Transforming Our World with the Help of Enlightened Beings

Listening to Extraterrestrials

Calling on Extraterrestrials

ABOVE
and
BEYOND

The Incredible **True Story**
of Extraterrestrial Contact

LISETTE LARKINS

RAINBOW RIDGE
BOOKS

Cover and Interior design by Frame25 Productions
Cover art © Albert Ziganshin c/o Shutterstock.com

Published by:
Rainbow Ridge Books, LLC
140 Rainbow Ridge Road
Faber, Virginia 22938
434-361-1723
www.rainbowridgebooks.com

If you are unable to order the print edition
of this book from your local bookseller,
you may order directly from the distributor.

Square One Publishers, Inc.
115 Herricks Road, Garden City, NY 11040
Phone: (516) 535-2010; Fax: (516) 535-2014
Toll-free: 877-900-BOOK

Visit the author at:
www.lisettelarkins.com

Library of Congress Cataloging-in-Publication Data applied for.

ISBN 1-978-937907-25-9

10 9 8 7 6 5 4 3 2 1

Printed on acid-free recycled paper in the United States of America

Author's Note

It was quite an undertaking to write this personal memoir and attempt to highlight some of my many extraordinary extraterrestrial and paranormal encounters spanning many decades. This is why I have written four previous books based on the spiritual practices of my extraterrestrial contact experiences that continue to inspire my interest in spiritual awakening. I literally have had tens of thousands of contact and paranormal experiences. There's a lot of information to convey, and it has taken many different books to articulate much that I have learned.

Consistent with my experience of evolved extraterrestrials over many decades, they continue to inspire and guide all of us, across many different domains of human experience.

In fact, it has been an incredible soul-searching endeavor to decide which experiences best serve the mission of *this* particular book while charting my spiritual development. As a result, I have omitted many personal and paranormal experiences covering many years. In some cases, those experiences that *are* included have been combined or condensed, or they may have even overlapped, due to space constraints.

In most cases, names have been changed to protect the identity of those difficult people in my life who, as it turns out, would later prove to be most responsible for my spiritual growth and present joy and happiness. I am greatly indebted to those beloved difficult people described herein, because they are the ones who have most served my soul's growth.

It is to them that this book is most gratefully and lovingly dedicated.

Prologue

It is the day that caught the world by surprise and is still considered to be the biggest news story of the twentieth century. It would usher in new political, military, technological, and scientific developments. Even sixty years later, it is still recognized as the day when humanity stopped to look skyward and consider its place in the galaxy.

~

On October 4, 1957, a speeding Chevy screeched to a stop and parked in front of a suburban hospital in Southern California. From the car radio issued the excited voice of reporter Walter Cronkite, announcing that "the world will never be the same." After switching off the ignition, a young man leaped out of the car, awkwardly clutching a bouquet of flowers in one hand and a newspaper in the other. Sprinting inside, he raced down the halls to the elevator, following the signs reading "Maternity Ward." As he passed the nurses' station, the nurses and doctors seemed shocked, bewildered, speechless—all mesmerized by Walter Cronkite's newscast.

As the father dashed past, Cronkite's voice continued, "This day will prove to mark the start . . . ," then the young man burst into a room occupied by a young mother holding her newborn.

The baby was peacefully nursing as her father rushed to her, red-faced, breathless, waving the front page of the *Los Angeles Times* at her as though she could read it. "Look, baby Lisette, an omen occurred on the day following your birth! The Soviet Union launched a surprise satellite—Sputnik! You've heralded the dawn of the Space Age!"

~

A few years later, now seven years old, Lisette was on her backyard lawn, playing "Barbie dolls" with her sister. The dolls were dressed in wedding gowns. It was a cloudless, warm summer day in Los Angeles.

Lisette's mother joined them on the lawn, commenting on the heat. As she applied sunscreen to the children's faces and arms, they squirmed at the cold feel of the lotion.

"Hold still, you don't want to get sunburned," the mother said to her children.

Suddenly a distinct, cool shadow from above passed over them. Only Lisette noticed and looked up curiously, smiling and scanning the cloudless blue sky overhead, but she saw no cause for the shadow.

Chapter One

MY OLD CAR IDLED NOISILY as I pushed in the clutch, shifted into neutral, and set the parking brake while checking my notes. I was on time for my job interview, but was this address the correct one? After checking the numbers on the wall of the front gate entrance, I was satisfied that I'd found the right place and veered down the hill. This sprawling Malibu estate had an expansive view of the Pacific ocean and the coastline southward that took my breath away. Wow, this was no ordinary house, even by Malibu standards.

Unlike the business environment of my last position—sales director of a small publishing company—this was a residence, but at least it smacked of mainstream Los Angeles success. I had loved my previous job, but, in the end, it was time to move on. I was tired of pushing the envelope and pushing upstream against an unwelcome tide of skeptical potential customers—readers of books who couldn't appreciate the cutting-edge nature of the nonfiction we published: books relating to metaphysics and paranormal phenomena.

Of course, mainstream book reviewers like *Publishers Weekly* considered our books pseudoscience. Such had been my previous professional challenge as sales director, to find a way to spoon-feed "new thought" to a largely jeering public and to book reviewers whose opinions held sway with bookstore buyers from Barnes & Noble to Amazon.com.

As if that weren't enough of a trial, added to my creative challenges and responsibilities was the fact that I was also an author. My own books on alien contact were included on our list. Defending my position that extraterrestrial contact experiences were spiritual experiences had no small part in my present jobless situation and my arrival at the property of my potential new employer of a normal mainstream job.

My résumé, crisp from my printer, lay on the passenger seat next to me. It didn't mention anything about my books or the fact that I used to do book signings and radio interviews about the spiritual nature of extraterrestrial contact phenomena. It didn't mention that I considered myself a specialist in this arena, or, at least, I used to think as much.

There were extraordinary obstacles to overcome in the process of "opening" to extraterrestrial contact, and as an "experiencer," I had felt that it was my mission to help prepare others for the inevitable difficulties that lay ahead. There were potential issues to overcome: emotional, psychological, physiological, interpersonal, cultural, and, last but not least, familial. When announcing to the world, or even to your own spouse, that you had seen, met, or even spoken with an alien from another world, you expected a skeptical reaction at best; at worst, being considered "certifiable."

Now, arriving for a new-job interview, I was ready to explain my move from Virginia back to my hometown of Malibu, California, as "job burnout," something I imagined a lawyer could understand.

As I pulled my car up to the house, I had to admire the beautifully landscaped entrance at the front door. Grabbing my résumé off the seat, I studied it for a moment, knowing that I didn't have any direct experience relating to the job description—property manager and administrative assistant—but I felt I could handle any position with "administrative" in the title.

I stepped out of the car and stood for a moment in the driveway, locked at the midpoint between unemployment and possible employment, and listened to my gurgling stomach. Am I nervous, I wondered? It had been a long time since I'd had any kind of a job interview, so admittedly, today was outside my normal routine, even weird—as if I hadn't had enough "weird" to last me a lifetime.

The view was breathtaking from where I stood in the driveway, peering over the bluff at the amazing expanse below me. I wondered what the UPS delivery man thought when he pulled up to deliver a package at this address. Just standing outside the front door was an almost spiritual experience in and of itself. It felt as if I were at the top of the world, looking down at the Earth's stunning beauty and the blue ocean, where white sailboats dotted the sea as a light wind chased puffy clouds across this seascape.

"What a view!" I gasped in surprise. "Who lives here?" I asked myself, wondering if maybe the mention of "attorney" in the ad was really a subterfuge for a Hollywood celebrity who needed personal help. I would find out soon enough if I could just make my feet walk across the driveway and knock on the front door.

As I continued to peer over the bluff, a light breeze caught my hair. Below me, as part of this same property, was a large grassy park, complete with a putting green and hole with a flag fluttering in the wind. Blinking into the midday sun, I looked hard at the park-like acreage and squinted in surprise to see several deer grazing there. Were those real, or were they bronze statues just placed there to be admired? It turned out to be both. I watched a large, regal buck with three-point antlers stand erect, peering up at me. To my astonishment, at that moment, the buck lowered his head and, turning to another buck at his side, rammed it with full force, and the victim toppled over—dead!

What was happening? Just when I was about to enter a "normal" life again, a wildlife scene from the Discovery Channel was playing itself out in the front yard of my job interviewer's house.

Walking closer to the edge of the bluff, I looked down in amazement, trying to discern what was really happening. As the proud buck trotted off triumphantly with his harem of does, I gawked at the poor dead deer, until I saw that the victim was actually a bronze statue that was so lifelike it had even fooled the real buck, who had mistaken it for a rival. As soon as my interview is over, I thought to myself, I'd like to drive down to the grassy area and get a closer look at the golf green and the "dead" bronze statue. It looked so intriguing.

As the buck nudged his does up through the sumac toward the top of the hill, I chuckled to myself, recalling my own power struggles with a few testosterone-charged members of the male gender. There was my first husband, Peter; then a previous employer, a well-known physician who had once been a benefactor of children's hospitals . . . only to be discovered as a perpetrator of insurance fraud. I was his billing supervisor, and, as it had turned out, a potential co-conspirator had I not found the backbone to say "no."

As I gazed at the toppled-over deer, I wondered if the buck would ever realize his mistake. Probably not, I considered. It took a great deal of spiritual maturity to avoid a sense of moral superiority over others when it came to the mind's habit of deciding who is right or wrong. For most of us, habitually condemning and judging others is part of the mind's normal sense of entitlement. This was part of my own spiritual challenge. Wanting desperately to seek and actually experience inner peace was often problematic because I, too, had to overcome this tendency. Particularly challenging was an environment in which there were many difficult people and circumstances.

Off in the distance, I could still see the proud buck prodding his does to follow him, and I chuckled at the display of the male ego. It's always strange to me how strong people, male or female—or even animals—will seek to bully the weak. Best-selling author Eckhart Tolle would have called that a demonstration of one's "pain body"—part of the analytical mind that wants to find fault and make others wrong, if only in our thoughts. Whether through physical confrontations, verbal attacks, or simply an unspoken sense of superiority, the judgmental mind is the biggest block to finding inner peace, according to just about any spiritual teacher over the last millennia.

Whether the buck's aggressive behavior in attacking a bronze statue that he had deemed to be an "enemy" or the constant mental chattering and "make-wrong" attitude that has become the daily mental habit of most humans, these were two sides of the same coin. We all have to learn to get along and coexist with one another. As I considered the fake deer now lying flat on the grass below me, I couldn't help but see the greater spiritual lesson that it represented: the need for humans to find a way to quiet the mental chatter and to find peace in the moment despite outward difficulties and the tendency to judge and condemn.

This was the same spiritual message brought to me by the strange and curious extraterrestrial beings I had come to know. Humanity's challenge was to become a living example of peace and joy, despite difficult people and challenging circumstances. The buck who had attacked his imagined opponent was urged on by his survival instincts. But was the bronze deer an actual threat? No. The real buck was reacting out of habit. It had no way of knowing that his instinct to name and label as "enemy" the fake deer was an illusion. The buck's demonstration was the perfect symbol for my own spiritual struggles: finding a way of living that would produce a sense of inner peace, despite problematic "others" in my midst. I wanted to solve the everyday problems of living with clarity, dignity, and an empowered sense of purpose.

I wanted to master *this* aspect of spiritual study because I constantly found myself in the midst of very challenging situations and difficult people. From my first husband to my physician employer, those past difficult relationships were directly related to my desire to solve the riddle of extremely challenging life problems.

Let's face it, we are all faced with difficulties and challenges. What purpose do they serve? Relationships can be particularly challenging because human beings squabble amongst themselves when left to their own devices. Ask anyone who has gone home for the holidays, and you'll hear testimony that spouses, siblings, parents, children, and grownups constantly "make" one another "wrong" and judge and criticize one another. Every job or school environment is the same: cliques, factions, competition, and enemies. It seems to be human nature. Or is it?

While the spiritual practice of examining the purpose of human struggles was first inspired by the ETs, I had sought to verify their ideas with other spiritual teachers. It was not a strange concept to me, as suggested by my otherworldly experiences, that the conundrum of human experience on Earth was to find inner peace despite outward circumstances while achieving the goals of the soul. Also, if we couldn't figure out how to get along with our parents, spouses, grown children, coworkers, siblings, and acquaintances, how could we ever expect to transition into a compassionate species?

War and conflict were our guaranteed future unless we could demonstrate how to get along with one another in our own homes and communities. There was no need to shake our heads in dismay at the conflict between Israel and Palestine if we ourselves couldn't create harmonious extended families.

Coincidentally, my own childhood home, where I was now living, was a mere several thousand feet as the crow flies from this very doorstep. Malibu, although beautiful, was not for the squeamish. If you lived over the hill in the San Fernando Valley or in nearby Santa Monica and commuted to work in Malibu, you were often late, missed work altogether, or just called in sick every time there was a delay or closure on Pacific Coast Highway due to wildfires, electrical failures, mudslides, or car wrecks. And you better not have an issue with rattlesnakes. So I knew to exploit this on my application by stating that I lived in Malibu and that the aforementioned would cause me no problems. It had worked. I had gotten an interview—at least during this particular round of 350 other applicants.

With confidence, I rang the doorbell and waited for someone to answer. There was no immediate response. This allowed me a moment to catch my breath and gather my thoughts as I again took in the rare beauty of the sea below me and the wild expanse of hillside spilling down to the Pacific ocean. From where I stood at the entryway, I could see part of an elaborate infinity swimming pool in the backyard. The setting was stunning and could have been something out of *Architectural Digest*.

What a crazy, circuitous journey, I thought, pondering the strange turn of events that had, almost thirty years earlier in Malibu, launched me into what I initially thought was a living twilight zone that got even weirder when I tried to explain it in my books. Now, on this front doorstep, I had come full circle—ready, or so I thought, to start over again.

My thoughts were interrupted by the sudden opening of the front door. Kent Charles, Esquire, extended his hand and invited me in. A fit, handsome man in his mid-sixties, he seemed nice enough. As he led me inside, I mused that except for the plethora of expensive art pieces decorating the foyer and living room, he could have been an average attorney looking for an ordinary assistant. He gestured me toward the couch; I took a seat and handed him my résumé. I patiently waited for him as he read through it.

Finally, he looked up. "I've already burned through five caretakers," he admitted, smiling sadly. I looked at him curiously, then at the lovely environment in which our interview was conducted, wondering what the cause was of his turnover.

"I need an assistant, but also a property manager," he said matter-of-factly, forestalling the obvious question forming on my lips.

"That sounds like something that I can easily handle," I replied, eager to fill an ordinary position at a spectacular house in a lovely community. "Why the turnover here?" I asked.

Ignoring my question, Kent looked over my résumé again, appearing to like what he was reading. "You're actually overqualified," he said, but there was a tone of hopefulness in his voice, as though he were considering the possibility that just maybe I could handle the job.

"I'm ready for a less demanding position," I responded somewhat defensively, wondering if I'd oversold myself on my résumé. It hadn't occurred to me that he might later Google me on the Internet and discover that I'd also been an author of extraterrestrial contact phenomena. I'll just have to cross that bridge when I come to it, I thought. In the meantime, there were real benefits to hiring me, and I intended to firmly point those out.

"I'm living just five minutes from here, back at my family home, so the commute's simple. And your ad said that you needed administrative help. That's definitely something I can handle. I'm used to a busy and demanding office but want something slower paced." I paused. "You also mentioned helping out your wife? Does she need an assistant, too?"

"We'll come to that." He glanced down at my résumé and came to the part about the job at the doctor's office. "So you worked in a medical office?" he asked brightly.

"Yes, although I'm not a nurse. I was billing supervisor at Dr. Helman's office. He's internal medicine. Century City. More recently, I was sales director at a publishing company in Virginia."

"When you were at the doctor's office, did you work with the patients?" Kent asked hopefully.

"Yes, in terms of their accounts and billing," I replied, wondering about this line of questioning.

"That name sounds familiar," Kent said. "Dr. Gerry Helman… where have I heard that name before?" He thought for a moment. "Oh, yes, wasn't he the medical doctor who went to prison for insurance fraud?" he asked, raising his eyebrows with curiosity.

"Yes." I said. "I wasn't there long."

Kent peered over his glasses at me as though considering this fact for a moment. He was a lawyer, after all. "I remember reading about that case in the newspaper," he said. "As I recall, he was quite a difficult guy to work for. It must've been trying for you," he said, almost to himself, clearly impressed that I had survived this position.

"Yes, but then I'm a survivor; always have been."

Kent nodded, perhaps thinking he'd found the right person for the job. But I could hardly accept the position before finding out the reason for his high turnover rate.

"But what about your employee turnover?" I asked again, trying to tactfully circle back to my original question. "What's the catch with the job?"

"Well, the main part of the job is property manager. I need someone to run the household, but there's another part to it. I'm a trial lawyer. I'm in the middle of trial, and I can't be late, no matter what kind of disaster happens at home."

"Disasters? You mean burst pipes, backed-up toilets, or what?"

Kent exhaled loudly, as though carrying the weight of the world on his shoulders. "This is where your survivor skills might come in handy," he said chuckling despite himself. "My wife needs a . . . companion."

"A companion?" I asked uncertainly.

"Somebody to . . . watch over her, while you run the household—but without her realizing it."

"Oh, I see," I replied, now realizing the reason for his turnover, but wondering why he needed a secret property manager. "Is she hostile to your staff?" I asked, expecting to hear that he was married to Imelda Marcos or someone as dictatorial as her.

Kent stood to answer my question, as though pacing would help him to explain his predicament. Suddenly, a woman strode into the room with all the authority of an armed state trooper.

Jeannette Charles stopped in her tracks as she spotted me sitting on the couch. Her expression froze into a grimace. In her early sixties, drop-dead beautiful with an athletic, well-toned body, she was exquisitely coifed, wearing a stunning outfit and an outrageously large diamond necklace. Sullen, arms crossed, a frown on her face, she stood back as Kent awkwardly introduced me. I extended my hand, but Jeannette ignored me, turned on her heels, and stormed furiously out of the room, slamming the door behind her.

Answering my shocked expression, Kent said, "She's been diagnosed with early-onset Alzheimer's disease." I nodded my head in commiseration. "The job also involves keeping an eye on her. The disease hasn't affected her that badly yet, but then again, she does things that require . . . supervision. I just want to know that someone I can trust is around, keeping an eye on her—and the house.

"She still has her driver's license, although those days are numbered. But she won't hear of losing it. Every time I bring up the subject, she jumps in her car and peels rubber out of the driveway. It's just a matter of time before someone gets hurt, if I don't insist . . ." he said, his voice trailing away as he sadly looked out the window at Jeannette.

"She looks great—physically *healthy!*" I said, surprised that such a beautiful, vibrant woman had Alzheimer's.

"That's everyone's reaction," Kent said sadly, sitting down again and holding his head in his hands. "It breaks my heart to see her so beautiful and vivacious . . . but on the inside . . . well, let's just say that the dementia is waiting inside her like a . . . *time bomb.*"

His words hung in the air, and I couldn't help but feel a chill run down my spine. "A 'time bomb'?" I asked him, swallowing hard, desperate for more clarification.

"I need a *very capable* person," he said slowly for emphasis. "Someone to manage this property, but also to manage her challenges . . . somehow you've got to find a way to take away her driving privileges and drive her everywhere . . . among other duties."

"Me? That would be *my job?*" I asked incredulously. "Can't her doctor write a letter or something?"

"It's not that simple," he said quietly and, again, sadly.

"Well, just take away her car keys and face her down like you would a teenager," I said rather forcefully.

Kent tipped back his head and laughed uproariously. "Great idea," he said, his eyes now sparkling with mischief. "I'd like to see you try that." Becoming serious again, he looked directly at me. "You sound very . . . capable. That's exactly what I need. Someone with some down-to-earth common sense . . . but compassionate!"

As the telephone rang noisily in the background, he rose from the couch, indicating that the interview was now concluding. He gestured toward Jeannette, who was outside near the azure infinity pool, then turned to face me as though delivering his closing remarks to a jury.

"So what do you say? Want to give it a try, Lisette?" he asked hopefully.

"Okay. I guess I know a thing or two about time bombs."

Kent smiled at me inquisitively as we shook hands, agreeing that I would arrive there in the morning at six o'clock. "Please don't be late," he said. "I've got to be in court first thing, and I can't leave her alone."

Kent walked me out to my car and waved as I backed out of the driveway. Below me, the park-like setting of the golf green glistened in the afternoon sun. Even as I waved goodbye, I considered my hasty acceptance of the position and the inherent challenge of starting yet another difficult relationship. What had I just committed myself to?

As I headed down the main driveway, I turned the car toward the putting green, feeling that my new employer wouldn't mind if I strolled for a moment on his freshly mowed grass. It would do me good to think for a moment about the huge decision that I had just made.

It seemed that my entire lifetime had been consumed by one difficulty after another in this exact regard. Did I really want to start another cycle with a meanie? My old boss, Dr. Helman, had eventually done prison time for his bad behavior, but there were other difficult people who had preceded and followed him, each of whom had been a serious challenge to my ongoing spiritual practice.

My marriage to Peter was a crowning example. As a young woman, a newlywed and full of hope, it hadn't occurred to me that a West Pointer and an officer in the US Army might be a bit edgy on the home front. As young parents, we disagreed on just about everything. He had a bad temper and a fierce need to control his environment. He was a prime example of a difficult person, and I had barely survived my marriage mentally intact. Did I really want to undermine my hard-earned peace of mind again?

But I needed a job, and as they say, "necessity is the mother of invention." With respect to Jeannette, she could no doubt prove to be the "mother" of all difficult people. Perhaps my destiny was to find a way to perfect a spiritual practice in the midst of such a challenging situation, moving me into the "necessity" for advanced spiritual mastery.

I pulled up to the golf green and stepped out of my car. I walked toward the funny bronze deer that still lay on its side. The green carpet of grass felt spongy under my feet, and after inspecting the bronze, I struggled to pull it to an upright position, but was unable to lift it. Looking around at the beautiful grassy setting, I breathed in deeply, smelling the warm salty air that blew in from the ocean. This setting was a feast for the eyes, pastel green sod against the deep blue of the Pacific ocean and the azure blue sky above. The sea sparkled brightly as the playful wind painted white strokes on the water's surface.

There was a wooden bench on the grass next to a sand trap, like the kind that you would see on a golf course, but this one was smaller, as was the putting green. Several putters lay next to a huge pile of golf balls.

I took a seat on the bench and leaned back in the sun, breathing deeply again and swirling the warm sand below my feet with my shoes. Ivory white seagulls squawked overhead, flying aerial cartwheels and hoping, I imagined, that their antics would incite me to throw them a tidbit of bread. It was downright meditative, sitting there in the sun with the ocean breeze playing in my hair, suspended in the magical beauty where emerald green grass melded with the cerulean beauty of the blue Pacific. My mind drifted back, slowly at first, to a similar bench in the sand, a long-ago respite that I had once enjoyed as a young mother.

The other bench, coincidentally enough, was also set on a large expanse of grass high on a bluff overlooking the sea, only a few miles up the coast from this very spot in central Malibu. How could more than twenty years have passed by so quickly? I wondered. As I breathed deeply, the salty smell of the ocean brought the memory right back to me as though it were just yesterday. Almost twenty-five years earlier, then a young and naïve new mother, I had been blissfully reveling in the exquisite joy of the little bundle I held in my arms, my then seven-month-old baby boy. As a young mother, I did not realize that I was about to enter the strange and mystical world of extraterrestrial contact phenomena: a wondrous, yet often misunderstood, spiritual opening on the initiate's journey.

Chapter Two

It was autumn, 1987. I made swirls in the sand with my shoes while I cooed happily to my young son, Walter, who, not yet a year old, was propped on my lap. Sitting on the bench next to me was Debra, my best friend and coworker, who also played with her own newborn. A dozen white seagulls squawked overhead, competing for morsels that we threw in the air. A light ocean breeze danced through our hair as we chatted about our babies and the excitement of being new mothers.

On Saturday afternoons, we always convened on this spot—a lovely park bench in the warm sand that looked out over the azure blue ocean from high on a grassy knoll at Malibu Bluffs Park. While our husbands were busy catching up from busy workweeks, Debra and I would revel together in the bliss of new motherhood. Our babies were in daycare all week while we worked, so this was our time to unwind and to be with our precious little ones, whom we now bounced on our laps, giggling like two teenagers. Tenderly, I kissed my little cherub on his chubby pink cheeks.

As Debra looked on with curiosity, I reached for the large diaper bag that lay next to me on the bench and pulled out all manner of things—a baby bottle, pacifier, diapers, blanket—trying to find something at the bottom of the bag. Finally withdrawing two beautifully wrapped gifts, I ceremoniously handed one to Debra, and her eyes danced with delight as she accepted the festive, ribbon-wrapped treasure.

"What's the occasion?" Debra asked in surprise, allowing her baby to grab the package.

"Motherhood," I said beaming. "Isn't it great? Both little darlings get one. Come on, unwrap it."

While juggling the babies, we let them help us unwrap the gifts and pulled from the paper and bows two colorful baby toys. Each was a vibrant butterfly the size of a dinner plate, made with different soft, colorful textures and fabrics, inviting young hands to explore. Debra and I both burst into laughter as our babies immediately grabbed hold of their toys.

"They're beautiful!" Debra said. "Butterflies! How lovely."

Turning my baby around in my lap to face me, I launched into the story behind the butterfly, pretending that mere infants could understand the symbolism of their new prizes.

"The butterfly starts its journey as an ordinary caterpillar; then, when it's ready, it spins a cocoon and disappears inside!" I said dramatically, taking the butterfly and covering it with the blanket. "Hiding there in the dark, it changes and grows. Then, over time, it emerges, completely transformed." Whipping the toy from its hiding place, I sailed it through the air, its wings caught by the breeze as though it were happily in flight.

I jiggled the butterfly so that the mirrored reflective fabric caught the sun, and it danced in the children's eyes, causing them to giggle.

"The butterfly is nature's perfect example of a powerful metamorphosis."

At that, the babies happily mouthed their new treasures, and Debra and I sat back on the bench, breathing deeply and enjoying the sun on our faces and the sounds of our babies playing in our laps. We gazed skyward at the cloudless blue sky, then at the grand expanse of the blue ocean that lay beyond us.

Suddenly, as though from above, we were instantly bathed in a cool shadow, and we again looked skyward, searching for the source of it. Seeing nothing, we looked at each other in puzzlement, then shrugged, just as the sun again shone brightly on our arms. With playful abandon, we lifted our little ones into the air.

Breaking the peaceful setting, I suddenly snapped to attention. "Oh, my gosh, what time is it?" I asked Debra in consternation.

"Let me guess," Debra replied dryly, as though intuiting my sudden upset. "You're late. I bet you can hear Peter calling you from way over here."

"I said I'd be back at three. We're eating early because he's leaving to go out of town right after dinner," I said breathlessly, defensively explaining the reason I had jumped up to gather up my things.

"Again?" Debra asked. "He sure travels a lot. You must hate that."

Not answering, I ignored the awkward silence, piling the baby's things into the bag. I could feel Debra studying my face. Standing to leave, I hugged Debra goodbye while our babies reached their tiny fingers out to each other as though they, too, were bidding farewell. Delighted by their antics, this started us laughing all over again, and, after looking worriedly at my watch, I rushed off toward the parking lot.

"See you at work bright and early Monday morning," Debra called to me.

"You sure know how to ruin a Saturday," I called over my shoulder in response. "Don't remind me. It'll come soon enough."

Now half trotting toward the parking lot, my baby bouncing happily on my hip, I sang out loud to him, "You are my sunshine, my only sunshine." His little hand clutched the toy butterfly. The beautiful bright pastels of the fabric and the butterfly's reflective material shone like a mirror, caught the sun's beams, and sparkled in the late-afternoon rays. I fired up the car, and we sped out of the parking lot. Peter would not be happy if we arrived home late.

Chapter Three

As I pulled up to the large stucco condominium, predictably Peter was standing there waiting for us. Ignoring the reason for his impatience, I jumped out of the car and tended to Walter's car-seat buckle, meeting Peter's glare with a cheery distraction.

"We had a great time at the park," I said happily. "Walter loves his new toy." I handed the baby to his father. Peter accepted the bundle, frowning at the toy that was still clutched in the child's tiny hand.

Softening somewhat but still clearly agitated, he looked at me hard. "We agreed to a budget, remember?" Peter said, pointing to the butterfly and shaking his head.

"I know, but it's just a small thing," I said defensively. "Debra and I are celebrating. You know, we're new mothers. It's fun." I didn't dare tell him that I had also bought one for her child.

"You're late," Peter said peevishly, apparently not willing to let my tardiness pass by without comment.

"Please don't start, Peter," I said firmly, feeling anger start to ignite in my belly. "We've had a perfectly lovely day."

Peter grabbed my arm, meaning business. "I need you to be a team player!" he said, furious with my flippant attitude. "We keep going over the same issues, but you never change," he said. "If we cannot agree on a few basics in our marriage, then . . ."

Wresting my arm free, I glared back at him, tired of his strong-arm tactics, at which point, little Walter burst into tears. Thrusting the baby into my arms and clearly disgusted with me, Peter snapped at me again. "It's not that difficult! Don't spend money; don't quit your job. See? It's simple. And I don't care how much you hate it!" With that last retort, he stomped off across the parking garage.

I headed for the kitchen and a quick dinner preparation; I knew that Peter had to pack and be ready to leave for the airport after dinner. He had another business meeting in a distant city; hopefully, this one would lead to a promotion.

Peter had attended West Point but later graduated from the UCLA ROTC program. We had lived the first years of our marriage in Germany while he served a four-year tour of duty as a US Army officer. Now, back in the States, his transition to civilian life had not gone smoothly.

For one thing, he was a man who liked order: Life was black or white, with nothing in between. He couldn't tolerate the gray areas of life, which meant that I, with my new motherhood challenges and sense of marital crisis, didn't fit into his idea of the loving, devoted wife. We were struggling, plain and simple, to adjust to a life in the States. Back in the civilian world with no young recruits to boss around, Peter seemed to use me to vent his hostilities.

Arguments deeply upset me, so I busied myself with cooking a meal, the clatter of pots and pans ringing through a glacial silence. Our scheduled five o'clock dinner would be a few minutes late. In those early days as a young wife and mother, it felt to me that all of our problems were my fault. Everything wrong in our lives, from the grease spot on

Peter's silk tie to the size of our electric bill and the problems at my job, had occurred as a result of my low self-esteem. It would be many years before I could tolerate the idea that I was responsible for my own experiences and that I alone was the "master of my life, the captain of my own ship."

As a result, until some spiritual maturity informed my thinking, I played the victim role perfectly. I had placed myself in this painful position, but it ultimately turned out to be the catalyst that would push me to wake up, to grow spiritually, and to change. Frequently, painful experiences motivate us to change for no other reason than our very survival requires it. That night at dinner, I had no way of knowing that a huge change was underway: a change that would come disguised as a giant *problem*.

By the time Peter had come back into the kitchen, I'd had a chance to calm down. I smiled at him weakly. Sitting down at the table, we swiftly segued from dinner to departure by chatting robotically through our salad and spaghetti. Beneath the table, I frayed circles in the carpet with the rubber soles of my tennis shoes.

For once, I was thankful that Peter had not allowed our rambunctious son to join us for dinnertime; he was in his playpen in the next room. Burying my anger was taking more of an effort than usual that night, and my first priority was to keep my problems and our marital turmoil hidden from Walter.

Peter kept telling me that I needed to be a team player. He demanded that I fuse with him completely, mimicking his tastes for everything from political opinions to breakfast fare. Images remained with me of my husband's cocked fist held hard against a table or wall. Although his knuckles never made contact with me, the balance of power between us was well established. A large colorful windsurfing sticker on our bedroom door hid a splintered hole the size of a grapefruit from an episode the previous week.

I imagined that he would have made an excellent five-star general leading a military coup. There was something extremely intimidating about him, and I was amazed by the way that he commanded respect, whether or not he deserved it.

It was following one such argument, after which Peter had left for out-of-town business, that I had first started to pray, not really knowing to whom I was praying. But I was humbled by emotional pain, by my wrecked marriage, and by my hopeless fear that nothing would ever be right again.

Even our bed had become an emotional boxing ring. Peter could notice the smallest flicker of ambivalence in my eyes, and he would react. He said that he felt as if I didn't desire him, and this made him angry, setting him off into a tirade.

Certainly this was true, since post-partum changes had taken away any enjoyment for bedroom play on my part. But as my own victim role was oblivious to me, his dominator role in our mess was submerged, like that hole in the door—safely hidden beneath a slick layer of amnesia. Holding a mirror up to him, or to me for that matter, would be reason enough to instigate another round of dissent.

Now sex and intimacy were all tangled up in my mind with loss and intimidation. Miserable in my marriage and my work alike, I didn't know how to fix either one, and as Peter kept reminding me, quitting my work was not an option.

It seemed impossible that even my professional life was riddled with the precise emotional dynamics that permeated my marriage. For that reason, it was difficult to get any sympathy from Peter about my job, and no matter how much stress there was at work, he always saw me at fault and forbade me to quit. Our mounting bills with a newborn and his fledgling new career undermined my case that I should find other employment.

I was unable to explain to Peter, to communicate just how unbearable my work situation had become. He could not understand my difficulties; perhaps he did not want to understand. Subjected to continual daily harassment at work, it seemed to me that all Peter cared about was the large paycheck I brought home. Strangely, all the staff in my office, and especially me, were highly compensated. We assumed our padded wages were a result of our abusive employer overcompensating, because without the high salaries, everybody would have left. This is why Peter wouldn't hear of me quitting, because it was unlikely that I would find another position that paid as well. The topic was volatile. He said that, no matter the stress at work, I'd just have to somehow deal with it.

The dinner dishes now having been cleaned up, it felt like an eternity before I could finally walk Peter to his car as he headed out on his business trip. A perfunctory kiss on the cheek and he was gone, gunning to the airport like a New York taxi driver.

Upon my return to the living room, our wedding portrait seemed to scream at me from where it was prominently displayed on our big coffee table. I looked closely into our smiling faces, wondering how much longer we could go on before someone else noticed the hysteria hidden just below the surface. Family, friends, and neighbors were privy only to our fleeting moments of composure. Having distanced myself from my own family out of embarrassment, all of our physical and emotional struggles took place in private. We had a certain image of ourselves to uphold, and appearances came first.

Peter was very photogenic—a handsome six feet five inches of self-confidence. He dazzled women and many a shutterbug. His white-toothed grin was set off perfectly by his olive skin tones. I knew few men who commanded such notice. But there were also few people, if any, who had witnessed how Peter could flip from soothing charmer to bulldozer in an instant. My weakness and lack of backbone fed Peter's temper tantrums. Just like our contrasting personalities in the fiery emotional tango we danced, my red-headed complexion contrasted sharply with his bold skin tones. We were a striking couple.

However, our physical differences were not responsible for the dire mess our marriage had become. Ironically, our growing troubles together fueled our desire to keep our problems to ourselves. As a couple with a strong sense of upholding an image, we were sensitive to others' judgment. With so much suspicion obliquely expressed by well-meaning family and friends about our apparent marital differences, we were determined to prove to skeptics that our marriage could work. Had we been able to admit to our difficulties early on, perhaps we might have received the help that we needed.

Despite our problems—or perhaps because of them—I had evolved into a superwoman in the housecleaning arena. As Peter had become more and more demanding and controlling, I had tried harder and harder to comply. I held down a full-time job I loathed, shuttled our son to and from daycare, and found enough time at home to perform domestic wizardry. Apprenticed to Peter, who closely supervised my progress, I became expert at organizing our home—with perfectly laundered and ironed clothes and flawless gourmet meals—while burning through cases of cleaning solutions. We were a wreck, but, by God, the house looked good. Our possessions were not heaved about and shattered against walls as they were by other sparring twosomes; we only used our fraying emotions as the battlefield. Except for the well-concealed hole in our door, our property remained intact.

With Peter now gone, I dusted the heavy picture frame of our wedding day, looking sadly at our photograph. The hard reality of our circumstances created more pain than I wanted to feel. After this recent argument, I had to admit that our marriage was a complete failure. The vivid memory of our wedding day no longer had any impact on us. The sunny breeze at the reception, my sisters' smiles—all of it was as clear as if our wedding had been just a week ago. But our smiling wedding portrait in the living room was from another planet, completely out of context.

Surprising even myself, I trudged up the stairs to hide the photograph on the highest shelf in the coat closet. There, Peter's stunning good looks and magnetic allure were turned toward the wall, hidden in the dark.

After I put the baby down in his crib, he fell asleep quickly. As he slept the sweet blessed sleep of the innocent, I took my disappointment to bed, where, perhaps, I too could find solace. After slipping under the covers with a good book, I was reading quietly when I heard a strange, almost inaudible sound.

At first it sounded like a low hum, barely a buzz, similar to the subtle white noise of an electric appliance. I hardly gave it a thought. But then it grew louder, and I froze. The book I was reading dropped to my side. I sat statue-still, holding my breath, with an eerie feeling that something was not quite right. A chill ran down my spine, and I almost wished Peter were home.

How ironic, I thought. Peter's frequent absences usually allowed me the space to collect myself and to find some peace in our otherwise roller-coaster marriage; I needed those time-outs. But now, as the humming grew louder and a distinct vibration permeated the room, I wished he were beside me. Just when I had thought there was nothing else to worry about, in the silence of the night, something was trying its hardest to present a new twist—a whole new set of problems had presented itself. As if I don't have enough to deal with, I thought angrily. What now?

Still relatively young at thirty years old and definitely quite spiritually naïve, I had not yet begun to step onto the path of growth that would eventually lead me to discover my own inner strength and fortitude. I was caught up in the deception of focusing solely on worldly concerns and blind to the nuances of spiritual life; this night would prove to be the Great Gift, the single event that propelled me on to a life of my greatest dreams *and* an ability to feel inner peace and joy despite challenging life circumstances. I felt that only a very wise sage could know *why* a particular problem or challenge has presented itself, and thus only the sage would be uniquely capable of solving difficult problems with understanding and grace This was my desire: to possess such a gift.

But I continued to suffer when confronted by difficult challenges and people. It was still early in the wisdom game, and like most naïve spiritual initiates, I couldn't recognize that the very invitation to become initiated was, in fact, the arising dilemma. I only perceived *problems,* and "resisting problems" is similar to the storied hero's classic resistance to embark on the journey that will allow him to find himself and the solution to his predicament.

Spiritual initiation does not happen in a vacuum but rather in the context of deeply painful and often "horrible" life events that are usually resisted and fought with every fiber of the initiate's strength. Ironic, isn't it? That which arrives to save us is the very thing that we angrily beat off with a stick. How could I have known that its arrival would at first appear to be something that would destroy me?

As the hum turned into a strong vibration that permeated me, it also grew louder. I could feel my skin prickle, as though I were being electrocuted. I tried to scream, but all that I could utter was a low gurgling sound deep in my throat. Because I had no context for what was happening to me, the depth of my fear at that moment was complete.

Desperately afraid of anything to do with death and dying, the very notion that I might actually die would have usually caused me to black out. But concern for my son's safety occupied me, and I tried to maintain consciousness, despite the ever-encroaching reality that some seeming evil was confronting my beliefs that the world around me should be problem-free and predictable.

My desire to run down the hall to Walter's crib to protect him was overruled by a need to contain the terror in my bedroom before it took over the entire house, my son included. So I stayed on the bed, waiting for the moment at which I could slay whatever material manifestation might soon follow the onset of this paranormal light show.

Intense fear gripped me, and an even greater anxiety about my human vulnerability caused untold emotional pain. Marital problems were one thing; this paranormal onslaught threatened to rewrite my life story as to what was and was not possible in the world of form and matter.

Right then, as I became flash-fried on my bed, I felt more
hopeless than ever. It takes great wisdom to recognize when
a crisis is actually an invitation, one that almost always first
presents itself as a great big, huge, gigantic emotional *challenge*. And it *hurts*. That's the nature of divinity's role in *thrusting us out of a rut*. The emotional pain squeezes us into a new
paradigm that most of us resist with every fiber of our being.

I was no exception, writhing there on my bed, unwittingly
being pushed and prodded into a new spiritual awakening. It
would prove to be the classic introduction to the training of
the initiate—yet, at the time, the only way I could respond
was to kick and scream at the heavens like a wild child.

As the humming turned into a siren pitch of a wail, I
carefully went over a checklist in my mind: I had closed the
bedroom curtains and had luckily remembered to lock all
the doors. Feeling suddenly conspicuous, as though a burglar outside might be watching me in my well-lit bedroom, I
switched off the lamp next to me and considered dialing 911.

Suddenly, I sensed that *someone or something* was very close.

Unspeakable terror gripped me, and I thought I heard
breathing. Through the dark, I strained to see the shadowed
corners of the bedroom. I saw nothing, but suddenly I knew
that someone or something was above me, near the ceiling.
My fear was so great that I didn't dare look up. Then slowly,
wishing I were invisible and dreading what I would see, I
turned my gaze upward.

At that instant, as though I were not yet ready to see
what was there, a blinding golden light burst from the ceiling
and enveloped me completely. The streak of bright light cut
through the darkness, a brilliant funnel contrasting sharply
against the dark bedroom wall. Accompanied by the continuing pulsing sensation of an electromagnetic current, the

blinding light held me in its grip as I tried to twist free. A zapping sensation pierced my entire body as though an electrical current were firing inside me.

The pulsing current held me as I gasped and struggled in fear, until sheer exhaustion stopped my useless attempts. Rapid-fire questions whirled through my head. The humming vibration in the room was so intense that I wondered briefly if a police helicopter had landed on the roof.

How has it come to this? I thought, as I lay there, dying—at least in my own mind. Everything seemed to slow down, as it is sometimes reported by those who believe that they are about to die. As if my death were imminent, my recent past replayed in my mind, and I felt sadness for my difficult marriage to Peter, despite the disaster that was taking place around me.

It was a particularly scorching evening in Los Angeles. Outside the window, eucalyptus branches rustled dryly, brittle leaves whipped by hot Santa Ana winds scuttled and swirled, falling into crumbles against the condominium's white stucco walls. I was awash in self-pity as I lay there in bed. I didn't know that I was being introduced to the initiate's path. All I knew was the pain from unsolved problems.

I was in my third year of marriage, and I felt hopeless. All of the agonizing workdays that had turned into bitter, edgy evenings replayed in my memory, recalling now how long I had been stumbling through on automatic pilot, vainly trying to sidestep the looming awareness that my marriage was dissolving. Life's purpose, if mine ever had one, seemed obscured by numbness and fog.

Yet, somehow, Peter and I had produced a lovely son, who hopefully was still sleeping soundly, despite the goings on in my room.

Then Dr. Helman came to mind. Despite my desperation to save myself at that moment, how could it be that my employer's face was so clear in my memory? Perhaps it was because my protestations over work created such fury with Peter. He felt that my quitting would undermine what little financial stability we had, although I had promised to get other work.

I was having trouble dealing with my job duties in the office, which appeared to me to be either unethical or, at least, legally questionable. Yet I was paid very handsomely.

As I lay there in my seemingly near-death state, I couldn't help but wonder: What does one event have to do with the other? Was it a coincidence that my imploding marriage and my imploding job had anything to do with my imploding bedroom?

As I asked myself that question, a momentary turquoise flash of light erupted at the far end of the room, as though a flashlight had been turned on and then off. As fast as a wildfire racing uphill, my life changed completely.

Chapter Four

THE SOUND OF VIOLENT sucking that rolled into a siren-pitch wail was so loud that I thought my eardrums would burst. As the bright golden light seared me, an icy blast of wind rolled my long hair into whirling tornadoes about my face. I felt my cheeks turn polar blue.

Through squinted eyes, I saw that the lampshade on the side table had not moved an inch. I was flabbergasted. The pastel curtains also lay perfectly still against the window just a few feet away. The wind tunnel somehow encompassed me without affecting the rest of the room in any way.

I tried to look around, but my body would not move at all. There has to be a logical explanation, I thought. The continuing crackling light intensified, until its brightness blinded me. I heard a gurgle from deep within my throat that was another squelched scream. My skin tingled, then throbbed with pain, as though I were being cooked. I wanted to run out of there but could not move. My mind raced, panicking, aching for my son, and hoping he was still safe in his crib. This is what death feels like, I thought. Silently, I called out to anyone at all who might intuit my need for help. My heart thundered.

Finally, feeling dizzy and completely drained, I closed my eyes and went deep down into myself, soon to become unconscious of my own depths. Everything became quiet and muffled, as if I had slipped under the foam of a warm bubble bath. All I heard now was my own breathing. Maybe I was finally passing out.

When I next opened my eyes, it was morning. I froze with the realization of what had happened. Warily, without moving at first, I looked around the bedroom. Then I carefully picked up the clock on the dresser and noticed that it had stopped working. Everything else was fine and bathed in an early morning calm, soft and quiet, as if my night of terror had all been a dream.

Moving cautiously, I stretched my limbs, which felt unusually stiff. Then a crimson drop of blood fell onto the pillow beneath me. Then another. By the time I reached the bathroom, steady drops of blood fell from my nose into a small lake in the palm of my hand.

That morning, and for a long time afterward, I could find no explanation whatsoever for the bloody nose, much less for any of the previous night's events. Fortunately, my son appeared to be just fine. While fixing Walter's breakfast, I pored over dozens of possibilities. I knew it wasn't all a dream. The dictionary was open on the dresser to the word "poltergeist." Was my house possessed? Were we safe? Should I leave? Where would I go, and who would believe me?

I moved through the rest of the day like a robot. If my relationship with my husband had been less combative, I might have tried to call Peter and talk to him. In fact, there was no one I could turn to. Debra, with her own baby to protect, would be easily frightened if I unburdened myself to her. Since my marriage to Peter, I had rejected the warm, nurturing support of family and friends to keep my marital problems a secret. It felt safer to stay away, avoiding any unwelcome scrutiny. I had hoped to fix my marriage first, then rekindle those relationships.

Besides, I could never discuss with my family the phenomena of lights and sounds I had experienced, since I had never known them to take seriously anything that could be considered "strange." In addition to everything else, I couldn't face the possibility of their rejection. Even as a grown woman at that point in my life, I still found it difficult to announce to others my own differing opinions and perspectives. There was no way I could share my strange new nocturnal experiences.

As night fell again, I was terrified of a repeat performance. Unable to sleep, I sat up most of the night, constantly checking on my son. I was afraid to stay with him in case it happened again, but I was also fearful for his safety if I left him in his room alone.

Nothing happened.

Another day passed in bewilderment as my mind continually returned to the experiences of that terrifying night. I began researching ghosts and paranormal phenomena. Not certain whether they could be the source of my troubles, I also tentatively began to research the signs and symptoms of stress. Maybe I was simply having nightmares as a result of the stress of my crumbling life.

Later that week, while Peter was still out of town and Walter was fast asleep in his crib, I went to bed after an uneventful day. Sometime in the middle of the night, I suddenly awoke and sat up in bed as I again heard the unmistakable low humming sound. Bracing myself for another onslaught, my heart started beating faster, and I looked around the room for somewhere to hide. As my eyes adjusted to the darkness, I saw the form of a man standing at the foot of my bed, and I gasped in alarm. A momentary aqua-blue flash of light burst in the air next to him.

A soft glow emanated from and surrounded his head like a halo, and although at first I was startled, fear gave way to wonder as I looked upon him; he seemed to be a very wise and learned man. There was nothing fearful about him; he had a gentle, loving gaze like that of a tribal shaman. However, it appeared that the man who stood before me was asking something of me. For a brief moment, I considered how odd it was that within a week, my bedroom had turned into an episode from *The Twilight Zone*.

The entire room began to glow, pulsating with a beautiful, golden light. I was transfixed by a feeling of love that swept over me despite my best intention to stay wary and alert. Almost in spite of myself, I slipped out of bed and approached the man as his crystal-blue eyes beckoned me to him. There seemed to be something that he wanted to show me, although he didn't say a word.

Obediently, I moved toward him, my fear having vanished. So saintly was his bearing that I could feel my eyes become misty with awe and respect at beholding his regal status. The gold buttons on his white robe shimmered with light, almost as though they were pulsating with living energy. Then he turned his head toward my open bedroom door as though he wanted me to follow his gaze and focus mine there also.

The dark carpeted hallway lay outside my bedroom; at the end of the hall was the front door to my condominium. There was something in the hall that this wise man wanted me to see. I went to the bedroom doorway, then I heard a commotion on the other side of the front door. Someone or something was coming inside. My heart began to pound. As

I stood inside the doorjamb, I grasped the wall molding and felt faint, almost too fearful to look down the hall. Slowly, I inched my head forward until I had a clear view of the foyer.

Like a hologram, a vision appeared before me: dozens of angry "people" passing through the solid front door, as real as if I were watching my own child walk toward me. Unfolding before me was a scene in living color out of a distant time that I didn't at first understand. It was like watching actors practicing a scene from the movie *Ben Hur*. Their "costumes" were richly authentic, but as the image unraveled and they made their way in my direction, I somehow realized that they were not actors at all, but real people out of a real scene from a life that I, myself, had once lived! I wondered how that could be, since at that time in my life, I didn't know much about reincarnation.

Then I saw sheep running in disarray, frightened by the mob. Little bells around their necks jingled as they scampered for safety. An old sheepherder lifted his cane and yelled out angrily at someone running straight for me, from my vantage point, down the hall.

The crowd was out of control, like unrestrained sports fans storming the field, as they chased after a young woman who was running for her life. Suddenly I focused on an older woman who was leading the charge. A huge cloud of dust was stirred up and enveloped them as the crowd roared after her. The older woman was inciting the angry mob with squeals of "Stop, witch," as she led the pursuit of the younger woman, whose eyes were wild with fear.

As the crowd rushed past me, I fell back, terrified to see that the mob had caught her and obviously intended to burn her at the stake. The crowd's hatred rolled over me like a thick ocean fog. The young woman's clothes had been ripped from her shoulder, and a stream of blood oozed from her nose.

The young woman was me.

She didn't look like me—her hair was long and brown, and she had olive-toned skin. But I knew.

Instantly I understood that I was being shown a previous lifetime of mine. I wondered why it was important for me to know this now and how on Earth the entire scene was being broadcast to me as though I were watching a video playing in my hallway.

Somehow I knew that the young woman was being persecuted as a witch because of her mystical abilities: her healing work with the villagers and her divinations and prophecies. The smell of sweaty terror had filled my nostrils with horror as the girl tore past me, running for her life. As the mob continued to surround her, the vision faded, and I looked back to the old man for an explanation, but he, too, began to fade away. I couldn't help but sink to the ground and cry; the scene was so violent and filled with such hatred. It was astonishing to realize that such distress had not only occurred in my past but offered a context of how my strange dance in relationships—persecutor and persecuted—still played out in my present circumstances.

If I was stuck in a repetitive victim role, it was incumbent upon me to discover my own weaknesses and reasons for remaining stubbornly blind to alternative solutions. But that night this concept had just been introduced to me. It would take many more years before I could integrate all that I had experienced that night.

Suddenly remembering my son, I rushed to his room to check on him. He was sleeping peacefully, undisturbed. I slowly walked back to my bedroom and eventually fell asleep.

The next morning, I discovered that I had overslept. I had to be at work in an hour and couldn't be late, or I would really hear it from my boss.

As I drove to work, perhaps for the first time in my life I had a hint of my own role in this sordid mess. I had grown resentful of my husband as the oppressor in our marriage, but what was my role as a victim wanting to teach me? What was I being asked to learn from our relationship? It was a strange feeling to allow myself to ponder as I drove through the early morning Los Angeles freeway traffic.

There was no doubt that Peter—who would be returning home that evening—was guilty of inappropriate temper tantrums. But what was I guilty of? In what way was I, too, refusing to change and to grow? Up until last night's hologram, I had assumed total wrongdoing by Peter and an almost presumed victimized innocence with respect to myself. But now it seemed as if there were something more to learn about this dance between enemies and victims. If the wise elder, who had introduced me to this hologram, had arrived to teach me something, surely it wasn't simply to have me feel more justified in my arrogant sense of self-righteousness. Had a karmic pattern been presented as a key to understanding my role and preventing similar repetitive cycles?

There was something deep and life-changing to glean from my past-life scene. There was more to know, the knowing of which might reveal the block in my awareness of the reason *why* we become entangled in difficult problems requiring our solutions.

As I parked my car and rode the elevator up to the eleventh floor and the office of Dr. Helman—the other bully who played a strong role in my life—I wondered how I could both retain my own sense of empowerment while simultaneously avoiding the pitfalls of avoidance by running away or by turning into a cold-hearted, doubtful cynic who avoids interpersonal intimacy. Perhaps this was the lesson being asked of me. Perhaps in some mysterious way, the bright lights and intense humming vibrations were connected to the next stage of my own evolution.

Chapter Five

As the elevator doors opened to the eleventh floor, I stepped out and took a deep breath, resolved to avoid a confrontation with my boss. I was billing supervisor for a wealthy physician of internal medicine, Gerry Helman, MD, who was the founder of an upscale Century City medical practice. The good doctor had been friendly and solicitous when I'd accepted the well-paying job; he was the sort of man who put his arm around you and complimented your perfume even when you weren't wearing any. He had an instinct for how to gain favor with the girls in the office by providing gifts and things that they themselves could never have afforded.

As I entered the lobby of the plush medical practice, I stopped to read the large framed award that was prominently displayed on the wall next to a framed newspaper clipping. Dr. Helman had made a large donation to the local children's hospital. The newspaper article displayed a photo of the ribbon-cutting ceremony, showing the mayor handing a ceremonial award to the good doctor. Dr. Helman was practically famous in this town for his generous donations to worthy causes.

The girls in the office also loved him because he showered them with jewelry and Lakers tickets and new clothes. It would have been nice to imagine him as simply a hardened

businessman, but I was beginning to suspect that something
wasn't right with the goings on in the practice.

As billing supervisor, it was my job to verify the physician's
charges, then submit them for reimbursement to a myriad of
insurance companies. But the paperwork never quite added
up in my analyses, and therein was the problem. The doctor
kept telling me to submit the charges as they came across my
desk and to stop over thinking my job duties. The problem
was that the descriptions of treatments provided to patients
often read as redundant and confusing. When I would ask
the doctor to clarify certain entries in the medical charts, he
would explode.

"Stop micromanaging me!" he would screech. "Do your
job and submit the charges to insurance companies without
wasting my time with a hundred of your feeble questions."

That morning, as usual, a schedule of charges crossed
my desk for procedures that I suspected had never been performed. With renewed inner strength as a result of the night's
vision, the huge pile of unsubmitted claims on my desk now
posed less of an inner conflict. Previously I had seriously considered that Dr. Helman's defensive response to my queries
could very well be justified, given my less educated analysis—after all, he was the trained physician and I only a mere
administrative supervisor.

But now that perspective was shifting, and for the first
time I was considering that my own discernment and intuitive analysis might just be accurate. Although I was dreading
yet another confrontation with another angry man, I nonetheless knocked on his door to ask for clarification once again,
wanting to solve our differences without having to resort to
the more difficult option.

I closed the door quietly behind me as I entered his large office. He smiled guardedly, insisting that I sit down. I took a seat, carefully balancing the offending files on my lap.

After arranging himself behind his big desk, Dr. Helman leaned forward on his arm and with an icy smile, he spoke to me in a clear but calculating tone. "Are you still having trouble performing your basic job duties?" he asked, clenching his teeth.

"These charges don't accompany any treatment entries. I can't figure out what treatments the patients received," I said, gulping hard.

Dr. Helman sighed heavily and grimaced, as though his patience were being tested to the limit. "As I've warned you before—and I'm noting this in your employee file—your lack of ability to comprehend the complex nuances of insurance billing will in no way dictate the processing of these claims." He scribbled furiously in my employee file. When he was finished, he slapped his pen on the desk, stormed to his door, and opened it, gesturing that I should now leave immediately.

As I walked from his office, Dr. Helman yelled after me down the hall, with the other employees gawking in amusement at my embarrassing rebuke.

Humiliated, unresolved inner turmoil began to rise to the surface of my awareness, with the doctor's shrieking voice sounding strangely like my husband's. How had angry, short-tempered men come to make up my primary male relationships? Frustrated, tears of rage filled my eyes as I rushed back to my desk, with the doctor yelling more insults at my back. Waves of revulsion swept over me as I attempted to control myself before these emotions overtook me completely. Sitting at my desk, I breathed deeply as Debra rushed over to comfort me.

"Just do what he says," Debra pleaded, taking my hand in hers. "It's just a job. Why turn it into a power struggle that you can't win?"

Amazed that my best friend couldn't see the truth of my dilemma, I looked back at her, my eyes filling with tears. "I know it's hard to question somebody in their field of expertise, but suppose that he's just plain wrong?" I asked her.

"Well, that's just it," Debra said beseechingly. "Are you sure that he is? I mean, you *are* kind of new to the medical field and, well, he *is* a physician after all."

"They're not gods, Debra. It's a matter of ethics. Either these are honest mistakes on his part, or he knows that I'm on to something underhanded, and I just can't figure out which. But either way, something's not adding up in this place."

At that moment, Dr. Helman could be heard charging down the hall toward our office. Sitting at attention, I tried to look busy as the doctor came up behind me and looked over my shoulder at the files I was working on. As soon as he left my office, I carefully added the files to a growing stack of problematic charges in the back of the file cabinet, where they could not be found or submitted for reimbursement.

There were plenty of other tasks requiring my attention, and I saw to them conscientiously. But whenever suspected erroneous charges landed in my "in" box, they were quickly "misplaced" to the back of the file cabinet.

At home that night, now trying to resolve my work problems with Peter, I gently posed to Peter my dilemma with respect to my concerns at work. Snapping his head to attention, perhaps believing that my work issue had already been solved, he slapped down his fork and glared at me.

"As usual, you're making too much of the situation. Be happy for your paycheck and do your job. The subject is closed."

Biting my tongue, I didn't respond. What was there left to say?

The next day at work, Dr. Helman seemed to have declared war on me. First, he moved my desk as far away from Debra's and the others' as office space allowed. Next, I was assigned a staggered lunchtime, so that I was the only one leaving for lunch at that hour, further isolating me. As another punishment, he personally selected complicated, meaningless tasks for me to perform, then shouted at me for wasting time. His intention, no doubt, was to demoralize me and hasten my resignation, since processing those potentially fraudulent charges required complete compliance in his billing department.

I wanted to run, not walk, from that office and never look back. That night at home, I sat Peter down and told him that I couldn't take it any longer. Looking up from his evening paper, Peter stared at me blankly as though not knowing whether to yell or to leave the house in a fury.

"We're not having this discussion," he said fiercely.

"But suppose the doctor really is running a fraudulent billing practice? I could be implicated."

"You cannot be held liable for simply following orders. You don't know what the bigger picture is in that office. You might be imagining things. Besides, no job's perfect."

Incredulously, I listened to Peter calmly instructing me to adapt to the dysfunction at work, which, I was beginning to recognize, was what I was doing in my marriage as well.

The next day at work proved to be Dr. Helman's angriest day yet, and his campaign to rein me in soon grew uglier. After another round of unreasonable demands from him, I left work that day knowing that it was time to tell Peter that, no matter the result, I had to quit. But dinner brought other challenges, and after getting the baby to sleep, I was just too tired to start another heavy discussion. We fell asleep early, and I vowed to bring up the subject the very next day.

Later that night, while deeply asleep, I was again awakened by the sound and feel of the telltale zapping and intense humming vibration of an electromagnetic surge. As it filled the room, I felt as if I were being electrocuted; but, strangely, Peter slept soundly next to me in the bed, undisturbed. Suddenly a new hologram appeared; this time it was the image of two men having a discussion near the foot of my bed! They looked like normal businessmen, each dressed professionally in a suit and tie, but they were floating in the air. Here was my chance to prove to Peter that something strange was going on in our home.

I shook him until he awoke. "Peter!" I said urgently, as he leaned on one elbow, bleary-eyed and wondering why I woke him up. "Look at those men!" I whispered, pointing to the end of the bed.

"What are you talking about?" Peter demanded irritably.

"Don't you see them? Those men; they're right in front of us!"

Peter looked at where I was pointing with a blank expression, then looked back at me. "You're dreaming; there's nothing there. What time is it anyway?" Grabbing the clock from the side table, he looked at it with annoyance, noticing that it was broken. "Our clock's broken, but it must be two o'clock! Go back to sleep." With that, he rolled over on his side, pulling the covers up to his ears, yelling, "And get a new clock, will you?"

I returned my attention to the hologram; the men seemed to be waiting patiently for me to finish with Peter. I now looked at them more carefully. They wore gold badges on the lapels of their suits that looked similar to FBI badges that I'd seen on television. Not sure of what to do or say, I simply listened to them talk to each other as though I were not there and they were not part of this vision in the middle of my bedroom.

As casually as if they were sitting in their office with cups of coffee, the men discussed my employer, the infamous Dr. Helman! Then, as if on cue, they suddenly turned and looked directly at me. I gawked at them in surprise as they addressed me as though they could see and interact with me.

"How can this be?" I said out loud, rubbing my eyes. Am I imagining this? I wondered privately. Then one of them spoke to me.

"Your help is needed with the doctor," he said in a crisp tone. "He—and you—are accountable for what you do and for what you don't do."

Recovering from my surprise at having a second apparition within a week speak to me, I cleared my throat to ask a question, glancing at the sleeping Peter beside me. Was I having a conversation with a ghost, I wondered?

"Accountable?" I asked, suddenly alarmed at his intimation.

"Each of you has a spiritual mentor who watches over you. They observe and monitor your progress. You are accountable for meeting or not meeting the goals of your soul."

"My soul? What do you mean?"

"Do your actions demonstrate that you care about others, that you engage in service to others, and that you feel compassion for others?" asked the other man.

"Well, I think so, but—"

"Are you trying new approaches to old problems or are you preoccupied with getting even for the wrongs done to you?"

"I don't understand."

"Are you forgiving yourself and others and responding to problems with temperance, tolerance, understanding, and compassion? Are you learning from difficulties and challenges? Are you helping society, despite the challenges you face, while living in Earth's chaotic physical environment?"

"Okay, so what you're saying is that Dr. Helman—"

"Our focus is on *you*. Your council will be looking to see if your actions reflect the integrity of your immortal soul in terms of values and ideals."

With that, he disappeared. The humming vibration and charge in the room immediately dissipated.

It took me a long while to fall back to sleep, as I replayed their questions over and over in my mind. Exhausted, I finally drifted into deep dreaming.

As soon as I awoke the next morning, I felt strangely energized. With renewed clarity, I practically danced through my morning chores, fixing breakfast for Peter and Walter. Then, with great enthusiasm, I dropped Walter off at daycare and headed for work.

Once in my office, I took a seat at my desk, and it wasn't long before Dr. Helman came in to badger me. When he stood over my desk and saw the stack of unsubmitted insurance claims, he glared at me, turned to Debra, and ordered her to process them. Intervening, I stated aloud that the charges had not yet been verified, so neither Debra nor I would be able to process them.

Debra glared at me, wondering what kind of trouble I was stirring up for both of us.

Angry at this perceived demonstration of unity, Dr. Helman stepped back to consider us for a moment; then, with an icy smile, he snapped, "You're both fired."

Debra started to protest, but I grabbed her hand and led her out into the hallway. Then a thought occurred to me; I turned around and stepped back inside to grab a few files from the back of the file cabinet. Dr. Helman, who had walked off, looked back and saw me take them. He now chased after us as we ran down the hallway toward the elevator. Dr. Helman bellowed after us, "Stop, thief!" The elevator doors opened just in time, and we dashed inside, the doors closing on the doctor who shouted, "I'm calling security!"

Once inside the elevator, Debra glared at me. "Are you crazy? Peter's going to freak out, and what am I going to do for a paycheck?"

"Don't worry, the doctor will be held accountable. You'll see. We've just gotta get to the parking lot before security finds us."

We snuck out the side door of the lobby. Safely inside my car, I burned rubber peeling out of the lot and headed for the freeway.

"Where are we going?" Debra asked, dazed by the ruckus.

"To an attorney's office," I said. Debra looked questioningly at me. "Somebody I've consulted with before. We can trust him."

An hour later, Debra and I were sitting in the attorney's office as I explained my suspicions about the doctor's erroneous insurance claims. Surprised to hear about the famous doctor's fraudulent practices, the attorney thumbed through the files that I had given him.

In a serious tone, he said, "If what you're saying is true, I'll take this case on contingency. If it checks out, I'll be filing a complaint on your behalf with the Department of Insurance Fraud. This could be a very big deal."

As Debra and I stood up to leave, the attorney turned to me and said somberly, "I hope you've got your facts right, because this doctor, he's a big fish. You don't want to be poking at sharks for no good reason. Do you understand what I'm saying to you?"

We nodded, and I shook his hand with confidence.

As Debra and I rode down in the elevator, I couldn't help but reflect on my life, and on the fact that I had been a coward—plain and simple—to wait so long to demonstrate courage and clarity in the face of opposition. "Debra, I've been a coward for most of my life. I'm just realizing that now. My husband and I were drawn to each other for some higher purpose that I haven't understood. I now realize that there must be something important that we're supposed to learn from each other."

As we walked together to my car, I thought how strange it was that the holographic men in suits had stirred something deep inside me that had been too long dormant. By calling attention to my inability to find my voice and speak my own truth, they had lit a match, igniting greater understanding. This had led me to holding Dr. Helman accountable for his apparent criminal behavior, but now my mind turned to my husband.

I hoped Peter would see that I was changing and growing. The guys from my hologram wore badges representing spiritual power and authority, and they had inspired me to take new action.

As I pulled up to Debra's house, she stepped out of the car, then suddenly turned back to me. "Can I ask you something?" I nodded. "How did you know that this was something we needed to do? I mean, he's a powerful guy, and you seem different somehow . . . it's a big deal what we did. It's like you suddenly have more strength. Why?"

I pondered Debra's question for a moment, dying to finally confide in someone. Could I dare tell her the details of the whole saga? What would she think? "Will you come over after dinner? Peter's heading out of town again, and we can talk then."

Debra agreed.

I stopped at the local drugstore, selecting a new clock from the dozens on display, then went to the cashier to pay. Feeling suddenly lighthearted after having just taken a step in the direction of my own empowerment, I was almost jubilant as I watched the young man place the clock in a bag. The world was suddenly my oyster.

"Did you know that planet Earth is a chaotic physical environment?" I asked, bemused by my own statement. "I guess that's why we *need* clocks!" I laughed out loud.

Sullen, he returned a surprised expression and shrugged me off, saying, "Have a nice day, lady."

I was late returning home, and Peter had already made dinner and was sitting at the table feeding Walter. I joined them and cheerily sat down myself, only then noticing that Peter was quietly fuming.

Trying to break the ice, I ceremoniously placed the new clock on the table and happily gloated over my purchase. "A new clock. The hands glow in the dark."

"I called you at work, but you got fired!" Peter spat out.

I was shocked that he had found out so quickly. I hadn't had a chance to prepare for his reaction. It felt like the wind suddenly got knocked out of me, and I held my breath, bracing myself for the inquest. "Dr. Helman . . . well he—"

"Don't say anything! There's nothing you can say to make this right," Peter said in a chilling voice. He slammed his fist on the table, and all the dishes jumped. Eyeing me suspiciously, he continued his tirade. "We can't afford this. You have to work."

"I know. I'm sorry. I'll get other work."

Peter, unfazed, continued his angry diatribe. "The thing that bothers me the most is the fact that you don't care about little Walter here. He's the one you're putting in jeopardy. Don't you realize that? I just mailed the check for his health insurance, but now that check's gonna bounce."

Glancing worriedly from the baby to my husband, I took a deep breath, wondering if perhaps I had been too hasty and had not considered all the repercussions. "I'll look for work tomorrow," I said, feeling guilty.

Standing up from the table, Peter looked at me sadly, shaking his head. "I don't even know you anymore."

Feeling helpless, I stirred the food on my plate, pretending to eat and hoping that Peter wouldn't notice my lack of appetite.

"Do you know how much weight you've lost?" Peter asked, as though reading my mind. "I'm telling you, something's not right with you, and I don't like it one bit. Make an appointment with Dr. Jones and get checked out."

As a result of my quiet concern for my sanity, given the nocturnal light show, sounds, vibrations, and visions, my appetite had indeed fallen off dramatically. I had eaten very little since the night weeks earlier when the lights had first appeared in my bedroom. It was true that I had lost quite a bit of weight; I was also pale and feeling sickly. I'm sure that I didn't look very healthy, but now Peter was going to use this as one more thing wrong with me.

"Did you even eat anything for breakfast?" he asked me accusingly. "How about lunch?"

"Sure, just look in the dishwasher," I replied, relieved that I had at least prepared for this particular line of questioning. "Look and you'll see my dirty dishes."

Peter opened the door of the dishwasher and, sure enough, there were the morning's dirty dishes.

At that moment, all the lights in the kitchen turned off, then back on, and then off again. Peter reacted, clearly annoyed, and after he fiddled with the switch, the lights came back on. I looked nervously around the room, wondering if another light show was about to erupt in the kitchen.

Taking a deep breath, I was relieved to skirt Peter's question for now, although I was sad at the lengths to which I had gone to cover my lack of appetite. It was easy enough to place food on a plate, then scrape it back off into the garbage disposal, and rack the dirty dishes in the dishwasher as proof I'd eaten.

After slamming closed the dishwasher door, Peter stalked out of the room, calling over his shoulder, "I'm leaving to go out of town. When I get back, you better have righted our financial mess."

Like a balloon stuck with a pin, my previous clarity and confidence dissipated, and tremendous guilt and shame settled in on me. What had I done? What was I thinking? After all, I had just taken action based on a vision that materialized in a firestorm cloud at the foot of my bed. Who did I think I was, Moses? What if I had imagined Dr. Helman's wrongdoing, and he responded to my lawsuit by counter-suing me?

I could only imagine what Peter would do to me if he discovered that I had sued the good doctor! Had I really just taken direction from some ghostly apparition? Was I really that suggestible? Was adding my name to the lawsuit the last straw that would destroy my family and upend my baby's health?

My thoughts were interrupted by the sound of a taxi honking its horn in the driveway. Peter rushed out the front door, pulling his suitcase, not bothering to say goodbye.

By the time Debra arrived later that evening, I was upset again.

"What happened since I last saw you?" Debra asked me incredulously, as I opened the front door to let her in. Thankfully, Walter was sound asleep, so I could now focus on this problem.

As we sat down on the couch with cups of tea, Debra took a deep breath and grabbed hold of my hand in sympathy, waiting for me to talk.

"Remember when I told you that I'd been having these strange dreams?" I said. "Well, they're kind of like nightmares, although not all of them are actually frightening. The point is, they seem so real and they keep coming!" I paused, and Debra squeezed my hand. "I don't know what's happening to me."

Debra noticed a large textbook on the coffee table and opened it. "What's this?" she asked, reading the title page with consternation.

"Oh, just a college psychology textbook I found in storage," I replied.

Debra flipped through the pages and then came across a yellow-highlighted chapter heading separated by a paperclip. Reading aloud, she said, "Multiple Personality Disorder?" Debra stared at me in alarm, as she continued to read. "Lapses in time, disruption in memory caused by trauma or stress, could signal the development of a second personality, or even multiple personalities."

She looked up. "Are you okay?" Debra asked me earnestly. I nodded my head. "Does this have something to do with your dreams?"

"If that's what they are," I said tentatively.

"I hope you're not suggesting that you're going crazy?" Debra asked with frightened concern.

"No, of course not," I replied defensively, reaching for the textbook and closing it, somewhat distressed by her reaction. "It's probably just stress from post-partum blues, that's all."

Debra was thoughtful for a moment before nodding her head. "I've got an idea. Call a babysitter."

"What are you talking about?" I asked.

"Call her," she said, standing up to leave and grabbing up both of our purses. "I know a woman who can help you figure out these headaches and how to better deal with your marital stress."

An hour later, Debra and I sat solemnly in a group of women in the living room of a house in a middle-class neighborhood. Leading the group in an opening meditation was Laura—mid-thirties, dark-brown hair, long earrings, and a bead necklace. After the meditation, Laura explained that she was a psychic and passed around a basket, asking the women to drop in a personal item that she would then anonymously "read." As the basket went around the room, the women dropped in a ring, bracelet, or hair clip. I deposited my wedding ring.

Laura took each item out of the basket and provided a quick reading to the anonymous owner. She's got talent, I observed, as evidenced by the fact that, following each short reading, a gasp of surprise erupted from the item's owner upon hearing Laura's accurate prophecy. She "read" all sorts of predictions from each piece of jewelry, addressing people's finances, a spouse's affair, and children's allergies. When Laura pulled my wedding ring from the basket, she frowned.

"Who owns this wedding ring?" she asked the group, looking from one guest to another.

Slowly I raised my hand. "I do," I said quietly. Everyone looked at me, and the entire room went silent. Debra smiled at me encouragingly and whispered, "This is great, your headaches are a gonner now."

"See me afterward," Laura instructed, placing my ring in her breast pocket.

When everyone had left for the evening, I waited patiently in my chair, wondering what Laura would have to say. I could see her at the far end of the room, drinking from a bottle of water. When she finished, she walked toward me and sat down in the chair at my side. I glanced across the room to be certain that Debra was out of earshot. Removing my ring from her pocket, Laura handed it to me and said soberly, "Your house is haunted."

"Meaning, what?" I asked her in an upset voice, glancing anxiously in Debra's direction. "Ghosts, or what, exactly?" I whispered quietly but urgently.

"Evil spirits, demons, and, yes, ghosts. You'll have to cleanse it." She paused. "I see that you've got a young son?"

Gasping, I nodded my head in surprise and leaned in closer, eager to hear her remedy.

"That will be two hundred dollars," Laura stated, and I caught my breath, realizing that there would be no free ghost-busting advice.

"Of course," I said nervously, looking around the room for Debra, but she had left us alone. I fumbled through my purse for my wallet. Laura watched as I withdrew some twenty dollar bills and counted them. Realizing I didn't have enough, I began rifling through my purse again. "Will you take a check and hold it for a week until I can make a deposit?" I asked Laura, figuring that I'd soon get a new job and all would be well.

Laura considered my question, then shrugged her shoulders. "Seeing as how you're a friend of Debra's, okay," she said, somewhat reluctantly.

I wrote out the check and handed it to her. Satisfied that I had paid her, Laura looked at me seriously and cleared her throat as though what she was about to say would require my utmost attention.

"At least three times each and every day for three months, you need to recite aloud the Bible's twenty-third psalm."

"Is that it?" I replied, surprised that my night apparitions would actually be chased away by the recitation of a biblical passage.

"I know it sounds simple, but once you set your mind straight and recite that passage, I will be working on your problem from my end," Laura said.

"Doing what?" I asked her.

"Clearing your house. I can do it remotely."

At seeing my less-than-enthusiastic response, Laura stood up, indicating that our meeting had concluded. "Don't worry; this won't be as difficult as you think. You actually came to the right place, and just in time, I might add." At that, she handed me an old Bible and opened it to the passage. "See, I've highlighted it for you."

She herded me out the front door. I walked down the path to my car, where Debra was waiting for me, and we drove off.

Upon my return home and after the babysitter had left, I settled into bed. As directed, I turned to Psalm 23 and began to read it aloud. Suddenly, a humming vibration started, and a strange shadow appeared, as though created from overhead. Looking up and all around the room, I could find no source for the shadow. Then an aqua-blue light momentarily flashed in the room approximately ten feet in front of me.

I read the passage again, and this time a little louder. But when the humming vibration did not abate, I reached for the phone.

I dialed Peter's hotel room, and he soon answered. He seemed surprised to hear my voice and asked me with a worried tone, "Is Walter okay?"

"Yes," I said, although now that he'd asked, how could I be so sure? "The babysitter got him to sleep an hour ago."

"Babysitter?" Peter practically bellowed through the phone line.

"Listen, Peter," I said, ignoring his anger that I had spent money on a babysitter. "I've been having these bad dreams, and I went to a psychic for help because everything's getting so intense."

"Psychic? Are you crazy?"

"Laura does ghost-busting. She's helping me."

"Don't waste your time with crackpots, do you hear me? Next thing you know, she'll be charging you for her time. I told you to make an appointment with Dr. Jones. He'll prescribe something to help you sleep."

I suddenly grew silent, not knowing what to say, thinking about the two-hundred-dollar check that I had given to Laura, and knowing that I would have to cover it before she cashed it.

"Get some sleep, will you?" Peter pleaded now, obviously hoping that I would see it his way.

"I'll be okay. Never mind. Sorry to call you so late," I said, hanging up the phone before I said anything else troubling to him.

Falling back onto my pillow, I gave up in surrender. All I could think to do was bury my head in the pillow. If there were shadows in the room, I didn't want to see them.

Suddenly, a strong electromagnetic vibration erupted, and the loud humming soon grew deafening. Looking around the room in terror, I saw a mysterious long, white burst of light explode from the ceiling, followed by a "firestorm" of paranormal phenomena. My hair blew around my face, but again the draperies lay still against the window just a few feet away. I could hear and feel the intense, zapping vibrations. Despite my obvious trauma, for some strange reason, I fell asleep in the middle of this onslaught.

I awakened early the next morning and rushed into the bathroom, where I vomited. With some difficulty, I dressed Walter, afterward noticing that I had put his left shoe on his right foot. At the breakfast table a few minutes later, the toaster ejected the toast with so much force that it smacked the ceiling.

The lights above us flickered on and off.

The phone rang, but there was no one on the other end. Frustrated by everything going haywire, I called the doctor's office. "Yes, I need to make an appointment with Dr. Jones," I said, almost breathlessly.

"Well, we have a cancelation for this morning," the receptionist said.

"Perfect," I said feebly.

An hour later, my son and I sat in an examination room when Dr. Jones stepped inside, extending his hand and smiling broadly at Walter.

"You're growing like a weed," Dr. Jones said to my son, picking him up and placing him on the exam table. After checking his heart and all his vital signs, Dr. Jones wrote a few notes and turned to me smiling. "He's right on target for his age. Keep doing whatever you're doing."

As he readied to leave the room, I realized that I had better speak up. "Dr. Jones, can I ask you a question?"

He stopped and looked at me inquisitively.

"I've been having bad dreams . . . and sometimes I think I see things in the middle of the night that seem so real. It's bothersome and affecting my sleep."

"Post-partum changes are perfectly normal," Dr. Jones replied. "In fact, your body will take at least a year to adjust to life with a new baby, and with all the hormonal changes relative to motherhood, it will affect your sleep pattern. If you feel depressed or particularly fatigued from lack of sleep, I can prescribe you something.

"As for bad dreams, many young mothers have nightmares associated with subconscious fears of motherhood, and the resulting stress that all of this puts on a new marriage." He pulled his prescription pad out of his pocket, scribbled on the page, then handed it to me. "Why don't you attend one of our support groups? I think you'll find that you're not alone."

Taking the paper from him, I shook my head, doubting that my story would find a friendly response amongst a group of exhausted new mothers. "Thanks Dr. Jones, but I think I'll just try to work it out myself. It's kind of hard to describe what I'm going through. People might get the wrong idea."

"Suit yourself," he said, turning again to leave.

Then, as though he were having an afterthought, he stopped and turned back to me. "At the very least, it might be a good idea for you to keep track of the frequency of your nightmares, and when you come in for Walter's annual exam, we'll discuss it again. I would expect them to decrease over time."

I nodded my head hopefully, picked up Walter, and walked out behind the doctor.

Chapter Six

NIGHT AFTER NIGHT, WHOLE chunks of sleep time disappeared in the dark. Following Dr. Jones's advice, after every late-night light show, I put one of my son's green marbles into a covered jar on my bedside table. The jar was starting to fill up.

Peter continued his hectic work schedule, leaving to go out of town somewhat regularly. During his absences, I had come to almost expect that the light show in my bedroom would blast me awake from a deep sleep.

Almost two years passed in this way. I watched my son grow into a three-year-old as I attended to my motherly duties in the best way that I knew how.

I had found other work, so Peter was somewhat appeased. I spent busy weekdays shuttling my son to and from preschool, while I earned a paycheck, then rushed home at night to prepare dinner.

Then, one day while picking up my son from preschool, an unusual thing happened. Walter's teacher, Mrs. Green, saw me gathering up his backpack and called over to me.

"Lisette, I wanted to show you something, if you can hold on a moment." She directed her assistant to keep an eye on Walter and motioned for me to follow her into a private office. She closed the door behind us.

"Everything okay at home?" Mrs. Green asked me in a friendly voice.

"Yes, why do you ask?" I responded, wondering about this line of questioning.

"Well, as you know, every afternoon we set up easels and paint brushes for the children, and they come up with some of the most extraordinary paintings. Even at this young age, they're budding artists."

I looked at Mrs. Green, now holding my breath. Although she was friendly enough, she had closed the door for privacy. Something had gone awry. I could feel it in my bones.

Mrs. Green paused, as though not quite sure how to proceed. Then, gesturing to a dozen easels set up along the far side of the room, she took me on a tour of the other children's paintings.

We walked slowly by each easel, admiring one painting after another. For the most part, they were "stick figure" representations of homelife that three-, four-, and five-year-old hands tried their best to paint. There was a painting of a house and a tree; one child had painted a large brown dog; another painting exhibited a three-year-old's version of a fire truck; one painting displayed an attempt to represent a little girl taking horseback-riding lessons. At that one we both laughed out loud, delighted by the way in which children interpret their world, despite their rudimentary hand/eye coordination. Suddenly, Mrs. Green's smile evaporated as we moved to the final easel in the row. She pointed to it, saying only, "Your son painted this. I thought you'd want to see it."

As large as it was striking, there on the easel was an unmistakable child's rendition of an alien: a large, black, inverted pear-shaped head with large black eyes. Together, Mrs. Green and I stood there in silence, my heart beating faster. After what seemed like an eternity, I looked up at Mrs. Green, realizing that there were tears in my eyes. My world had practically been turned upside down in that one moment. What did this mean? Why was my son painting pictures of aliens? How could I explain it without revealing too much of my own secret nocturnal life.

Mrs. Green spoke, "Naturally, sometimes children sneak in and change the TV channel when nobody's watching. Just thought you might want to know. Obviously, frightening sci-fi shows are not appropriate for young children."

"Yes, of course!" I responded, concerned that Mrs. Green thought that I had lost all sense of appropriate parental controls. "I don't have a television. We don't go to movies," I said. All of the saliva in my mouth suddenly disappeared at the implication of my statement. Where had he gotten the idea for the portrait? Under any other circumstances, this child's fantasy would not have alarmed me. But now, my mouth was so dry I could barely swallow.

"Well, there are books like *Communion* with such images on the cover."

"Not my type of reading," I said rather forcibly. "Thank you for showing this to me," I said, gently removing the page from the easel.

"As you know, open house is next week, and we normally display the children's paintings," said Mrs. Green with some authority. "But under the circumstances, I feel that you'd agree that this particular . . . masterpiece is best dealt with at home."

"Of course," I said. "I'll see to it that my son paints something more appropriate, and we'll get it to you in time for the open house."

At home that evening with Peter, I avoided all discussion about my conversation with Mrs. Green and of our son's alien rendering. For now, the painting was folded up and hidden inside my dresser drawer. I planned to ask my son about it later that evening. As we cleared up the dinner dishes, I took a deep breath and turned to Peter with as casual a tone as I could muster.

"You know, I've been thinking. Perhaps it would be a good idea if I attended that new mothers' support group that Dr. Jones recommended a while back. It's on Saturday mornings at the local rec center," I said matter-of-factly, not wishing to call too much attention to my motivation for seeking help.

Lost in his newspaper, Peter looked up momentarily and shrugged. "Suit yourself. As long as there's no charge for attending," he said emphatically.

On Saturday, Walter and I headed to the new mothers' support group at the recreation center in the middle of town. As I entered the room with my son, the coordinator motioned toward the playroom where I dropped off Walter with a group of children his age. After being directed to the room hosting the support group, I walked inside, and a dozen smiling faces looked up and invited me to join their circle. I took a seat.

The meeting had already started, and I listened attentively as all manner of complaints got voiced. It seemed that this was a rare opportunity for exhausted new mothers to vent their frustrations. A therapist supervised the process, wherein each person took a turn talking about whatever was bothering them. There were problems relating to the stress of giving birth, marital snafus, and sleepless nights. Mothers described their toddlers' supermarket tantrums, sibling rivalries, unreliable babysitters, and discipline issues. Nodding in commiseration and feeling comfortable amongst like-minded others, when it was my turn to share, I dove right in.

"I can really relate to everything that's being said here," I said smiling, looking around the room at all the compassionate, friendly faces.

"To be honest, though, my biggest worry has to do with nightmarish dreams that seem very real. It's hard to explain, but my nights are filled with some kind of . . . phenomena. I don't really know how to describe it. To tell you the truth, I don't know what's happening to me except that sometimes I get awakened to bright lights coming through the ceiling and super loud . . ."

Suddenly I noticed that the room had gone dead silent, and the other mothers were fidgeting uncomfortably in their chairs. Others were staring blankly at their hands, embarrassed. Sighing deeply, I looked from one surprised or awkward expression to the other. Feeling a hot surge of anguish welling up from my belly, I grabbed my purse, rushed into the playroom to retrieve Walter, and we exited the building.

After buckling Walter in his car seat, I drove off, feeling numb, confused, and utterly alone. In attempting to find a safe haven to express my unique new-mother experience, I had taken too big a leap and expected too much of these suburbanites; that was now clear to me. I would have to find a different strategy for finding solace and a place where I, too, could vent my worries and concerns.

Although I had avoided returning home to my mother's house in an attempt to keep my private agony to myself, clearly I had nowhere else to turn. Maybe it was time, I thought, to allow my mother and my siblings, those who loved me, to help.

"Do you want to play with your cousins?" I asked little Walter, thinking that it might be nice to spend an afternoon with family members, hoping all the while that I wouldn't alienate myself from them, too.

As we headed onto the Pacific Coast Highway toward my mother's house, the car's electric windows went up and down by themselves.

Thirty minutes later, we pulled up to my mother's place, a modest house in the low foothills of Malibu. As I lifted Walter out of the car, we were greeted with cheery applause, and I grinned sheepishly, recognizing that this was an attempt to convey their surprise at seeing us.

"Look who's here," my mother said happily, embracing Walter and me. "Come on into the backyard. We're all set up on the lawn, barbecuing chicken."

My mother led us around to the back of the house where a few of my grown siblings were lounging in chairs, tending to a barbecue, or setting the picnic table. Several of my young nieces and nephews were also there, and they jumped up to embrace me. The smell of cooking chicken filled the air. My siblings called out their surprised and delighted greetings, and my sister took Walter by the hand and led him over to a group of his cousins playing on the grass.

I settled down amongst the adults with a glass of lemonade, and we all caught up with the latest family news. I tried to remain interested in the details of everyone's lives, but my mind kept wandering, wondering about the source of the light show in my room and unable to dismiss the strange alien portrait that my son had painted.

I recalled the conversation I had had with Walter earlier in the week about his alien masterpiece. "This is a very creative painting," I had said, smiling to Walter while looking at him intently. "How did you get the idea to paint an alien?"

"I don't know," he replied, shrugging his shoulders in disinterest. "I had a dream."

Sitting down on a chair, I motioned for him to come over and I looked deeply into his eyes. "Well, I'm so happy that you painted it. Always listen to your own inner voice, even if others might not like what you do. Sometimes it's hard to be brave, but promise me you'll always try, okay honey?"

"Okay, mommy," Walter replied, giving me a big bear hug. "I promise."

Now as Walter played with his cousins on the backyard lawn, I could only stare off into the distance, wondering what happened to what I had hoped would be a fairytale life with Peter and Walter? My mother kept trying to draw me into the family discussion by asking me to catch her up on all the latest news with me and my husband. I talked about Peter's promotion and my new administrative job, but everyone could tell I was distracted, and they didn't press me for details. I preferred to sit and think, to try to sort out the mess that my life had become.

I couldn't help but slump back against my lawn chair and watch Walter playing happily on the grass with his cousins. Up to this point, my son had apparently remained untouched by my maelstrom—if you considered his pop art as a mere flight of imagination. Other than that, he went about the business of being a curious three-year-old with blessed, self-centered oblivion. He was the reason that I needed to figure it all out. It was my love for him that created a context for my life. Where he was concerned, life made sense.

Had almost two years really passed, and I still did not know the reason for these nocturnal visions? Thankfully, my son was now a three-year-old spitfire. His sweet, plucky nature was rambunctious and sassy. I chuckled at the way he giggled and laughed at just about everything. He was pure bliss, and I could lose myself in that whimsical, fairytale-inspiring crop of hair. I cherished every moment with him.

Watching Walter play on the grass with his cousins allowed me momentarily to push aside the terror of my suspicions that perhaps my mind was unraveling. I envied his gleeful innocence. Bored with his cousins, he ran across the yard to play with the other toys strewn around. I watched him smile, as every new discovery delighted him.

Suddenly, a young kitten ran out into the yard, and I laughed in spite of myself as I watched Walter play with it. He was fascinated by the way the kitten's throat buzzed when it purred, which was an endless source of fascination for him. Squatting on his tiny heels to peer under a lawn chair at the kitten, which had run for cover, Walter picked a small caterpillar out of the grass, then gently looked at it with innocent curiosity. I was mesmerized by this symbolic demonstration of life in its utter simplicity. I had to stay strong for my son.

Recent events turned over in my mind as I thought about everything that had happened up to this point. The sun was glaring down on me, so I reached over to adjust the umbrella next to me to better block the strong rays. I looked over at Walter, who was now happily kicking a rubber ball across the lawn, and it occurred to me that I should put a hat on him before he got sunburned. At that moment, taking the initiative herself, my mother scurried over to the kids and applied sunscreen to their faces. My son squirmed at the cold feel of the lotion. "Hold still, you don't want to get burned," my mother said to him.

As I heard her words and watched this scene, I remembered myself as a young seven-year-old girl playing "Barbie dolls" with my sister. We were sitting here on this very backyard lawn where I also had once played. So many years ago, my own mother had lathered me up, and I, too, had squirmed with the cold feel of the sunscreen as she had applied the lotion to my face and arms.

Then I remembered the shadow on the lawn, and how I had scanned the sky to find the source of it. How curious, I thought, now remembering that long-ago memory, submerged until this very moment. What did that childhood shadow have to do with my current life mystery? Was the invisible source of that shadow connected to my nighttime firestorm?

Life had seemed so simple back then, I mused. My son was now in my old place on the lawn, himself an innocent young child filled with all the hopes and dreams of a fulfilling future. What would I have thought back then if I could have known that I would later grow up and be facing a paranormal conundrum? For a child, the visions, strange lights and sounds would have been fascinating, but for the adult, each succeeding mystical event seemed to cause a dissolving of my denial that the universe—and by association, me—was bigger and grander than anything I had ever imagined it to be.

I could only shake my head at the irony of this situation. It's funny, I thought. As a child, when change happens, we are more able to adapt to it because we face it with curiosity and adventure. As a married adult with a family and a child, suddenly change appeared so threatening. As a young girl, a mysterious backyard shadow was a delightful, curious mystery. As an adult, these shadows were unnerving. Why did this have to be the case?

Did my nighttime lights and electromagnetic vibrations reveal some great, wondrous, universal mystery, the essence of which remained elusive due to my fearful reactions? Why had the lights and vibrations started now that I was an adult? I pondered these questions, wondering about their connection to my childhood experiences. What was unfolding?

Why did it feel like *someone or something* was trying to get through to me? What were they trying to say?

The lights and sounds seemed to have arrived at the apex of my troubles with my husband. Debra's friend, Laura the psychic, had seemed to think that the solution was a simple one; that my problems were due to garden-variety, household demons. Could she have been right? Could all my midnight difficulties with the strange lights and electromagnetic vibrations be written off as something as bizarre as ghosts and poltergeists running amok in my bedroom?

Perhaps it didn't really matter what the reason or cause was. Maybe I would never know what ghosts were actually running through my mind or if I had multiple personalities.

I was just now beginning to recognize how fully I had allowed myself to become trapped: trapped by my upset reactions; trapped by my fears; trapped by my own self-imposed powerlessness. I couldn't even tell myself my own truth, let alone tell anyone else my truth. I was just too plain afraid: afraid of my husband; afraid of the lights and their electrical zapping sensations; and, most of all, I was afraid of the whimpering, disempowered woman that I had become.

What would it take, I wondered, for me to become fully alive and to feel joyous; to have the personal confidence to choose a different way of living? I had become a frightened woman, afraid of shadows that were not, in and of themselves, doing me any harm.

As I watched my son, sitting there in my old place on the lawn, I saw him shiver at the touch of the cold sunscreen on his grandmother's hands. I looked skyward, all these years later, wondering if *someone or something* had caused that long-ago shadow on the lawn and what connection it had to my present situation. And, as I gazed into the deep-blue sky, I wondered what it would feel like to be free.

Chapter Seven

I WAS CHILLED WHILE standing outside in the night air. Peter kissed us goodbye, then got into the waiting taxi. He was going out of town again. I was growing accustomed to his frequent trips away, so I used my alone time to nurture my son and to try to clear my head of life's stresses. I turned to Walter, who blew kisses to his father, then I led him into the house. "Okay, sweetie, let's get your pajamas on. It's past your bedtime."

Cuddled up together on Walter's bed, I read aloud from a children's book until he fell asleep. After quietly kissing him on the cheek, I turned off the light and left the room.

While reading in bed later, the unmistakable humming vibration and strong electromagnetic surge started to fill the room again. My scalp crackled with a piercing electrical current that felt as though it were running right through my body and out the top of my head. My hair seemed to crackle with sparks. I shot upright in bed as I noticed a form emerging in the darkness at the foot of my bed. In complete disbelief, I beheld a small being, no more than four feet tall, staring back at me with large, black, almond-shaped eyes!

Gasping in fear, I shrank back, horrified to realize that what I was seeing was an alien being of some type. His large, inverted, pear-shaped head was similar in size and shape to the terrifying images I had seen on book covers and in horror films. In fact, the alien's image was similar to what had been

painted by my own son in his preschool class! With a terrible sinking feeling, I wondered if Walter's painting had been
inspired by his own visitations.

I could hardly bear to consider that my child had been
terrorized in the same way that I had been for these past three
years. I could hear and feel my heart beating loudly in my
chest. The unmistakable and, unfortunately, familiar zapping sensation filled the room. I felt as though I had entered
another dimension in time and space. I was extremely dismayed that the appearance of the alien might be the reason
for my continual light shows; this was almost more than I
could tolerate. Is this what it all came down to: *aliens?*

Just then, as though my eyes had been playing tricks on
me—or perhaps because my mind could no longer comprehend the incomprehensible—the form shifted its shape. It
morphed slowly at first, then it changed completely; in the
place of the alien was a man sitting on the end of my bed and
looking at me.

Where had the alien gone? How had one form seemingly
turned into another?

Shocked and surprised, I could not catch my breath at
first, nor could I utter any word or sound. We sat there staring at each other for what seemed like minutes. When he
continued to stare back at me without moving, I regained my
composure and demanded to know his identity. After all, at
least I knew how to deal with a human being.

"Who are you?" I asked him breathlessly, surprised at
myself for trying to chat with an apparition. Or was it a
shape-shifting alien, a burglar . . . or maybe a . . . ghost? He
did not respond.

"How did you get in here?" I demanded again. Now that
he looked like an ordinary citizen, he was subject to our laws

forbidding breaking and entering. Certain that I had locked all the windows and doors and had not heard any break-in attempts, I challenged my vision, daring him to explain his presence here.

"All my doors are locked," I said with emphasis.

He only looked at me and smiled engagingly.

His apparent lightheartedness lessened my fright somewhat. As my eyes adjusted to the dark, I saw that he was not acting in a way that suggested he meant me any harm, although I did not know about the alien's intent. Wanting to get a better look at him, I reached over and switched on the bedside lamp.

He didn't look like a ghost, not that I had ever seen one. He appeared to be a regular person, with the exception of the crackling vibration that surrounded him. Was that a sudden flash of aqua-blue light near his head?

Despite the weird lights, he looked rather normal—as solid as my own hand in front of me. There was obviously something unusual about him and his visit, and I wondered if I was acting inappropriately friendly. Thinking that I may have been brainwashed into passive submission, I reached for the phone to dial 911.

Looking at me with the phone in my hand, he smiled and didn't seem threatened by the prospect of a flotilla of police cars arriving at my door. In fact, he appeared rather amused by it all. Frankly, his response disarmed me, and I hung up the phone. Expecting some move on his part, I looked at him guardedly. Before anything else happened, I picked up the clock on my side table to note the time: 10:10 p.m.

Still gawking at him and noticing my own diminishing fear, I wondered who he was and why had he come? How convenient, I thought, that Peter was always out of town during my nighttime skirmishes, and tonight was no exception—a scenario that was probably planned by my visitors.

Looking the man up and down, I searched for clues as to his identity. He was approximately forty-five years old and had hair so black and thick that I stared at this considerable mane for a moment. His locks seemed to dance on his head. He was wearing a navy jacket, and he gently moved his hand to withdraw something from his pocket; this immediately startled me.

Instead of a weapon, he withdrew a strange business card; then, surprising me further, he simply stretched out his arm to offer it to me. I could hardly contain my confusion and concern that perhaps I was losing my mind. What kind of apparition is this? I wondered. First I had seen an alien in my room, then it had morphed into the astonishing character before me. Was I merely dreaming?

"What's going on?" I asked, more to myself than to him, incredulous at the way I was patiently awaiting his next move. I was flabbergasted that some kind of paranormal interloper was sitting on the end of my bed in the middle of the night, offering me his business card!

Despite myself, I grabbed his card, exasperated that I had been pulled down some warped rabbit hole and was now cooperating with my own crazy imagination run wild.

As I read it, he spoke. "My name's George Graysuff."

Startled, I jumped in fright at my apparition now talking to me. Like the hair on his head, the business card seemed alive—the engraved letters on the card were actually pulsing with a sort of energy. Entirely perplexed, I stared at my bogeyman, trying to sort out the whole scenario.

Strangely enough, the letters on the card that spelled out his name formed an outline of a fish. There were other words, too: "carpenter," "fisherman," and a few other professions that I didn't recognize. I looked at him skeptically, as if to say that just because a phantom put a few biblical references on a business card didn't mean that he was worthy of my trust. I handed the card back to him.

"Why list so many different professions on one card," I asked dryly, not really believing that I was having this conversation. At any moment, I knew that I would wake up from this crazy delusion.

"It represents the way and the manner that each person returns here to live life, again and again, in different roles, to learn and to grow."

"Oh, really," I said doubtfully, shaking my head and wondering why he was talking in riddles. "I don't remember making such plans."

"No, of course not. Otherwise you couldn't be tested by increasingly challenging circumstances that serve to spur your growth; and also, so you won't try to get even with those who have previously hurt you."

"I'm just trying to master the basics of living."

"There's more to living than that."

"What do you mean?"

"Each lifetime requires that you stay true to the goals of your soul. Your responsibility is to discover what you came here to do, then to embark on that path with courage and discipline, no matter how impossible it seems. The more challenges you face, the more rigorous the training. For example, many advanced souls deliberately volunteer for imperfect bodies with physical handicaps."

All I could do was stare at him, shaking my head, as though by denying the conversation I could will it away. I rubbed my eyes and, for a moment, held my head in my hands, disbelieving my own senses. Then I looked up, almost angry with my state of confusion.

"Well, what *is* my path?" I blurted out, frustrated by his ability to suck me into this fantasy.

"We'll give you a hint: The goals of the *soul* are often contrary to the goals of the mind and those pursuits that are highly valued by a competitive culture."

"Well, how can I discover the goals of my soul?"

"You already have."

"What are you saying?" At that moment, he held up a finger as if to quiet my further queries.

Okay, I get it now, I thought to myself. These questions and answers make no sense, so any second now, I'm going to be roused from this silly dream.

He just looked at me calmly.

"I know you're not real," I said with conviction, almost daring him to disappear. "Because if you *were* real, I could touch you and feel something solid. But you're either a dream, or you're a ghostly apparition."

He continued to be unruffled by my skepticism.

"Okay then, I *am* going to touch you . . . all right?" I asked.

I was taken aback to see him respond by bowing ever so slightly, as if to say, "go right ahead."

Taking a deep breath, I moved slowly toward him, chiding myself for not having done this with my previous apparitions and holograms.

Intuiting that I wanted to touch his thick mop of black hair, he lowered his head, as though he were a gentle pony accepting a bridle. At first cautious, I gingerly touched the top of his head. Then, satisfied that his hair felt real, I ran my fingers through his thick mop.

"Wow. You feel so real!" I said in amazement, even if this didn't explain what was happening to me.

"Okay, so you're not a ghost," I said wearily, wondering what or who he was.

George Graysuff only beamed a gentle smile, as though patiently indulging a young student who had just begun an arduous tutelage.

"You must eat," he said, changing the subject. "Come with me, and I'll show you what food will be good for you."

Surprised at his suggestion, I got the feeling that he wasn't going to give me a tour of my own refrigerator. Instead, there was something downright mystical about the offer. I glanced down at my skinny figure. Was my health in such question that this being would show up in the middle of the night just to encourage me to get nourished? And his invitation was ridiculous.

"I can't go anywhere with you," I objected, given that I would be leaving my sleeping son alone in my house to go on a picnic in the middle of the night. "My child's asleep. I won't leave him alone!"

The words had barely left my lips when, despite my protests, I felt myself inexplicably following him as he walked out of the room. Smiling gently and compassionately, he gestured for me to continue down the hallway toward my son's bedroom. "Let me show you something," he said, his blue eyes sparkling with delight.

I followed after him, noticing that his feet didn't seem to be making contact with the floor. As we entered Walter's room, it was awash in a mystical white light. Surrounding the entire bed was an arc of golden light, cradling my child in peaceful slumber. It was the most serene and lovely sight that I had ever seen or ever hope to see again. My child's cherubic face expressed pure bliss. The man and I stood there viewing the mystical scene as though we were in a theater somewhere watching a good movie.

His words broke my seeming hypnosis as he gestured toward my sleeping child. "Memories of previous lives usually become suppressed by the second or third birthday. But this is no excuse. At the conclusion of each life, you each will still have to answer to your council as to how your host body and mind either served or hindered your soul's spiritual progress."

Jolted out of my peaceful reverie by his bold statement— one that intimated there was something that I wasn't doing right—I turned to him, upset. "What is it I'm supposed to be doing that I'm not doing?"

"What is your soul's intent in this life? How is your soul interfacing with your human body?"

"I'm not sure that I know—"

Suddenly, I was disoriented by a blur of lights and sounds; my eyes closed momentarily as I experienced a strange sensation of movement. It felt as though I were lifting into the air. I opened my eyes, and I was rushing feet first through a tunnel of light, a vortex of energy. In the distance, there appeared to be a white light, similar to what has been described by those who have survived near-death experiences and returned from the spirit world, their bodies having been resuscitated. I wondered if I, too, was dying, and I sadly thought of my child and my foolishness at leaving him alone.

Abruptly, the tunnel opened up, and I began to descend into what seemed like another world. Below me was a city of extraordinarily exquisite buildings. Their roofs appeared to be made of solid gold. Never had I imagined that such splendor could exist. Had I entered another dimension? Or was

I simply on another planet? I next found myself standing in a room with a long table on which were various food items.

My apparition, who had suddenly appeared at my side, gestured toward the arrangement, saying only, "Here are some of the foods that you can eat." It was as though he were trying to remind me of the human necessity to nourish oneself by eating. It occurred to me just how long it had been since I had last eaten a full meal.

On the table was an assortment of foods, including brown rice, vegetables, fruits, nuts, and seeds. There were no packaged goods. Several items were not familiar to me, and a few vegetables and fruits were clearly not from my neck of the woods. "We don't have that type of vegetable," I said matter-of-factly to the gentleman, pointing to a huge red pumpkin-like vegetable that resembled a tomato in texture.

Soon I was directed to another room, which had a home-theatre atmosphere. Several elders there smiled graciously and gestured for me to observe the screen, on which a scene was just beginning to play. It was as though we were all standing around watching a home movie.

I was shocked to see that the movie actually contained scenes of me as a seven-year-old girl. I observed the incident from my early childhood in which I was playing with my Barbie dolls in the backyard with my sister. My mother was applying cold lotion to my arms when the mysterious shadow passed overhead. Why were they showing this scene to me now? Not only was I curious about the shadow, but the scene also reminded me of my as yet unrealized longing to be part of a bonded family.

My marriage to Peter suddenly filled me with regret. I looked from the screen to the assembled elders, who were all studiously observing me, and I asked for an explanation. "Why am I seeing this? *How* am I seeing this?" I asked incredulously, realizing that dozens of questions needed to be answered.

"This is the precise episode that we showed you when you were in spirit prior to choosing a body for your upcoming life. You were offered several choices of families, but you specifically chose this one."

"But what about that shadow? Was *someone or something* creating it from overhead?"

Without responding, they suddenly switched the movie scene, and I was viewing my wedding day to Peter; the scene made me catch my breath.

The elders considered my sad reaction; one said, "You each choose beforehand who will make up the main cast of characters in the life to come, and they in turn choose you. It's a joint decision, and a grand plan in which we are all involved. In this way, you make agreements with one another as to the experiences and events that will best help your soul to grow and mature."

"You mean I knew that my marriage to Peter would be so disastrous?" I asked in amazement. "So I deliberately chose to marry him to experience the hardships of being—"

"Thwarted."

"Thwarted?"

"Yes, and to grow wiser, stronger, and more confident despite it. You must learn and then demonstrate how to solve difficult problems, rather than avoiding them, or running away from them."

"And this is how we grow through adversity?" I asked.

"Every time you face discomfort, ask yourself an important question: What am I learning as a result of this situation that I would not have learned had I missed the opportunity?"

"So every challenge in life is, as you say, a prearranged problem that serves to test our emerging ability to master it?"

"Yes, to learn how to find your own inner strength despite hurdles and setbacks. You knew that you'd be presented with rigorous obstacles and challenges. That's what the fast track *implies*," one of the elders explained. "How you respond and react is what your period of testing is all about."

"It doesn't seem fair that we can't remember actually agreeing beforehand to get involved with difficult people and problems to challenge ourselves."

"It's the most effective training imaginable; that is, if you are up to meeting the challenges of your soul's goals. Not everyone is. In that case, your growth comes to a stop."

"But what about the light show in my room late at night? Why the strange visitors, and what about that *alien*?" I asked urgently, referring to the strange being who had morphed into their messenger. "How can all of *that* be part of a mutual agreement?" I was unbelievably relieved that I had finally stumbled upon someone who had some real answers for a change.

"All events, experiences, and occurrences are subject to the same laws."

"What laws?" I asked incredulously. "You mean we all chose one another in the same way, by mutual agreement before we were born?"

"Of course," another elder replied with a smile. "Earth is not the only learning environment available for an incarnating soul, but when you *do* choose Earth, you are choosing one of the most difficult, if not *the* most difficult, learning environments possible. Usually you reconnect with others on Earth whom you once knew in your past from elsewhere.

No matter your origins, all reconnections serve as reunions, although, admittedly, you may not perceive it that way."

"But why would we choose to come to Earth with all its suffering and problems and have a hard time?" I asked, not sure that I believed him.

"The Earth plane is a dense and chaotic physical dimension. It is competitive and not governed by fairness and equality. But that's why the incarnating soul attempts to make the world a better place. But not everyone meets their training goals, because they get caught up in material accumulation or the satisfaction of authoritarian power over others. Those are tests built into the program. Earth is not for the faint of heart. As we said, your incarnations are not limited to Earth-type worlds, as many of you meet one another again in various other 'worlds,' some of which are much less challenging than Earth."

"So are you saying that while on Earth, many people meet aliens from other dimensions, ones that we've actually known before in other lives?"

"Yes. You return with your primary soul group, each taking turns playing different roles, whether or not you remember those agreements. Your choice of roles all depends upon what your mission is. What is the goal of your soul? In your case, you've met up again with friends from your previous incarnations in other realms to test your emerging confidence and power. Some of those beings are human now, and others are other than human, but alien or human, you've all agreed beforehand as to where, and with whom, you will incarnate."

"Are you saying that a person who sees an alien is actually seeing someone they've known before, in another life, but have now forgotten?"

"Naturally. Soul groups reunite, again and again, no matter what your present role is."

"So we're all one big happy family?"

"Some of you do meet up with old enemies from your past, but even so, it's your responsibility to respond and to act with compassion, tolerance, and kindness as you calmly uphold your empowered highest ideals and values. You are all growing and evolving, but each of you started out as rank beginner, often displaying discourteous immaturity."

"So I don't have to be best friends with everybody?"

"Life offers you relationships and experiences that the soul is calling to itself so that it can master certain lessons, no matter how seemingly impossible or challenging those relationships and experiences may be. Your soul group assists you in meeting your stated goals. These arrangements are made prior to your incarnation. Members of your soul group—whether human or alien—take turns providing one another with opportunities for growth.

"Because free will is always honored, overly dramatic responses and reactions *are* one potential choice, but this need not be the case. No matter how much you dramatize the effects of those challenges, fear and anger are always just that: a choice. However, if you continue to make that choice, you will have to repeat that part of your program. Why not notice your stubborn refusal to find creative solutions to your problems so that you don't have to repeat the experience?"

"I'm entitled to feel the way that I feel," I replied defensively.

"Again, all experiences—and especially experiences involving the heart—are deliberate tests in life. If you are stubborn, you will remain closed to alternative solutions and you will continue to deceive yourself. But your council knows you very well, and you can't fool us as you would your counselors on Earth. Your council is looking to see if you remain true to your *soul's* ideals and values, despite outside pressures that impinge upon your desire to achieve your learning goals for this life."

All of my failures flashed through my mind, from my teenage rebellion to my difficult marriage to Peter and all of the fear that I had felt up to that point.

As though reading my thoughts, the elder said, "Strong compulsions, illusions, and attachments cannot be used as an excuse for poor conduct, even the illusion of fear. Each of you will be held accountable for your choices in the face of the 'false trials' that are presented and must be overcome. Those false trials test your emerging strength. Naturally, fear is the hardest habitual response to overcome, because of its power as a false trial in encouraging you to submerge your inner voice and convictions."

"You make it sound like I've previously agreed to difficult conditions to provide a test of my progress. I don't remember any of this, or any of you."

The elders exchanged looks amongst themselves as though they were considering letting me in on a big secret, but said nothing to me.

"Even the aliens—if any actually exist—*couldn't* be part of this same agreement. It's hard to believe that I actually set out to choose to have problems and upsets and *complications!*" I insisted.

"You choose to be *challenged* in order to grow; that is, *if you are on the fast track.* No challenges, no growth opportunities. If you choose merely to tread water, that, too, is your choice, but eventually stagnation becomes unsatisfying. Everyone has the opportunity to coast now and then, in one lifetime or another, but even in that case, eventually you will be encouraged to choose more rigorous opportunities for growth. Although you can move as quickly or as slowly as you like, you'll come to recognize that 'higher learning' is ultimately more satisfying."

"But am I to take your word for all of this? I don't remember making these decisions before I was born as to what parents I chose and what guy I wanted to marry—and, for that matter, what alien I wanted to blast me out of my bed!"

The elders smiled as though they were somewhat bemused by my stubborn clinging to what they seemed to perceive as ignorant bliss.

"*Of course* you don't remember," one of them said emphatically. "There's a deliberate suppression of memory imposed by the Divine and your master guides so that you can avoid discomfort—an amnesic block. How else can you be truly tested? Life *is* the test. You are not given the answers beforehand, although you are often provided with clues and inspirations that encourage you to stay on track. You must make fresh choices without the benefit of knowing that, at each crossroad, you are being observed and evaluated; you either progress or are held back based on your reactions and responses."

"But what are we being evaluated *on*?" I asked.

"We look to see what the *result* of your soul's previously stated intent for this lifetime is," he said. "Are you missing or avoiding opportunities for growth by being afraid to take risks, or taking paths that might damage you? Did you find your own inner power, then use that power wisely? Was your influence positive or corrupted by the need to dominate or exploit others? Were you led astray by the convictions of others, demonstrating no personal courage, or did you make original contributions? Are you allowing 'problems and obstacles' to detract you from your original commitment? Then there's the single most important question of all."

"Which is what?" I asked nervously.

"Are your decisions and your actions aligned with compassionate values and ideals? Or has fear diminished your capacity for courageous conviction?"

"Are you saying that I'll be punished if I don't demonstrate courageous and compassionate conviction of my values and ideals?"

"No one punishes you. But there are consequences when you allow fear or an addiction to power or money to continually submerge your values and ideals. It's much more painful than any imagined punishment."

"Consequences?"

"You will break your own heart."

"I don't understand what you mean by that."

"Yes you do. There is no greater pain than when your own heart is crying out to you, and you try to silence it, again and again."

"Then it breaks?"

"It weeps. The pain is extraordinary. That is, unless you have become so submerged by your mind's immature dominance that you are deaf, dumb, and blind to the goals of your soul. In that case, you are treading water, virtually wasting a lifetime."

"And I can prevent that kind of pain by listening to my heart?"

"By *feeling* its guidance and by remaining open to alternative solutions to life problems. Your heart yearns for the fullest expression possible from the deepest part of you. Its desires are inspired by your soul."

"I don't want to abandon the call of my heart."

"Then you must continually ask yourself an important question: Does fear or the desire to control others prevent you from making decisions or taking action in a compassionate way that would have you violate your values and ideals?"

"Why is it so difficult for us to stay true to our own hearts?"

"Because most of you have submerged your own truth for someone else's. Of course, you may *believe* that your truth is your own. You may *believe* you're upholding your *own* values and ideals, when instead, you're upholding someone else's, such as your parents', children's, spouses', or friends' values and ideals. A strong cultural belief is one of the hardest to overcome, even when it is false and disempowering."

"So if we remain true to our own hearts—and achieve our previously stated goals—then we will have lived satisfying lives?"

"Yes."

"Then we grow old and die?" I asked sarcastically.

"Let's just say that you cannot leave until you have passed on what you've learned—assuming, of course, that you've indeed learned something of value. That's also part of the agreement. Once you've mastered a major phase in your training, you agree to pass on what you've mastered. You cannot move on until you've completed that aspect of your agreement. You must demonstrate proficiency in helping others to overcome adversity and obstacles as part of your student teaching assignment."

"Are you saying that I am a student teacher?"

"We are teachers. You are still in training, otherwise you would no longer be incarnating."

"But suppose I don't learn anything that I'm supposed to, and I get to be eighty or ninety years old—then what?" I asked.

"In that case, your learning trials will be carried over to the next incarnation, and you'll repeat that level, so to speak. As I said, you can move as quickly or as slowly as you want. Among you, there are slow-learner souls and those who are on the fast track, and you're all mixed up together. That's precisely what makes Earth such a coveted environment for higher learning: Spiritually speaking, your kindergarteners are on the same playground with your PhDs.

"That's why there's such a grand opportunity for testing your progress. Sooner or later, each of you comes up against difficult people and difficult problems that challenge you to your core, that challenge you to respond with compassion, yet firm conviction. How you deal with difficult people and difficult problems demonstrates your mastery or the need for further counsel. If you lose yourself in emotional drama, you will lack the perspective of all that we are now discussing, and you'll call yourself 'victim.'"

"Are you saying that we will become aware of these ideas in the afterlife? Most people wouldn't believe that what you are saying is actually happening."

"Eventually failure in finding solutions to stubborn repetitive problems brings awareness over many lifetimes, which can begin to dissolve your blocked memory of past lives. The very definition of spiritual expansion means becoming aware of that which was previously unknown to you but is now known. Just because you are not aware of the grand plan of the universe doesn't mean that it's not in effect."

"Then *show* me the grand plan," I begged, suddenly desperate to understand the inner workings of the cosmos.

"When you can handle the truth of the universe, more will be made known to you. 'When the student is ready, the teacher will appear.'"

"That doesn't make sense," I objected. "I'm afraid *because* I don't understand. If you'd show me more so that I *could* understand, then I *wouldn't* be so afraid."

"No, you've got it backward," the elder replied in a serious tone. "You don't need to fully understand the rhyme and reasons for your trials to meet them with grace, courage, and compassion. But don't feel bad; almost everyone's got it backward."

"Meaning what?" I asked.

"When you really, truly grow *beyond fear*, allowing the call of your heart to guide your decisions and actions, *then* you will see more and know more so that you *can* truly understand."

"Well when will *that* happen?" I implored them. "You should try living in my life. It's *frightening*."

"Try curiosity instead of fear."

Suddenly, before I could respond further, I was sitting back on my bed at home, and the strange man was standing nearby.

He withdrew something from his lapel pocket. I expected that he would again offer me his business card; instead he took a deep-blue, velvet pouch from inside his jacket. As he handed it to me, he said, "We want you to have this."

"We?" I asked, surprised at his use of a plural pronoun since he was all alone. "You mean my elders, from my soul group?"

He nodded yes.

Happily reaching to accept the gift, I loosened a delicate, mustard-yellow drawstring and gently removed from the pouch a stunning wooden object slightly larger than the size of my hand. It was inlaid with bronze. Two wooden "Ts"— one larger than the other—were connected by one horizontal bar as if they were forming the letter "H," but the left vertical line was longer than the other. "What does it mean?" I asked.

"It's a symbol from long ago," he offered.

Strangely, his form seemed to be slowly fading away, becoming lighter and lighter until he was gone. Amazed at what I had witnessed, I said aloud, "This is amazing. I must have been gone half the night."

Opening the small drawer of my bedside table, I took another green marble out of the bag and dropped it into the large jar by my bedside. There were so many marbles inside that I was losing count.

Suddenly grabbing up the clock to verify the passage of time, I was astonished to see that the clock read 10:11 p.m.— only a single minute had elapsed! Impossible! How had a whole night's worth of experience transpired in a matter of seconds? This was a very upsetting development, because I felt that the lost hours would be the sole evidence of anything having actually occurred. But wait, I suddenly remembered the contents of the purple satchel.

Evidence! I thought, smiling happily at my prize, finally feeling victorious. I could hardly wait to show it to Peter and to tell him of my wondrous adventure with the elders and the tunnel of white light.

I jumped up, went into the bathroom, and looked in the mirror. I stood there for a moment staring at my reflection. "How do you have a near-death experience when you didn't die?" I asked myself, deeply puzzled as to how I had experienced all that I had.

I returned to my bed and held the satchel in my hand. Touched to have received a gift, but having no idea of its significance, I thanked the stranger out loud, even though he was no longer there, grateful for all that I had learned.

Chapter Eight

WHILE IT WAS ONLY yesterday that I accepted this position in Jeannette and Kent's house, my mind was still brimming with the memories of my early spiritual struggles and my current need to find a safe haven and a normal life again. I knocked on Kent Charles's door that first morning. It was day one of my brand-new job: 5:45 a.m. After the previous day's job interview, Kent had impressed on me the importance of arriving on time, because Jeannette's Alzheimer's required constant supervision. So I had done better than that and had arrived fifteen minutes early.

Expecting to see him dressed in a suit and tie ready to leave for the courthouse, I was surprised when the front door swung open, and he greeted me in jeans and a T-shirt.

"Hello," he said cheerily, motioning for me to come inside. "I know I told you I had to be in court this morning, but we had a difficult time last night. Under the circumstances, I thought it best if Jeannette sees her doctor this morning. The judge isn't going to like it, but I was about to call the courthouse and postpone the hearing."

"Is Jeannette okay?" I asked warily, looking around for any sign of his wife. Kent motioned for me to follow him into the kitchen.

"Yeah, she's doing better. With Alzheimer's, body control starts breaking down as the mind deteriorates. She keeps choking on her food, and she stumbles and falls more than ever. It upsets us both," he said with concern. "I phoned her doctor last night after a bad choking spell, and he said to bring her in first thing this morning."

"I'd be happy to take her to the doctor," I offered.

"That would be great," Kent replied, "but I'm not sure she'll let you."

Suddenly, an angry voice bellowed to us from down the hallway. "It's my car, and I'm driving it myself!" Jeannette yelled, entering the kitchen.

Both Kent and I turned to watch Jeannette stride angrily into the room. Dressed smartly in matching slacks and sweater and perfectly coiffed, she looked annoyed but determined. She marched over to the refrigerator and began to pull out eggs and butter, apparently preparing to make herself breakfast.

"Jeannette, this is Lisette," Kent said, introducing us for the second time in two days. "She's going to be working here, helping me with administrative stuff. If there's anything you need help with, I'm sure she'd be happy to—"

"I don't need help!" Jeannette snapped, avoiding my glance.

Kent sighed deeply, then took out his cell phone and punched in a number. After explaining his predicament to the court clerk, he clicked off and shook his head.

"I won't be able to postpone the hearing," he said, giving Jeannette a nervous glance. "I'd better hurry up and get ready before I'm held in contempt of court."

Jeannette ignored him and continued to butter a pan and make herself some scrambled eggs. Kent turned and walked back to his bedroom, and I stood in the kitchen unsure of what to do or say.

After pouring herself a glass of iced tea, Jeannette carried her plate of food to the table and sat down to eat. Wanting to make myself useful, I put the eggs and butter back into the refrigerator and started to wipe down the counter. At that moment, Kent called out from his bedroom, "Please help yourself to some breakfast. You've got a long day ahead of you."

"Can I fix you a breakfast burrito?" I called back to him.

"Yeah, thanks, that would be great. But I'm dashing out of here in three minutes."

While I quickly prepared Kent's breakfast, Jeannette ate her eggs in silence, stopping occasionally to glare in my direction. After rolling Kent's scrambled eggs in a burrito, I wrapped it and placed it in a lunch bag that I found in a bottom drawer.

Just then, Kent rushed into the kitchen wearing a blue pinstriped suit and red tie. He grabbed his briefcase, lunch bag, and cell phone, then stopped to kiss Jeannette goodbye.

"Give me back my cell phone," Jeannette said dryly to her husband.

"Jeannette, this isn't your phone; it's mine," Kent explained in a soft tone. He walked to the other end of the counter, unplugged another cell phone from the wall socket, then stepped back and handed it to Jeannette. "Here's yours," he said, kissing her goodbye again and giving her a hug.

As Kent headed out the front door, I noticed that he had left his phone on the table next to Jeannette. Despite her Alzheimer's, Jeannette was aware of her surroundings and had spotted Kent's phone on the table. She quickly picked it up and walked out the sliding glass doors to the patio, coveting her prize. I, in turn, walked briskly out the front door and called to Kent as he backed his car out of the garage. "If you need your cell phone, Jeannette took it out to the pool."

Kent stopped the car, jumped out, and ran into the house. He grabbed Jeannette's cell phone off the table, then hurried out the sliding-glass door in pursuit of his wife. She had gone around to the far side of the Jacuzzi and was guarding the phone, obviously afraid that Kent would take it from her. I stood back watching the scene, not sure how I could help.

"Jeannette," Kent cajoled her in his most pleasant tone, "I told you, that's *my* cell phone." He slowly approached her. "Here's yours. Let's trade." At that moment, he lost his balance and fell into the Jacuzzi. He brought his left knee up to break his fall, and his knee hit the edge of the Jacuzzi, followed by a loud groan. Kent grabbed his knee, clearly in great pain, and steadied himself, waist-deep on one leg, the water soaking his very expensive suit.

Jeannette and I both ran around the Jacuzzi to come to his aid. Amazingly, he still held Jeannette's phone in his hand, fuming but speechless, and rubbing his painful knee with his free hand.

"Are you okay?" I asked him, looking around the poolside for a towel. Sheepishly, Jeannette handed him his cell phone and took hers, clearly not quite understanding the sequence of events that had caused his fall but seeming to understand that she'd had something to do with it.

Kent slid the phone into his wet jacket pocket, and Jeannette and I helped him out of the Jacuzzi and onto a nearby lawn chair.

"Please get me some ice," he said in a pained voice. "There's some in the freezer." Jeannette and I rushed into the kitchen and piled ice cubes into a large baggie. After I sealed the bag tight, Jeannette grabbed it from me in annoyance, then headed outside to give it to her husband.

Two hours later, Jeannette and I sat at opposite ends of Kent's doctor's waiting room; she glared at me from across the suite. I wondered if she was thinking that Kent's accident was my fault, that if only they'd been left alone, none of this would have happened. Just then, the door to the examination room opened and out hobbled Kent, wearing a leg brace from his thigh to his ankle and leaning on crutches.

Meeting our shocked expressions, Kent said sadly, "My patella is fractured."

Jeannette rushed to give him a hug, and I stood back in shock, wondering if I had taken on too much with this job.

Kent's doctor came out and handed him a prescription. "This is for pain. You'll have to take it easy," he said. "No golf until further notice."

Kent groaned.

"When the swelling goes down, you'll have to start physical therapy. I know you're a busy lawyer Kent, but find a way to lighten your load, will you?" the doctor pleaded, glancing from Kent to Jeannette and back again. "Do you have somebody who can help you at home?" the doctor asked earnestly.

"Yes," Kent replied, pointing in my direction. "This is her first day on the job. I hope she doesn't quit on us."

I sheepishly shook my head.

With some effort, the two of us helped Kent hobble down the hallway, into the elevator, and down to the parking structure. When the valet pulled up the car, Jeannette grabbed the keys from the attendant and rushed to sit in the driver's seat. The car was a two-door Mercedes coup with a small backseat. I wondered about the seating arrangement now that Kent had broken his knee.

"Jeannette, Lisette is going to drive the car, okay?" Kent said.

Jeannette didn't respond but started the engine. Raising my eyebrows, I looked at Kent in dismay, wondering what would happen next.

Leaning on his crutches and grimacing in pain, Kent took a deep breath and tried again. "Jeannette, I'm not getting in the car until you get out of the driver's seat."

Furious, Jeannette turned off the engine, leaped out of the car, and threw the car keys at Kent. He grabbed them in midair. Nothing was wrong with his reflexes. He then handed me the keys and said, "Get in the driver's seat, please."

I did as I was told and awaited my next direction.

Seeing me in her coveted driver's seat, Jeannette started yelling. "Why does she get to drive?" she cried in anguish.

Kent responded firmly but calmly. "Jeannette, please get into the backseat and let's get me home."

With that, Jeannette stomped around to the other side of the car and sat down in the front passenger's seat, slamming the car door behind her and leaving Kent outside. I started to get out of the car myself, but Kent told me to stay put.

"Jeannette, please get into the backseat."

"No, *you* get in the backseat," Jeannette said in rebuff.

Yelling now and clearly in a great deal of pain, Kent bellowed, "I can't get in the back because I can't bend my knee!"

Considering this for a moment, Jeannette looked at Kent's leg brace; then in anger, she flung open the car door and reluctantly climbed into the backseat. After gingerly easing himself into the passenger's seat and closing the door, Kent turned to me and said, "Let's go home."

Later that day, I made some lunch for Kent and carried it into his bedroom, where he sat upright in bed with his knee propped up on a pile of pillows. Legal pads and papers lay strewn around him in piles as he read a legal brief and used a yellow highlighter to mark it up. As I handed him a tray with the plate of food and a glass of iced tea, he gratefully accepted it and put aside his brief to take a break and eat his lunch.

"The judge granted me a postponement after all," he said with a grin. "As soon as the swelling goes down, I'll be back to court and out of your hair."

"That's okay," I said. "But what shall I do with Jeannette? She won't talk to me, much less allow me to help her."

"I know," Kent replied. "Just try to keep an eye on her and do the best you can. I've got a ton of work to do, and my leg hurts like hell." Raising his glass, he saluted me with great flourish and said, "General, I'm leaving you in charge."

I closed the door to Kent's bedroom and returned to the kitchen where Jeannette was sitting at the table eating a small cheese quesadilla. "May I join you?" I asked her, wondering if she would ever grow to accept me in her home.

Surprising me, she nodded; before she could change her mind, I sat down opposite her. Just after Jeannette took a bite of her snack, she began to cough as though she were choking on her food. I jumped up from the table and rushed to her side. Despite her loud coughing, Jeannette swatted me away furiously, continuing to sputter and cough as though gasping for breath. To my dismay, she grabbed the glass of iced tea and took a big gulp before I could stop her, which doubled the logjam in her throat.

Her throat rejected the additional load, and she spurted iced tea and food all over the table. Relieved that I didn't have to attempt the Heimlich maneuver, and speaking without really thinking, I said, "Your doctor wanted to see you this morning for a checkup, and for this very reason."

Still coughing but recovering from the worst of it, Jeannette shot me a harsh glance as though remembering something. She now stood up, strode over to the counter, and fumbled through Kent's jacket pocket. She pulled out the car keys, grabbed her purse, and headed out the front door.

"Where are you going?" I called after her, jumping up myself and grabbing my purse, knowing exactly what she had in mind.

Ignoring me, Jeannette hurried off to the garage, pushed a button on the wall for the garage door, and jumped inside the coupe, starting the engine. As she backed out of the garage, I froze, not knowing what to do or how to stop her. My mind raced through all the possible solutions. If I stood in her way, I had a feeling that she would simply mow me down. As I yelled for her to stop, she ignored me, and shifting the car into drive, she peeled rubber out of the driveway.

What am I supposed to do now? I asked myself, confused and bewildered at how my "normal job" had turned into another trying test with the most difficult person yet. By this point in my spiritual journey, I realized that this was no coincidence but was motivated by what is called the goals of the soul. It was important for me to apply what I had learned from my guides and to develop a firm spiritual practice that would allow me to find inner peace despite the problematic people and challenging circumstances in my midst. I had learned to be open to alternative solutions to my problems. I had been told that all the difficult people in my life were part of a previous agreement to teach me something important.

With new resolve, I got into my own car and started the engine. Flying after her down the hill toward Pacific Coast Highway, I had no idea how her compulsion to drive was going to help my soul to "grow and mature." But it's all okay, I thought. Somehow, in some way, all of this would later make sense. As I caught up to Jeannette on the road, I could see her look back at me in the coupe's rearview mirror, then she flipped me the bird out the window.

"Just great," I said to myself, careening around one corner after another, smiling in spite of myself, while trying to keep up with the speed demon in front of me. This is one heck of a soul agreement, I thought, hoping that I was up to the task.

As our cars wound down the two-mile-long hill and approached a stoplight ahead of us, I began to worry. Would she run a red light? Barely able to keep up with her, I followed closely behind as she slowed down at the light. After stopping only for a second and before the light turned green, she veered her car to the right and ventured onto Pacific Coast Highway.

I made the turn myself; now in hot pursuit on a busy four-lane highway and having no idea where she was going or what she had in mind, I kept her car in sight, hoping that the traffic would stay light and that no pedestrians would cross her path.

Two miles down the highway, she slowed down and pulled into the left-hand lane, clearly intending to turn into the large shopping center. I followed her into the parking lot as she drove around, apparently looking for a place to park.

She exited her car, and I watched her from a safe distance until I could figure out where she was heading. Then, as she quickly ducked inside a grocery store, I parked my car and ran across the parking lot and into the store after her. Circling the aisles of the market, I looked for her in vain, until suddenly I discovered her pushing a grocery cart down the candy aisle. I grabbed a cart of my own, and we met halfway down the aisle. I stopped, joining her nonchalantly as she selected one candy bar after another, piling them into her cart. I did the same.

Discovering me standing next to her, Jeannette stared at me as though remembering my face from somewhere but not able to place it. Then she smiled and wheeled her cart down the aisle. I followed after her. As she passed the stationary aisle, she stopped and sorted through a selection of colored paper and crayons, made a few selections, then placed them along the shelf to inspect them more carefully.

Catching up with her again, I, too, made selections of the very same items. Suddenly, she looked over at me and the contents of my cart, then to hers, and smiled.

"Hi, Jeannette," I said in as casual a tone as I could muster, as though we were great friends who had just bumped into each other.

"Hi," she responded in return. At that moment, another customer passed us, pushing her own cart down the aisle. I moved my cart to the side to give her room to pass. Jeannette studied the woman for a moment, then in a loud voice said, "There goes a *fat* puppy!"

At that, the other woman spun around, despite her large frame, saw Jeannette and me looking at her—my mouth had dropped open—and charged down the aisle toward us as though she were about to strike Jeannette.

Stepping in front of my ward to protect her from the charging linebacker, I implored the woman earnestly. "She didn't mean it," I said to the stranger, ready to start a fist-fight in the coloring book aisle of the local grocery store. Then leaning forward, I whispered in the woman's ear. "She's got Alzheimer's. I'm so sorry."

Glaring at Jeannette, then at me, the woman spun her cart around and charged off down the aisle, shaking her head.

I looked over at Jeannette, who simply looked back at me, and I wondered if she had any awareness of what she had just provoked. I was trying to ascertain the degree of Jeannette's disability, but because I did not know her nor did I know the nuances of Alzheimer's, it was a mystery to me as to what Jeannette was likely to do next or what I should do. We stood there for a few seconds, continuing to make eye contact.

"So you like to color with crayons?" I asked her hopefully, remembering that my mission was to gain her confidence and steal her car keys.

Jeannette nodded, smiling at me. "Well then, let's buy some coloring books, shall we?" I said, grabbing several of each and dropping them into each of our carts. I could see Jeannette's car keys sticking out from a side pocket in her purse, and I hatched a plot.

Distracting Jeannette, I pointed across the aisle at a colorful set of markers. "Hey, look, Jeannette, let's get a packet of those markers, okay?" Falling for my ruse, Jeannette took a few steps away from her cart to reach the markers on the far shelf. When her back was turned, I gingerly grabbed the car keys out of her purse and placed them inside my pants pocket with my own set of car keys.

Satisfied with her selections, Jeannette pushed her cart down the aisle toward the checkout counter. I followed close behind with my own cart, relieved that she hadn't noticed that her keys were missing.

As we neared the counter, Jeannette tripped. Instinctively, she grabbed on to the side of her shopping cart, but it couldn't withstand her entire weight. To my horror, Jeannette and her cart tumbled noisily and bumped into a large display of boxed crackers, which cascaded on top of her. I rushed over to help her up, but Jeannette swatted me away. She was furious, but now crying and confused.

"It's okay, Jeannette, don't worry about the crackers. Are you all right? Here, let me help you up." As I righted her grocery cart and bent over to pick up its contents, I heard the sound of something drop to the floor. Jeannette heard it too. There, on the floor next to her, lay two sets of car keys, which Jeannette grabbed with all the speed and treachery of a hawk snatching its prey. Glaring at me as though intuiting my evil motive, she clambered up off the floor and, with renewed determination, pushed her cart up to the cashier.

In dismay, realizing my fatal error in dropping both sets of keys, I followed after her, placing my selections on the conveyor belt behind hers. When the cashier completed ringing up Jeannette's items, she said aloud, "Sixty-seven, ninety-three."

Smiling at her, Jeannette nodded, reached for her wallet at the bottom of her purse, opened it up, and handed her a five-dollar bill.

The cashier patiently accepted the five and waited for more. Jeannette smiled.

The cashier waited.

A long line of customers in line behind us watched the transaction with curiosity.

Suddenly realizing that Jeannette had lost the ability to count money, I opened my purse and handed the cashier a pile of bills, which Jeannette angrily intercepted, grabbing it herself with a loud protest. "This is *my* stuff!" Jeannette said loudly.

"I know. I'm just helping you pay for it," I responded, noticing the cashier's confused expression. Considering that Jeannette looked so youthful, was dressed so smartly, and carried herself with so much authority, no one would have imagined that she was suffering from the late stages of early-onset Alzheimer's disease.

Thrusting the money at the cashier, Jeannette scowled at me, waiting for the bagger to place her things in a carryout bag. When he handed it to her, she snatched it from him, as though he were complicit in undermining her efforts. With a strange glance at me, the bagger stepped out of her way as Jeannette stormed passed him, heading for the door and the parking lot outside.

Realizing that Jeannette had both our car keys, I ditched my cart, my items still on the conveyor belt, and raced after her, calling her name. "Jeannette, wait! Please, stop!"

Ignoring me, Jeannette opened the trunk of her car and put her bag inside. Gleefully hopping into the driver's seat, she started the engine and squealed out of the parking lot, leaving me standing there in the midday sun.

Chapter Nine

PERFECTLY MANICURED, MAGNIFICENT beach houses zoomed past as I gazed at the opulent setting from the backseat of the taxi.

"Turn left here," I instructed the driver; we exited Pacific Coast Highway and headed up the hill toward Kent and Jeannette's house. I had failed my first mission of this job by allowing my charge to leave me stranded in a parking lot, and I now felt embarrassed and humiliated. What would Kent say? I wondered.

Nothing I could do about it now, I told myself, prepared to accept the consequences of my poor performance. Jeannette was a handful, I now realized ever so clearly. Spiritual fast track or not, what had I been thinking to take on the full-time job of caregiver on top of that of estate manager? What did I know about Alzheimer's and brain disease?

My head now in my hands, sad and frustrated at my predicament, I leaned back against the car seat, wondering what my next step would be. I might have to find other work, even if Kent didn't immediately fire me. I really didn't sign up for this.

Then I recalled the little speech I had given myself only an hour earlier about soul goals. Perhaps there was indeed another way to view my present circumstances. I had once learned that there was always another perspective available to those who suffer—namely *me* at that moment—when faced with a "problem" that's causing mental suffering. "Okay, how can I put this into a different context? What can I learn from Jeannette?" I asked myself out loud, challenging my own assumptions. "What is the appropriate way to respond?"

"What's that?" the taxi driver asked, calling to me over his shoulder. Embarrassed, I now realized that my private musings had spilled into his ear space.

"Oh, it's nothing, really," I responded, sighing deeply. "I've had an opportunity to learn a few things over the years, but *applying* those teachings in real life is a different matter altogether," I said, chagrined at my status as a failed caregiver.

"Gimme an example," the driver said, smiling broadly at me in his rearview mirror.

"Do your behaviors and actions demonstrate that you care about others?" I asked him in response. "Do you engage in service to others? Do you feel compassion for others?"

The cabbie nodded his head thoughtfully, as though pondering my words.

"That's what I'm asking myself right now," I said. "While in my care at the grocery store, my Alzheimer's patient ditched me and drove her car home alone. I know that these kinds of predicaments can serve as spiritual lessons, so I'm sitting here wondering just how it might apply to me right now."

"You sound like my old philosophy teacher," he said, chuckling.

"Well, this is real-life stuff, not just theory. Each of us is accountable for our behavior. They'll be looking to see if we maintain the immortal character of our soul and its integrity in terms of values, ideals, and actions."

"They?" asked the driver. "Who're we talking about? You mean God?"

"The wise ones who watch over us. They're divinely inspired."

The cab driver shook his head as he pulled up to the front door. "If you say so. That'll be fifteen dollars and thirty cents, lady."

After paying the driver, I shuffled my feet across the wide driveway and knocked on the oversized front door. Taking a deep breath, I waited for Kent to open the door and fire me.

The big door swung open and Jeannette stood there. We faced each other for a moment. I smiled at her and was delighted to see her smile back at me. Extraordinarily relieved, I took a step toward the threshold when the front door was slammed hard in my face.

"How's your first day going?" I heard from behind me.

I whirled around to discover Kent standing in the driveway. He was smiling wryly and leaning uncomfortably on his crutches. "Challenging in many ways," I said, shaking my head. "Sorry for the snafu."

Kent tipped back his head and laughed. "Sounds par for the course around here." I nodded my head. "So what do you two have planned for the rest of today?" he asked, looking directly at me.

Momentarily surprised by his gracious response, I quickly collected myself and said, "Well, I confirmed her doctor's appointment for this afternoon; after that, I thought we'd get a bite to eat," I replied hopefully, recognizing an opportunity to redeem myself. Then I remembered that my car was still stranded at the grocery store.

"First, I've got to get my car," I said woefully, chagrined to be requesting help from him.

"Don't worry. I'll send a tow truck to retrieve it," Kent said, waving off that issue as relatively unimportant. "You've got enough on your plate. Your car will be here when you get back."

Just then, the front door swung open again, and Jeannette appeared, hands on her hips, her large purse dangling over her shoulder.

"Jeannette loves bike riding," Kent said, grinning at both of us, as though waiting for just the right moment to spring this new idea on me. Then, looking directly at his wife, he said firmly, "After your checkup with Dr. Kantor, you gals can hit the bike path." He handed me a sheet of paper and the keys to Jeannette's car. "Here's all the contact info you'll need, including her doctor's address. Don't be late."

At that moment, the sound of the telephone ringing could be heard in the foyer. "Sorry, I'm working at home until the swelling goes down. You're on your own." With that, he hobbled inside the house and closed the door behind him.

"Okay, let's get going," I said to Jeannette. Without waiting for her response, I walked through the side door of the garage and pushed the button to open the large garage door. Noticing two bicycles standing nearby, I quickly wheeled them over to the car, placed them on the bike rack, and strapped them down. As Jeannette continued to glare at me in stunned silence, I opened the coupe's door, slipped inside, and closed it. "Come on, Jeannette, let's go."

"That's my car!" Jeannette yelled at me angrily, pounding her fist hard against the passenger's side window.

Undeterred, I spoke to her calmly. "I can either drive your car, or we can take the bus to get mine." I paused to let her consider these alternatives. "Sorry, Jeannette, you can't drive—doctor's orders—but I'll take you anywhere you want to go."

Jeannette stood there fuming, not moving at all. I considered my options, then slowly backed the car out of the garage onto the driveway, shifted it into drive, and inched forward, so she'd know I meant business.

Intent on remaining calm, I looked back at Jeannette with a neutral expression, allowing her to realize that I would not engage in a screaming match with her. "You can stay here if you want, but I think you'll get awfully bored. As for me, I'm heading into town for lunch, then I'm going bike riding along the beach."

The car idled while I waited for her to decide. She soon recognized that the last thing she wanted to do was to be stuck at home with nothing to do.

Jeannette now charged up to the car, then begrudgingly swung open the car door and slumped into the seat. She buckled her seat belt, then crossed her arms in a huff. Without a word, we drove off, heading down the hill to Pacific Coast Highway. As we stopped at a red light, Jeannette barked at me. "Get going," she said, angry that I had stopped the car.

"It's a red light. Just as soon as it turns green, we'll go."

With great force, Jeannette angrily slapped her hand on the dashboard, and I jumped in my seat in surprise. The light turned green, and I drove off breathing slowly and deeply.

Jeannette unbuckled her seat belt.

"We've got to keep our seat belts buckled," I said in a firm but calm voice. "Please put it back on."

Jeannette ignored me, took a gulp of water from a plastic bottle, pushed the button that lowered her window, then tossed the plastic bottle outside.

My mouth dropped open, and I glanced over at her. She was determined and defiant. My head leant back in dismay, and I breathed slowly and deliberately, pulling the car over to the side of the road and stopping.

"What are you doing?" Jeannette bellowed at me. "Why are we stopping?"

Without saying a word, I removed the car keys, stepped out of the car, walked down the highway to pick up the plastic bottle, and came back. Cars whizzed by us, not slowing at all, as I stood next to the car. I tossed the bottle onto the back floorboard, got back in, and looked at Jeannette. "No littering," I said. "Also, you're going to have to buckle your seat belt."

"Get the car going!" Jeannette yelled at me, again slapping her open hand on the dashboard, more furious than ever.

I reclined in my seat as if I were thoroughly relaxed. "It's the law. You have to buckle up. While you're with me, I'm responsible for your safety."

In response, Jeannette crossed her arms as if to say that she'd rather die than buckle up.

I gazed out the window at the ocean that lay just beyond our reach. Since we were parked on the shoulder of the Pacific Coast Highway, the ocean waves lay just a few hundred feet from our car. White seagulls and brown pelicans were swooping over the water, darting to catch small fish, then soaring again into the sky.

"We're so lucky to live here," I said to Jeannette, admiring the expansive beauty of the Pacific ocean. "Look out there," I said, pointing to the gulls and the pelicans dive-bombing into the sea. Despite herself, Jeannette smiled, surfacing for a moment from the mental chaos of her misfiring brain synapses.

Without speaking, Jeannette buckled her seat belt. I had learned my first lesson on how nature could offset some of the effects of her disease.

I started the car.

Half an hour later, we were sitting on the other side of a large oak desk. Dr. John Kantor flipped through a medical chart, then peered at Jeannette over his bifocals. "Jeannette, how've you been feeling?"

Jeannette snapped back, "Fine."

Directing his questions to me, the doctor asked, "Any problems?"

"Well, uh, she's been choking on her food and tripping a lot. She took a fall earlier this morning." Jeannette glared at me, apparently not wanting me to speak for her.

"Yes, that's all pretty typical at this stage," the doctor said in a somber tone. "Start switching to a liquid diet. Protein drinks, milk shakes, yogurt. As for the tripping, do the best you can. Take her arm when the surface is uneven. Sorry, but a decline in motor skills is inevitable." Turning to Jeannette and pushing back his big chair to stand up, he said, "Come on, Jeannette, let me take a look at you."

He walked around to her chair. Using a small medical flashlight, he shone it in her eyes while giving her instructions. "Look up to the ceiling, please." Jeannette looked up. "Now look down at your shoes. Good job."

Then, taking a few items out of his white coat pocket, he held the first item up to his patient. "Jeannette, what is this?" he asked, showing her a simple ballpoint pen.

"It's a . . ." Jeannette cleared her throat. "It's a . . . thing that you write with," she said matter-of-factly.

"Good, now tell me, what is this?" the doctor asked her, holding up his wristwatch. "That's a clock," she said, pointing to it and smiling.

"Excellent," the doctor responded. "Now tell me, Jeannette, do you know what month it is?" Jeannette thought for a moment. "Of course," she said with an irritated tone. "It's November 20, 1942!" she said emphatically.

"Well done," Dr. Kantor replied. "That's your birthday, isn't it?" he asked, smiling at her. "You've got that date down pat," he said, winking at me.

"Now stand up, Jeannette," he helped her to a standing position. "I want you to walk across the room for me. Just take your time and walk slowly."

After a few strides, it became obvious that Jeannette's left foot dragged behind ever so slightly. I hadn't noticed it before. The doctor made eye contact with me, as though wanting me to understand the reason for her instability when walking.

Dr. Kantor pulled a walker over to Jeannette. "Here, why don't you try holding on to this as you walk. It will help steady you."

"I hate that thing!" Jeannette said defiantly, shaking her head and walking back to her chair, sitting down with a thump.

Dr. Kantor shrugged his shoulders and looked at me. "You can only do what you can do," he said, writing notes in the medical chart. "I'll see you in three months, okay, Jeannette?"

Walking us to the door, Dr. Kantor smiled and said to me, "Call me with any questions. Please give my regards to Kent."

Now back in the car, I asked Jeannette if she wanted to go to lunch and she agreed. After eating quiche at a small French café, Jeannette surprised me:

"Ready to go bike riding," she said with a smile. I was thrilled that we seemed to be making some progress. We drove out of the parking structure and headed toward the beach.

Twenty minutes later, we pulled into the parking lot of Temescal State Beach and parked the car. Famous for a long, uninterrupted bike path that was situated along the bluff above the sand, Temescal's path attracted bike riders from all over L.A.'s Westside.

We unloaded the bikes. I handed Jeannette a helmet and strapped my own helmet onto my head. Jeannette threw hers back into the car. "Jeannette, you've got to wear a helmet, for your own safety. Look, I'm wearing one, too."

Ignoring me, Jeannette grabbed her bike, jumped on it, and started peddling away. Jumping on my bike, I rode after her, calling to her from behind. "Jeannette, we've got to ride on the bike path, not through the parking lot!" Veering my bike up onto the narrow path that swept along the bluff and followed the Santa Monica coastline for miles, I was relieved when Jeannette followed my lead.

The bike path was divided in half to allow for two directions of travel, but Jeannette would not stay in her own lane. Several other bike riders approached us from the opposite direction and swerved sharply to avoid hitting her. "Jeannette, stay on this side with me, okay?" I asked.

Annoyed that I was giving her directions, she steered her bike off the path altogether, and rode into the middle of the parking lot. Following along behind her, I was now frantic. Cars drove quickly past her, beeping their horns, annoyed that some crazy bike rider couldn't stay on the path.

"Get out of the way!" a male driver yelled at her out of his window, just missing Jeannette as she crossed directly in front of his moving car.

I sped up to catch her and pulled alongside, breathless from the hard peddling. "Jeannette, please move over with me to the bike path. We're in the parking lot. This is for cars only!" Jeannette ignored me, peddling all the harder.

Becoming angry myself, I yelled after her, "Jeannette! Listen to me, *please!*"

As we both tore down the incline of the huge parking lot, cars passing us on both sides, I could hear these words from long ago echoing in my mind.

"Earth is one of the most difficult of all learning environments for the incarnating soul. It's a chaotic physical dimension; that's why it's one of the most coveted places of learning available. Free will is your great freedom, but you're still responsible for what you choose. Faulty decision-making is always honored."

The meaning of the words swirled around inside me, and I relaxed a bit on my bicycle, surrendering to the chaos of my present predicament. I was directly behind Jeannette, still peddling furiously to keep up with her, but I breathed more deeply now, realizing that I could not control her, not right now. I would do the best that I could to keep her safe, but I was just one person. Jeannette, too, had been endowed with the freedom of choice and faulty decision-making, even if her muddled brain was not capable of choosing wisely.

Suddenly, I veered sharply to the side, pulled up, and got off my bike. I looked calmly at Jeannette riding away. Noticing that I was no longer chasing her, she slowed down and also came to a stop. She walked her bike toward me. I smiled at her, and we stood there next to our bikes. I had learned another lesson: Don't react to her willful displays or get drawn into them; it only feeds her rebellion.

Again I replayed the words in my mind, "Earth is the most difficult of all learning environments," and I thought back to the most traumatic period in my young life and how my strange dance with Peter had led me down the dark path where I found my own tunnel of light.

Chapter Ten

THE STRANGE VISITOR, George Graysuff; the tunnel of light; and the wise council of elders were still on my mind as I lay in bed contemplating all that had occurred. How had I survived a seeming near-death experience without having died? The wise elders' words of wisdom and the lifelike videos they had shown me of my childhood were almost too amazing to believe. How could it be true that we actually choose beforehand our own soul group and the main cast of characters who will make up the primary people in our lives?

I closed the mustard drawstring of the purple satchel that contained the special wood and bronze talisman and tucked it under my pillow. With that, I settled down to sleep, patting the lump under my pillow where the velvet pouch was hidden.

The next morning, I was straightening the bedroom when I heard the sound of Peter's voice as he opened the front door. I could hardly wait to tell him about my mysterious trip down the tunnel of light, and how I had lived to tell him about it.

"I thought that you were going to be away for a week," I said to Peter, surprised but delighted to see him. Finally, here was my chance to show him the recent evidence of my nighttime escapades. I rushed out to greet him with a happy kiss.

"I'm so excited that I can finally share this with you," I said, pulling him back to the bedroom. "Last night, this guy came to visit; he wasn't a human being but a special visitor from I don't know where, and he . . ."

I trailed off. Peter's concerned expression alerted me to just how nonsensical I must have sounded. I tried a different tack.

"Look, a lot has been happening over the past two years. It all started with your out-of-town business trips. These crazy bright lights and this electric zapping sensation would wake me up from a dead sleep. Sometimes I see a beautiful, aqua-blue burst of light that shines in the room, only to immediately disappear."

"What are you talking about?" Peter asked me, frowning. "Are you still having those nightmares?"

"Have you ever heard of a near-death experience?" I asked him, noticing his startled expression. "Sometimes it starts out like that, except I never died. Somehow I'm straddling other dimensions, going behind a veil of some sort."

"You're not making any sense, as usual," Peter said, walking away from me.

"Wait, I want to show you something," I said, taking his hand again. "The sound of my experiences is super loud, and, initially, I was terrified, but I soon got used to it and would fall back to sleep afterward. Then came the next thing . . . these two guys arrived at night wearing FBI-type badges, and they told me that Dr. Helman—and all of us, for that matter—are accountable for what we do and for what we don't do."

"What are you getting at?" Peter barked defensively.

"The visits have been unrelenting for two years, but also, they have some ability to take me with them to other dimensions. I know, it sounds nuts."

"Yes, I agree with you for a change," Peter said.

"Let me finish, *please*," I begged Peter, and he allowed me to continue. "Every time something mysterious happens, I add a green marble to my jar to keep track. Then, just last night, this new guy appeared to tell me I haven't been eating that much—which is true—and . . . well, I didn't want to leave with him, but he showed me Walter, and he seemed just fine, so I went down this tunnel of bright light to another realm where I met the elders, and they recommended—"

Losing his patience and now horrified at my words, Peter's frozen expression said it all. "You sound absolutely crazy," he said.

"I know, I know, it sounds too weird, and at one point, I consulted with a professional ghost-buster of sorts, but look . . ." I stepped over to the bed. "Right here under my pillow, finally, the proof that I need to show you that it's all real . . ."

The pouch was gone. Throwing the pillow aside, then the sheets and blankets, I started ripping all the bedding off the mattress in a fury, certain that it had been misplaced in my sleep. When only the bare mattress was left, Peter could only shake his head in dismay.

Not knowing what to say, I could only collapse on the bed as Peter walked slowly from the room, calling over his shoulder, "I'm not sleeping here tonight." The last thing I heard was him slamming the front door as he left the condominium.

Pausing to catch my breath, I stood up and looked around at the mess I had made, then sank into a chair, dumbstruck. Either I was going mad, or some parade of paranormal phenomena, visions, or otherworldly beings were making a home of my bedroom. I would have to approach this predicament systematically, I thought. First things first. For now, I would take the position that I had seen something real. If that were the case, then it was best for my sanity and best for my marriage that I get it to stop—but how?

On the other hand, if I really had a serious mental problem with psychotic delusions, then ultimately I was facing the end of my life as I knew it: Peter would leave me; my son would be taken from me, and I would not be able to provide for myself and be a self-reliant, responsible person. My old age might even find me homeless and delusional.

In the meantime, my first priority was to turn my homestead back into a normal living environment where aliens and time travelers were kept at bay. Although there may have been several ways to address this transition, first I would exhaust Laura's solutions. Psychics may not be perfect, but neither were my options, and I didn't dare tell my strange story to my doctor or my friend Debra. My second-rate ghost-buster was all that I had.

I picked up the phone and dialed her number. "Laura, I know it's been a while, but I need to see you. It's kind of an emergency. Can you come over?"

We met in my living room later that evening. Laura and I sipped our tea while I described my experiences since the last time I had seen her.

"I've begun reading Psalm 23 again, like you said before, but to tell you the truth, nothing seems to change, back then or now. In fact, if anything, things are stranger than ever. Peter thinks I'm crazy, and, to tell you the truth, I'm not so sure myself. Either I have an extraordinary imagination, or my mind is playing tricks on me, and I can't tell the difference between fantasy and reality. *That's the part that upsets me the most.* The visions are becoming friendly enough, but suppose they're a result of some personality disorder. How can I know for sure?"

"Frankly, you *cannot* know until you first do a full-blown exorcism of your house," Laura said in an authoritative tone.

"You've consulted with the right person. It's my expertise," she smiled confidently. Standing up, she waived her hand around the room as if daring the evil spirits to take her on, and said, "Let's get started."

"The first thing to know is that there are no half measures here. You have to confront what you don't want to consider. That's why, in your case, Psalm 23 didn't work. You have to be brave and really face down demonic influences that threaten your sanity. You have to mean business. Intention is everything."

"Okay. What do I have to do?" I asked her earnestly. "I really don't think that I can keep going on like this."

"I understand," Laura nodded, agreeing with me. "But if you keep waiting, doing nothing, they'll next attack your son. If you think *you're* confused and upset, how do you think a little child will be able to cope with all that hysteria?"

"Yes, that's exactly what I'm afraid of," I said, remembering Walter's art class masterpiece. "What do we do first?" I asked again.

"Well, you need to pay me another two hundred dollars," Laura said without blinking an eye.

Upset at hearing her price to help me, I balked, leaning back in my chair. "I can't afford your rates."

"I can't work for free," Laura said. "I've got my own husband to answer to and child to support."

"I don't know," I replied, imagining what Peter would do to me if I bounced another check.

"It's your life," Laura said, impatiently, collecting her things to leave. "You can try other methods, like moving from your apartment, but at some point you'll have to confront them head on to protect you and your child."

"Okay," I said, desperate for a solution to my nightmare. Whatever the cost, it was money well spent. I fumbled through my purse for my checkbook, then scribbled out a check and handed it to her.

"All right then," she said smiling, folding the check and tucking it into her purse. "An effective exorcism means that you'll need to take frequent salt baths. In addition, light incense and candles and keep them burning in each room of the house—and keep them lit twenty-four/seven for protection. Go out and buy everything right now to stop their momentum. Then call me tonight before you go to sleep—"

At that moment, a very subtle electromagnetic pulsing erupted in the living room. I froze, and Laura's wide-eyed expression showed that she felt it too!

"It's here!" I said breathlessly, jumping up from my seat on the couch and rushing to sit next to Laura for protection. "What do we do now?" I asked her, my eyes darting all over the room.

As though caught off guard, Laura seemed to be startled, but rapidly regained her composure. "Don't panic," she instructed. "This is your house, not theirs. You've got to demonstrate who's in control."

"Okay," I replied, returning to the couch and awaiting my next instruction, thankful that my expert was right here in the room with me.

The vibrations greatly intensified, and Laura's long hair was suddenly brushed aside as though a breeze was blowing through the living room. Clearly alarmed and without saying a word, Laura jumped up, grabbed her purse and ran out the front door before I could stop her. After following her outside, my loud protests were answered by the sound of her car's ignition starting up as she sped out of the parking lot. Gulping, it took me a few moments before I returned to the living room, confounded by her retreat.

I didn't know what else to do, and so I rummaged through an old closet until I found my stash of candles and incense, then carefully laid them all out, lighting all of them. This caused a soft glow to emanate from every room in the condo.

My heart was racing, and after checking that Walter was still asleep, I fell into bed frightened, confused, and yet thankful that Peter was staying at his friend's house.

I scooted down under the covers, alarmed that my long nightmare was nowhere near its end, and worried that my *son* might still be confronting his own nocturnal drama.

At that moment, the paranormal firestorm started up again. A strong electromagnetic surge permeated the room, and bright lights burst through the ceiling. The lit candle on my bedside did not flicker one bit. Despite my alarm, and feeling increasingly sleepier, I crawled out of bed and into my clothes closet. The long coats draped over me and glossy boxes of shoes now became my pillow. My eyes closed, and I went deeper and deeper, despite my best efforts, until I could feel myself falling asleep.

Early the next morning, I became vaguely aware of someone shouting my name.

"Lisette!"

I walked to the bedroom door, cracked it open, and peeked out. Peter was standing in the living room viewing the array of lit candles and burning incense bowls and fuming. He picked up a candle and went to throw it against the wall but hit the side window and broke it. Shattered glass flew everywhere. I closed the bedroom door and heard him calling the police and reporting a domestic dispute. Afterward he walked down the hallway to Walter's room.

"Are you okay, son?"

"Yes, daddy."

He now headed for our bedroom and I hurried back to the closet. He opened the door. "Lisette!" he shouted. "What are you doing?" Peter yelled at me, grabbing me up by the arm and yanking me to my feet. He knocked into the bedside table, at which point my jar of green marbles spilled out onto the carpet.

"Marbles? What the . . ."

"Dr. Jones told me to keep track of every time I had a bad nightmare. I add a marble to the jar when the bright lights burst on me."

"This is crazy, Lisette. You're crazy."

Before I could answer, the doorbell rang and Peter stomped off, and I followed after him stopping at the bedroom door to peek out again.

"Yes, Officer."

"I'm Officer Nicholas. You called in a domestic dispute?"

"Just look at this place, look at all these lit candles. It's crazy. My wife's crazy."

"Please calm down and explain what happened."

"What happened? I came home this morning and found a broken window and lit candles and my wife conked out in the closet. She could've burnt the place down."

"Was she intoxicated?" the officer asked.

"No. She's crazy, trying to chase off demons or something."

"Mr. Larkins, be that as it may, I'm writing this up as a nonviolent domestic dispute, but will note that your wife broke a window and her . . . reported erratic behavior."

The officer wrote out the police report, handed Peter a copy, and left.

Peter charged back to the bedroom waving the police report. "Lisette, it's on record now. I want you to clear this house of these candles and occult paraphernalia. I'll not have my son exposed to this nonsense."

Before I could answer, the doorbell rang again and Peter stomped off to see who was there. I followed close behind him, hoping it was the police officer and I could tell him my side of the story.

To Peter's astonishment, a process-server stood outside. Looking past Peter to me, the process server asked, "Lisette Larkins?"

I nodded my head, and he handed me a stack of papers, saying, "You've been served." The man turned and walked off.

Grabbing the papers from me, Peter read aloud, becoming angrier by the second. "The State of California versus Gerry Helman, MD?" he bellowed at me incredulously. "What have you done? A lawsuit? You risked this without consulting me? What if the doctor sues you for libel? For God's sake, who advised you to do this?" he demanded.

"I've been trying to tell you. I've been seeing . . . spirits. They tell me we're all accountable for what we do and for what we *don't* do. It's my spiritual and civic duty."

Peter stared at me, speechless, unsure of how to respond to what he must have considered pure gibberish. Glancing over the court documents, he said, "Your appearance date is next Monday. Keep track of everything that you say, all right? I want a full report."

At Peter's insistence, I cleared the house of all the candles and incense bowls, but I stored them at the back of my closet. We both made a concerted effort that week to be civil to each other, and while Peter was in town, the light show was in abeyance.

After I dropped Walter off at preschool early the following Monday morning, I wove through the downtown traffic and headed to the courthouse. An hour later, I was sitting on the witness stand as the grand jury proceedings were explained to me by the prosecutor.

"The purpose of this grand jury is for the US Attorney's Office to decide whether there is probable cause to prosecute Dr. Gerry Helman for the felony crime of insurance fraud," he said. I nodded in understanding.

"The benefit of grand jury proceedings is that they are secret, which provides a safe environment for a witness to come forward. Here, you may speak freely without fear of retaliation. If this grand jury finds probable cause, then it will return an indictment, which is a written statement of criminal charges. In that case, the accused goes to trial, where a verdict of guilty or not guilty will be established. Do you understand?"

"Yes," I replied.

"Okay, good. After a five-minute recess, we'll get started."

Taking advantage of the break, I scanned the room, noticing that unlike the proceedings of a regular courtroom, in which there are twelve jurors, here there were twenty-four members hearing evidence. Looking more closely at the jurors, I suddenly blanched and caught my breath. Amongst them were the two men from the hologram of two years earlier! They were dressed exactly the same as I had seen them in my vision, and I leaned forward in my chair, hoping to catch their eye.

Just then, both of them looked directly at me and nodded, as though acknowledging my presence. I wonder how I'll be able to explain this to Peter, I thought wryly. The ghosts from my past now seemed like friends. Where was Laura to confront with this fact? Now, here they were again, appearing as real as my own lawyer, sitting in front of me during an official court proceeding!

Next thing I knew, the proceedings got underway.

"Were you the office supervisor reporting directly to Dr. Gerry Helman?" the district attorney asked me.

"Yes," I said, nodding.

He wheeled an enormous pile of medical files toward the witness stand. From the pile, he withdrew one particularly large file and opened it, no doubt preparing to ask me questions about the entries. Amazingly, even after two years, I remembered that particular file from my last day at work.

"This file was confiscated by the Department of Insurance Fraud," the prosecutor said to me. "It was prepared as though it was about to be submitted for reimbursement, but it never was. Can you explain why it was never submitted?"

"I had reason to believe that the charges were false," I responded.

"What caused you to come to that conclusion?" he asked me pointedly. Glancing at the two men in suits from my hologram, I swallowed hard and shifted uncomfortably in my seat.

"It's okay, you're not on trial. Just answer my questions as best as you can," he encouraged me.

"What I read in this file and others just didn't add up. For one thing, some medical procedures would've taken longer to perform than the visits themselves, or could not have been performed on an out-patient basis. There were constant discrepancies between what Dr. Helman wanted me to submit for reimbursement and the services actually provided."

"Please continue," the prosecutor instructed me.

"Although Dr. Helman got furious with me for stalling, I stacked those files in the bottom of my file cabinet, hoping that at some point I could get the doctor to help me reconcile the issues. He fired me before I could get any resolution."

The prosecutor made some notes on a pad and, for another two hours, asked me one question after another relating to the medical files and the exact details of my job duties. I answered the lengthy barrage of questions to the best of my ability until he excused me with a final word of caution.

"Please don't discuss this matter with anybody, and make sure that you don't travel out of the state until further notice," he said looking pointedly at me. "You may or may not be needed again, but in either case, you're our key witness."

I had taken the whole day off from work, so I spent the afternoon at the park with Walter and later took a long nap. I then cleaned up the house and prepared dinner. I was emotionally numb from the stress of it all.

That night, Peter announced that he was going to sleep at his friend's house so that they could catch up over a few beers and watch a Lakers game together. I could see that he needed some time to think things over and to talk to his friend about our crumbling marriage. I didn't offer any protest. However, I did put out a few candles and incense bowls, sensing a static charge in the house. Were the visitors coming again?

After putting Walter to bed, I retired, turning on the radio to help me relax. I listened to quiet music and took several deep breaths. The new clock's neon dials glowed, showing the current time as 9:20 p.m. There was plenty of time for a long restful sleep before Walter sounded the morning alarm.

I fell asleep but was awoken almost immediately by the vibrations and the bright lights bursting through the ceiling, again enveloping me completely. Soon, the initial low humming grew louder until I could hardly stand it. Where was the guy with the black mop of hair? Where were the hologram jurors? Would I soon enter another tunnel of light? I was trembling with fear. What was happening to me?

I had left the radio on and now clicked it off, wanting to listen closely for any other sounds that might erupt in the bedroom. There was a floor lamp next to the bed, and I switched it on, creating a very bright reading light that seemed to give me some level of comfort.

Then, *someone or something* passed between the lamp and me.

A shadow was cast, and a beautiful aqua-blue light suddenly appeared then disappeared. I could not detect what was blocking the lamp's light and creating the shadow at my end of the room. Instant panic overcame me, and I was too frightened to breathe. More shadows moved across my face, undoubtedly caused by some ethereal presence in front of me—but what? Quick as a flash, and just as bright, the crisp, golden illumination emblazoned me from somewhere above my head. It pierced my body like current. My skin danced on my bones.

Although I wanted to shout, "No!" I could only manage a very faint whimper. I tried to scream again, then, like anesthesia being administered, a woozy, drug-induced feeling came over me. I seemed to fall deeper, then still deeper into a dark, silent abyss. Although I was confused, I became overwhelmingly sleepy. All vigilance disappeared as a whirling, dreamy state washed over me and my tingling body.

A crackling, high-frequency sound accompanied by a radiant light shone against my closed eyes, bathing my whole body in dancing particles of energy that prickled my skin. Despite my closed eyes, I marveled at the brilliance of the light, until the prickling intensified, causing me to moan in pain. It was as if I had been plugged into an electric socket and left to die. The sound and the light seemed to vibrate right through me. I wasn't able to open my eyes.

Then rapidly—seemingly only seconds later—I was again alert to an echoing thump, and I sensed my body fall onto my bed as though I had been dropped from above onto the mattress. The headboard slammed hard against the wall.

Remaining on my back for a moment, I tried to calm my somersaulting stomach and slowly opened my eyes. Nausea rushed over me in waves, and I hung over the bed, vomiting onto the Oriental rug on the floor.

The clock on the bureau glared at me with its unbelievable report: 2:20 a.m. That's impossible, I thought. What had appeared to have happened in just seconds had, in fact, taken almost five hours. Where has the "missing time" gone? I wondered in desperation.

Struggling down the hallway to check on my son, I thankfully found him sleeping peacefully. Dazed and confused, I returned to my own room and stepped gingerly into my muffled, musky bedroom closet. Pulling my long, woolen winter coat down over my head like a tent, I huddled there in a numb heap beside my glossy shoeboxes and my jar of green marbles. I added another marble to the jar as the high-pitched frequency echoed in my ears and tears streamed down my face.

The next morning, I could hear Peter opening the front door and yelling for me in his usual angry tone. He yanked open the closet door in a state of fury, again finding me inside clutching the jar of marbles.

"Get out of there, woman!" he yelled at my huddled form, then walked around the room, blowing out the candles on the table and bedposts and throwing them into the wastepaper basket.

"I told you to stop this nonsense. And now this?" He withdrew a document from his pocket and waived it at me angrily, which I could see was our recent checking account statement. "You've gone too far this time, writing a check to that crazy psychic woman and overdrawing our account?" He picked up the wastepaper basket and headed back to the living room, no doubt to toss the candles there. With great effort, I tried to follow him. I made it as far as the bedroom door, where I stopped, holding tightly to the door jamb. Feeling dizzy and queasy, I waited there a moment to steady myself.

I could hear the sounds of Peter racing around the living room, snuffing out candles and incense bowls as though they threatened to catch the house on fire.

Calling to him from the bedroom, I implored him to stop. My pleas were falling on deaf ears. "It may look silly, I agree, but it's my feeble attempt at an exorcism," I said weakly. "I don't know what else to do to stop the nighttime onslaught."

The only answer was the sound of glass shattering as he dropped one glass candleholder after another into the trash.

"Come on, Peter. Is that really necessary?" I asked, taking one slow step then another as I headed to the living room on wobbly legs. Suddenly, I tripped over an end table and fell onto the wooden coffee table, now cleared of the books on the occult and some old psychology textbooks I had left lying there—Peter must have tossed them, too.

The sound of my bony arms hitting the table momentarily distracted Peter from his mission, and he stepped over to check on me, perhaps frightened that I had broken my arm. "Are you okay?" he asked, carefully lifting me up and setting me on the sofa.

"My elbow . . ." I said in a muffled tone, exhausted and spent from the long night and now the hard fall.

Peter rushed into the kitchen and made a phone call, speaking in hushed tones. Then he grabbed his car keys and wallet and returned to my side. He picked up my limp form and carried me out the front door.

After loading me into the backseat of the car and buckling Walter into his car seat, we drove off down the street. Broken in body and spirit, I was too tired and confused to care where we were headed.

Chapter Eleven

I WAS HUDDLED ON the backseat of Peter's car and had no inclination to sit up and check out my surroundings. We reached our destination and parked. Rubbing my tender elbow at the point where it had smashed into the coffee table, I expected to hear my mother's voice call to me from outside the car. I assumed that Peter was dropping Walter and me off at her house, that he was fed up with my strange experiences and our failing marriage.

I suppose I didn't blame him, expecting to hear him tell my mother that it was her turn to deal with me. I lay there quietly, admitting to myself that my experiences were incomprehensible from Peter's point of view. Unless he himself had been confronted with the same dramatic worldview shift, there was little hope that he could relate to the intensity of my inner shift.

I was exhausted from trying to reconcile my everyday life, the normal uneventful world of child rearing, working a job, and managing a household, while straddling an otherworldly dimension in which the normal boundaries of time and space dissolved.

It was easy for Peter to be judgmental, I considered wryly, given his conventional, myopic perspective. If all I'd had to reconcile was my checking account statement and what to cook for dinner, I, too could have enjoyed the bliss of vapid ignorance. I realized how much easier it would be to live life in a fish bowl as Peter did, with no comprehension or appreciation of otherworldly experiences. And here, in fact, was my quandary: Had I *really* opened up to something transcendent? Had I actually been introduced to another aspect of the greater cosmos? Or was it just something my imagination had contrived as an escape from the problems of this world?

My great fear was that perhaps the hard truth of it all was nothing more than a slow wearing down of my psyche. Suppose that I had *not* been exposed to multiple dimensions, but instead I was confronting the confusion and stark madness of dealing with multiple personalities? How could I know for sure? Maybe the truth was that I was nothing more than a mentally fractured woman, wanting to believe the truth of my illusions, ignoring the real plight of my husband and his well-meaning but awkward attempts to help me.

But all Peter had to do was get up in the morning and go to work, then repeat the process. At night, when he closed his eyes for sleep, that's all that happened: sleep. Ah, to be ignorant to the grander vista of human experience, I thought—if that's what it was. Crazy or not, my inner dilemma provoked excruciating heartache, a struggle with which few others could relate.

To behold evidence that one is potentially unraveling mentally is a very personal and horrifying possibility. I couldn't even imagine the degree of emotional struggle that patients with Alzheimer's must undergo, or others having similar experiences to mine but being less equipped to deal with them.

A loud crack exploded overhead, jolting me out of my reverie. Normally, I would have assumed that it was the sound of thunder on a stormy day, but now, huddled in the backseat of this car, I took nothing for granted. Sitting up, and half expecting to greet an alien or some other version of a galactic busybody, I noticed that it was raining outside. I looked skyward; streaks of lightning lit up the heavens and a steady downpour soaked the ground.

Peering through the rain-speckled car window, I could see Peter standing under the eaves of what appeared to be an emergency room entrance, talking to a physician. I didn't recognize the hospital and wondered why Peter had not taken me to our local emergency room to have my throbbing elbow checked out. Where were we? I watched as ambulances arrived and nurses dressed in scrubs entered and exited the building.

Wearing a physician's white jacket with a stethoscope dangling around his neck, the doctor periodically glanced in my direction, as though needing a visual to accompany whatever Peter was saying. The doctor wrote a steady stream of notes onto a form as he listened to Peter, who was waving the police report, and I could only wonder what horror story my husband was telling him.

While the doctor looked on, Peter, accompanied by an orderly, turned and walked briskly in my direction; Peter opened the car door. Without saying a word, he picked me up as though I were a mere infant and carried me toward the sliding doors of the white stucco medical center. The orderly waited by the car, keeping an eye on Walter. It was not until I passed under the eaves of the entrance that I caught site of its name: Brentwood Neuropsychiatric Hospital. I shook my head in disbelief. What was happening to me?

It had never occurred to me that my husband might take such a drastic step in an attempt to extricate himself from his *own* nightmare. I twisted in Peter's arms to look up at him for some explanation. He ignored me as he carried my limp body through the waiting room door and across the lobby into a treatment room. The doctor motioned for Peter to lay me on an exam table in the corner. I looked up at them through the steady stream of tears.

"Don't *worry*," Peter said to me tenderly, taking my hand in his. "We're just going to get you checked out, okay? I'm going home now to get your toiletries and pajamas, then I'll be back. Dr. Ventura here will examine your elbow. You took a hard fall."

Having no doubt previously rehearsed this seamless orchestration while chatting in the parking lot with the doctor, Peter briskly walked from the room just as Dr. Ventura took his place at my side. He nodded to a nurse, who joined him as though for reinforcement, after parking a medical cart in the doorway to effectively block me from bolting through the door.

"You've come to the right place," the doctor said reassuringly, glancing at his clipboard. "My nurse will get your vitals, then I'll examine your elbow."

After the nurse completed her preliminary examination and guided me to and from the X-ray room, Dr. Ventura read the X-rays and explained the diagnosis to me.

"You've bruised your elbow and the radius bone of your forearm, but there's really no specific treatment other than keeping it immobile. In the meantime, rest your elbow and forearm on this pillow, which will help ease the pressure. We're moving you to a private room soon. Tomorrow we'll start the intake process in earnest."

"What do you mean?" I asked in alarm. "What intake process? Why am I here?"

"We'll discuss that later, but you're here for now, so just take it easy," he said, patting my shoulder kindly, as though reasoning with a weary soldier who had just returned home from combat. "You must be exhausted."

Despite being upset at my presence in a psychiatric hospital, no truer words could have been uttered. I sank down, resting my head on a pillow covered with white tissue paper. I had not slept well the previous night—seeing as I'd spent it in the closet—so I decided to just rest there for the afternoon. I'd straighten this whole thing out with Peter when he came back. The nurse came over with a syringe to inject me.

"Don't worry, it's also a vitamin boost; you look undernourished," she said.

I stared at her to make sure she wasn't part of my nighttime retinue, then nodded my head in agreement. She left, and as the doctor followed, he called over his shoulder that he'd be returning later in the hour. I fell asleep almost immediately.

When I awakened, I was tucked under blankets in a proper bed, lying in a darkened room with bars on the window. Where had the day gone? A small night-light created just enough illumination to enable me to examine my new wardrobe and room. How had the nurse managed to transfer me and change me from street clothes to a maroon hospital gown without my knowing? I then realized that the vitamin shot had also been an anesthetic. A thick plastic ID bracelet was wrapped snugly around my wrist.

I wondered what had happened to Peter and the pajamas that he'd promised to bring me? I pulled the blankets up under my neck, trying to warm myself against the chill of the room's air conditioning. Unusually tired, I rubbed my sore elbow and figured that I would sort it out the moment that Peter arrived to pick me up and take me home to my son.

Terribly missing my child and our ritual bedtime stories, I realized just what a blessing a young child's tender snuggling could be. Where is Walter? I wondered to myself. I could only assume that Peter had become delayed, probably by our little boy's needs, and that thought helped me settle down; I headed into dreamland and a good night's rest.

The next morning, I awoke with a start to a woman's loud wailing through the walls. Looking around the room in surprise, I struggled to recall the events that led to my arrival at the hospital. I jumped from my bed and began searching for my clothes. They were gone. Only a pair of bedroom slippers lay on the checkered linoleum floor. While sliding my feet into them, I felt a draft of cool air on my buttocks. I could only assume that my backside was exposed in the hospital gown. Fumbling with the ties, I tightened the gown as best as I could.

An intercom outside blasted an urgent announcement, an apparent "Code Blue." I shuffled to the door in my floppy slippers and poked my head cautiously outside to see what the commotion was about. Suddenly, the woman who had awakened me hollered again, and I saw that the noise came from the room across from mine. Down the hallway, I could hear a thudding of shoes, and I turned to see a group of huge men barreling in my direction. When they reached her room, they pushed open the door and rushed inside.

Through the open door, I could see two medics attempting to resuscitate a naked woman who was lying on the floor. She was not moving. Soon after, they stopped their efforts and, after checking her pulse, shook their heads somberly.

Next to the medics was the hysterical woman, an old Hispanic hospital maid, who seemed shocked and teary-eyed, gazing sorrowfully at the woman on the floor and anxiously twisting a white towel into knots. The burly attendants escorted her from the room, but not before she and I exchanged glances—hers a compassionate nod of understanding. That's weird, I thought, wondering why she was looking at me with such pity. As the distraught maid was comforted and led away, I could hear the medics talking in subdued tones, and one of them held up what appeared to be an ordinary white bathrobe emblazoned with small red lettering.

I was able to hear one of the medics as he spoke into a walkie-talkie. "The patient in room 103 has expired. She stuffed her bathrobe sleeve down her throat, resulting in suffocation," he said in a flat tone.

Reacting to his message, I backed up slowly into my own room, now frightened, and softly closed the door. I stepped into the bathroom, thinking I might vomit. I leaned over the toilet momentarily, waiting for my stomach to settle. After catching my breath, I stood up again, noticing that there was no shower in the bathroom. That's strange, I thought, wondering how a person was supposed to keep themselves clean.

Then, noticing a similar bathrobe dangling from a hook, I lifted it off. Examining it more closely, I turned the robe over and found the same red lettering that spelled out three ominous words: "Suicide Prevention Ward." Blanching in surprise at the reality of my situation, I wondered exactly what Peter had told Dr. Ventura.

Frowning at the lettering on the robe, I realized that I, too, was a patient assigned to the SP Ward, but my worried thoughts were interrupted by a loud knock on the door. A strong female voice said, "Excuse me, shower time."

The orderly directed me to follow her down the hall where we entered a large room with many individual shower stalls. She motioned for me to undress in the private changing area, and I entered the enclosure and without protest removed my gown and slippers. Modestly stepping out from behind the curtain,

I was directed to the nearest shower stall. The orderly turned it on and adjusted the stream to an appropriate temperature.

I was growing impatient for Peter to come back and clear up this misunderstanding. Wait until I give him a piece of my mind, I thought angrily. I now glared at the orderly, as if to say that she had mistaken me for an imbecile. I was perfectly capable of managing my own shower without her close supervision. I figured that a shower might feel good under the circumstances, especially in light of the fact that, at any moment, I expected my husband to bring me a fresh change of clothes. The maroon hospital gown was for in-patients. I, on the other hand, had been examined and was now ready to leave.

"There's no soap in here!" I called to the orderly through the heavy spray of warm water. She was closely watching me bathe from her position on a stool.

The orderly reached into a bucket and handed me a bar of soap, but stood at the ready, as though expecting me to lather up then hand it right back to her.

"You gonna use a stopwatch?" I asked her, since she was acting as though I couldn't be trusted with a bar of soap.

"It's just orders," she said dryly. "Patients eat it. They do weird things to get out of here."

Frowning at her intimation, I handed her back the bar of soap, then rinsed my entire body. I turned off the water and looked around for a towel. She tossed one in my direction and I grabbed it, drying off and dressing again in my maroon hospital gown. Where was Peter?

After she handed me a plastic comb, I straightened out my hair and slipped my feet into a pair of newly assigned rubber slippers. She then motioned for me to follow her. Once in the hallway, another orderly approached us, and the two got to chatting, exchanging gossip relating to the morning's suicide.

After a while, another orderly approached us. The women broke off their conversation and turned to him.

"She's got a visitor," the burly orderly stated, glancing at the burst of enthusiasm that lit up my face. "Both of you follow me."

"It's about time!" I retorted, heading down the hallway, two staff members now escorting me. "Peter, you owe me big time," I said out loud for their benefit, wanting them to know that my husband had it coming for abandoning me for an entire night in this hospital. As we turned the corner, the burly orderly guided us over to a uniformed police officer in the middle of the room.

"Where's my husband?" I asked impatiently, looking around the crowded waiting room.

"He sent this," the officer replied, and I turned to face him, expecting to receive a note from Peter explaining the reason for his delay. Instead, the police officer handed me a stack of white papers.

"You've been served," he replied, almost sadly, noticing my maroon hospital gown.

"What's this?" I yelped, growing weary of Dr. Helman's legal battle and wanting nothing more to do with him. "I've *already* testified," I said in a firm voice. "Send this back."

Holding out the papers for the policeman to accept, he shook his head and turned to leave. I then glanced down at the court papers, trying to clear up this confusion. My son's name caught my eye, and my whole world stopped. Incredulous, I scanned the document, hardly believing what I was reading. My brain threatened to melt down as the raw truth screamed at me from the pages. Feeling my eyes close, the lobby floor came up to meet me as I collapsed in a heap onto the checkered linoleum.

Chapter Twelve

HAVING COLLAPSED ON THE lobby floor of the psychiatric hospital, the next thing I was aware of was the strong odor of smelling salts filling my nostrils. Soon after, my eyes fluttered open as the orderlies tried to bring me around. Petrified, I felt as though I would never arise, and I fought off the orderlies' attempts to get me up on my feet. Rolling over onto my side in the fetal position, I felt numb and speechless, the full impact of my husband's betrayal hitting me.

"What happened here?" Dr. Ventura asked the orderlies as he rushed over to me. The female orderly picked up the strewn papers and handed them to the doctor. After reading over the document, he summarized his findings to the curious group of people.

"She's temporarily lost custody of her child due to her hospitalization here. She missed yesterday's hearing and was deemed a no-show," the doctor said in a hushed voice, nodding his head as if this explained why I had fainted. He assumed I could not see or hear him, but I'd already read the fateful words. My son had been taken from me by my own dearly beloved spouse.

"He's also filed for divorce, and the follow-up custody hearing is in three weeks," Dr. Ventura explained, shrugging as though such news was a common occurrence here. He handed the papers back to the orderlies. "See that she makes it to my group meeting. She'll need to be acclimated as soon as possible."

After the doctor walked away, the orderlies huddled over the court documents, discussing them as though I wasn't even there.

"She'll never make it to this hearing," one of them said.

"It'll take that long for her to complete her intake interview," said another, nodding in agreement. "And family law judges want glowing recommendations, not AMAs."

"Come on, let's get her to 'group,'" the burly orderly instructed, as they all converged on me, lifting me to my feet.

"Dr. Ventura's expecting you," the female orderly said to me as I walked a few wobbly steps forward, dazed and confused. "Just take it one step at a time," she said patiently, nudging me in the direction of a large set of double doors that opened on to a spacious carpeted room. Once inside, the nurse pointed to an empty chair, and I shuffled across the room and dropped into it. She handed me the court papers somewhat tentatively, unsure if I might faint again. Grabbing the legal documents from her, I rolled them up into a tight wad, noticing that two dozen patients were watching me with interest.

I looked around the room, trying to ascertain my new status and the purpose of this gathering. All the patients sat in a large circle, dressed similarly to me in gowns of various colors.

"Dr. Ventura will be here in a moment," a nurse said to me, motioning for me to stay seated. "The session will start soon."

"How long's the meeting?" I asked, wondering how fast I could get back to my room.

"One hour, three times daily," she said, looking at her watch and turning to leave. Then she called back to me over her shoulder. "It's mandatory," she said, hustling out of the room.

"And you'd better not be late," said the man next to me, doing his best to mimic the nurse. I turned to receive a friendly handshake.

"I'm Scott," he said. "Are you okay? You look a little stunned."

Smiling weakly, I nodded. "Yeah, I'm all right." Then remembering the orderly's comments in the lobby, I leaned closer to ask him a personal question. "Can you tell me what 'AMA' means?" I asked, wondering about its relevance in child custody hearings.

"Against Medical Advice," he said with emphasis. "It refers to the status of someone who has left here without their doctor's blessing. Avoid *that* at all costs," he said soberly, as though he were speaking from personal experience.

"What does it take to get their blessing?" I asked earnestly.

"Dr. Ventura determines whether or not you're a threat to yourself or anyone else. Translated? It means he gets to decide if you're sane."

"How can he determine that in a couple of weeks? Isn't it rather subjective, without benefit of meaningful therapeutic analysis?" I asked him nervously, wondering how the good doctor would diagnose me after I told my tale of aliens and cosmic interlopers on my bedspread.

"Yes, and a lot of people out there see it his way," Scott said to me nodding. "Unless you're one of these poor suckers facing down a child custody hearing in family law court."

Upon hearing this pronouncement, my eyes filled with tears, and I realized the monumental challenge I faced.

Scott looked at me thoughtfully, guessing why I was now flushed. "You lost custody," he said as a statement, not a question.

"It's that obvious?" I asked, nodding sadly.

"If that's the case, you'll never get your kid back unless your release is approved. They've got to sign you out and fill out the judge's form that you're *capable* of custody."

I looked away, not able to bear him seeing the torrent of tears rolling down my cheeks. Glancing at the court document in my hand, I felt a sense of complete and utter shame. I was disgusted with myself. Why hadn't I simply taken sleeping pills and slept through my nighttime light shows? Why had I insisted on trying to figure it all out? Obviously, I was a nut. And now, I was in the nuthouse.

Sighing deeply, Scott leaned closer and said, "Most of us have lost our kids. I know how you feel."

Upon hearing his admission, I looked more closely at him, then around the room at the sea of empty, sad faces. Feeling tremendously forlorn, I turned back to Scott. "How do I get them to approve my release?" I asked almost frantically, needing to figure this out and expedite my departure.

"It's not that simple," Scott replied, looking up at the doorway as Dr. Ventura entered the room. "Rumor has it that there's a direct correlation between the quality of your health insurance benefits and your doctor's pen."

"What do you mean?" I asked, completely confused.

"If your insurance is really good, they'll find a way to keep you here," he said. "If it's lousy, they don't want you, and you're a goner. It just takes one signature from *him*," Scott said, motioning to Dr. Ventura as though pointing out the devil.

Dr. Ventura took a seat and began organizing his medical files. "Hello, everyone. I've just got to tend to a bit of housekeeping, so please come up when I call your name. We'll get started in a few minutes."

"You mean it's all up to *that* guy?" I whispered to him incredulously.

"His recommendation sinks you or sets you free," Scott said.

Scott and I looked at Ventura as though beholding the head of a mafia family. Realizing how much power he held over me was enough to take my breath away. I was stunned to hear that monetary politics dictated a patient's length of treatment. Unfortunately for me, Peter had purchased the best health insurance policy that money could buy. When was I going to a catch a break? I wondered hopelessly.

"But don't patients have any say as to when they leave?" I asked desperately.

"Hello? This is a psychiatric hospital!" Scott reminded me. "Here, we've got addicts, weirdoes, and psychotics, or so they say."

"Well, I don't care what his uninformed opinion of me is," I replied defensively. "Unless he can prove that I'm crazy, I have rights."

"You're awfully flippant for someone facing a child custody hearing," Scott needled me. "The *judge* goes by what the *doc says*—don't you get it? The doc's opinion of you is all that's standing between getting your child back and supervised visits, one afternoon every other week."

"And if I just make a run for it and bolt out the door?" I asked.

"No one ever got custody with an AMA. You'd do well to remember that. Everything we do here is based on *hedging* against that fact. Behave yourself. It'll get you much farther."

"I can see that it's done you a lot of good," I gently responded, more as a genuine question than an insult.

"I've learned the hard way. No reason for a nice girl like you to go through what I have," he said sadly.

"But if it turns out that there's nothing wrong with me, then the doctor should have no reason to withhold a glowing recommendation."

"I keep *telling* you. This place, it's a *business*," Scott said with emphasis.

Having completed his conversations with a few of the patients, Dr. Ventura sent them back to their chairs, then looked across the room and nodded at me. I managed a cool smile, nodding politely. This was no time to alienate my supervising psychiatrist, considering that I'd just learned that he held my future in his corrupt little hands.

"Okay, as soon as I get through the roll call, we'll begin, shall we?" Dr. Ventura said to the group, looking carefully at each patient and checking off names on his list.

"Just because it's a business, that can't be *legal*." I whispered to Scott. "They can't delay someone's release for no good reason," I said, furious at the intimation that I was now facing another corrupt medical practitioner, when I hadn't even finished with Dr. Helman.

"You gotta see it from their point of view. Whatever *you* did to get yourself in here, well, *that* wasn't legal. It's tit for tat. Who you gonna complain to anyway?" Scott seemed to dare me. "Most people in here broke some kind of law."

"I haven't," I retorted with pride, wanting to run out of the room and never look back.

"Well, that's good" Scott said, looking me over approvingly. "You'll do okay then, as long as you don't claim to be Jesus or Marilyn Monroe come back from the dead. What're you in for, anyway?" Scott asked me directly.

"Lisette Larkins?" Dr. Ventura announced out loud, interrupting my private conversation with Scott.

"Yes," I replied, raising my hand hopefully as though I were being called upon by the doctor to be the first one to leave.

"Why don't you start by introducing yourself and telling us why you're here?" he said, as the rest of the group turned to look right at me. "You're the new one in the group, so when you're done, they'll all introduce themselves to you."

Shifting in my seat, I looked out at the sea of faces, trying to find an appropriate place in my story to begin an introduction. Observing my discomfort, I was grateful when Dr. Ventura interrupted me.

"Our style here in 'group' is pretty informal," Dr. Ventura explained, smiling at me. "We keep an open format, so each participant can feel free to comment or ask a question. The only requirement is that you stay in your seat and remain appropriate. No 'poor me' stories, got it? Just stick to the facts when saying how you feel."

Nodding, I then shrugged, wondering how to explain my present situation, embarrassed that I was now being confronted with an audience of potential skeptics. Faltering, I looked at the papers in my fist, still not knowing where to begin.

"Anything that you'd care to share is just fine," said Dr. Ventura, encouraging me to say anything at all. "Believe me, we've heard it all, right?" he asked, and the entire room burst into laughter.

"There's nothing to be embarrassed about," Dr. Ventura continued, addressing my continued silence. "Long-term addicts, recovering alcoholics, and those with borderline personality disorders—there are no secrets here. Everyone's thrown in together." He paused and looked at my compadre. "Scott, why don't you start; warm up the room a bit."

I turned to face him, relieved that my turn had been skipped.

"Most of you know me. My name's Scott, and I've been struggling with cocaine addiction my entire adult life," he said, sighing deeply and looking at me questioningly, as if wondering if he'd just lost a new friend. "Most of you know my story. I lost my job—*again*—and I lost custody of my two kids." He sighed again, kicking his shoes against the legs of the chair. "They're *great* kids," he said, his voice breaking with emotion.

"Hey, man, you're cool," a loud voice called to Scott from across the room. A man in his mid-thirties sat up straight in his chair, now ready to take the hot seat. "I beat your problem, Scott," the man said, "so I know you can do it, too. I got off the white powder, and there's no lookin' back."

He brushed his nose, then sniffed, as though recalling only too well the inevitable dangers to his sinus cavity. "Only I fell back on an old drinking problem, and the *bad behavior* started up again." A few patients in the room nodded their heads in agreement.

"My name's Shelly," said a fortyish woman with purple tattoos on her wrist. After gulping a long swig from a water bottle at her side, she started in with her story. "They say I'm bipolar," she said rather shyly, darting her eyes around the room ready to head off a verbal attack. "My medicine stinks. I don't like taking it cause it gives me headaches and a super-dry mouth. But then, if I *don't* take it, stuff happens, and I go all haywire inside."

Dr. Ventura looked up from his clipboard and cleared his throat loudly to express his displeasure at her complaint.

Shelly settled down a bit, correcting her tone. "This last time I stole a diamond bracelet. I did jail time, but now I'm trying to clean up my . . . compulsions, trying to get my head on straight."

"Good job," said Dr. Ventura, making a note on his clipboard and smiling at Shelly as though approving of her ability to self-correct.

"I'm Susan," said a young woman, approximately twenty-five years old. "I'm depressed; attempted suicide three times. My dad told the cop to fifty-one/fifty me."

I shook my head, not understanding the terminology. Susan spotted that and responded. "It's a police code for a crazy one on the loose. It's someone who's a danger to property, others, or themselves," she said, looking straight at me. "Now it's like I'm stuck in here." She scowled at Dr. Ventura.

"Susan, remember the rules. No whining," Dr. Ventura reminded her. Susan nodded and slumped back in her chair.

Dr. Ventura looked at me, motioning that it was now time for me to introduce myself. Wanting to cooperate and earn the doctor's favor, I tried to sound as enthusiastic as possible.

"My name's Lisette," I said reluctantly, having hoped to avoid this inevitable speech. "I've been seeing bright lights and three-D images in my bedroom. People seem to appear out of nowhere, and I lose track of the time, minutes become hours, hours become minutes . . . It sounds crazy, but it's probably just nightmares," I said, peering at Dr. Ventura and noticing that he was writing something on his clipboard. He nodded, encouraging me to continue.

"When I tried to 'clear' my bedroom on advice from an expert on paranormal phenomena, my husband thought I was nuts and brought me here."

"So, what's the big deal with seeing ghosts? Doesn't anybody watch TV?" another patient challenged me. I swallowed hard, bracing myself for an in-depth inquisition.

"Your name?" Dr. Ventura interrupted him.

"My name's Lenny," he said, answering the question then returning his attention to me. "Just curious to know how bright lights and seeing ghosts landed you in the loony bin?"

A few patients chuckled, until Dr. Ventura shot them scolding glances.

Nothing good could come from this type of dialogue. Trying to recover lost ground, I tried another tack. "It mostly happens at night. I'm still able to hold a job, take care of a child, and deal with a . . . demanding husband."

There, I thought, satisfied that I'd said my piece and would be left alone. It wasn't as though I was acting like a stark raving lunatic.

"I also have hallucinations," another woman said, nodding at me in understanding. "I know just how you feel," she said, looking from me to Dr. Ventura. "Schizophrenia's a bitch without proper medication." The other patients looked directly at me, as though waiting for my response.

"They're *not hallucinations*," I said defensively, although it was true that I couldn't know that for certain.

Ignoring my response, another woman spoke up. "Yeah, sure," she said, pointing at me in an accusatory tone. "You could have a whole other personality walking around in your head, you know, like Sybil."

The room broke into laughter, then Dr. Ventura brought everyone back to order. "Okay, that's enough for now. I'll see you all again right after lunch; for our next session, we're going to explore feelings of betrayal—family members who've tried to help, but it feels like a stab in the back."

Almost the entire sea of faces nodded in understanding. How ironic that I actually had this very complaint in common with all of them. However, that's the end of my monologues, I vowed to myself. Following the herd of people out into the hallway, I turned to Scott and asked him where everyone was heading.

"Dispensary," he said flatly. "Lunchtime meds. Follow me."

Wanting nothing to do with medication of any sort, I nonetheless followed the group to the dispensary in hopes of slipping into my room unnoticed just as soon as everyone became distracted.

Getting into line behind a dozen other patients, Scott and I fell silent as we inched forward. Two women in front of me were talking about their own upcoming child custody hearings, so I moved in closer, hoping to pick up some tips.

"My custody hearing's tomorrow morning," the first woman said, dejected and teary-eyed. "It's just not right. Of course I don't stand a chance if I'm not even there."

"I know what you mean," the second woman said. "It's criminal. They refused to give me a decent recommendation, so what was the judge supposed to think? Then, they wouldn't even let me out of here long enough to show up and fight for it. My own kid thinks I've abandoned him."

"I know," the first woman said tearfully. "Talk about a conflict of interest."

I had heard enough. I broke out of line and rushed down the hall toward the main administrative offices, leaving Scott to wonder where I was going. Off to one side of the main hospital lobby was the counter of the administrative secretary. I stepped up to her.

"I need an appointment with Dr. Ventura," I said, wishing she'd at least give me the courtesy of turning around in her chair to face me. "A *private* appointment," I said emphatically.

"He's pretty booked," she said rather dryly. "I can get you in with someone else as soon as this afternoon," she said, flipping through her appointment calendar.

"No, thanks. I need Dr. Ventura. It's really important," I said. "When's his next availability?"

"Next week," she said, turning to me.

"That long?"

"Sorry. Do you want the appointment or not?"

"Yes, please," I replied. The secretary wrote something down on a large calendar, and then wrote the date and time on a small appointment card. When she handed it to me, I stared at the date, feeling that seven days away might as well be seven years. What was I going to do with myself for that long?

Looking around the lobby, I saw a row of pay phones against the far wall. "Excuse me," I called to the secretary, interrupting her again.

"Yes?" she responded, somewhat annoyed.

"I'm sorry to bother you, but when I arrived here, I didn't have my purse with me, which means I have no money, no credit cards, *nothing*. I'd like to use the pay phone over there, but I don't have any change. Is there any way that I can get a small line of credit so that I can call my family?"

"No," she said. "We're not set up to loan money."

"Well then, how do you suggest I contact anyone?" I asked, frightened at the idea of being completely cut off from everyone I knew.

"Borrow from another patient," she said dryly, turning back to her typewriter.

I walked slowly back to my room, wondering who would loan me enough change to make a phone call. I needed to call my mother and also the lawyer who had brought suit on my behalf against Dr. Helman. It had been two years since the complaint was first filed, and it wasn't completely out of the realm of possibility that an award for damages might come my way. Maybe the attorney could give me a small advance against that future award. In the meantime, I hoped I could scrounge up enough change to make at least one call.

Passing me in the hallway were several patients in wheelchairs, pushed along by bored orderlies. I didn't think it was right to stop and ask just anyone for a loan. Other patients passed by, talking loudly to themselves as if they were stark raving mad. No, they weren't good candidates, either. Then, up ahead, I saw Scott.

"Scott! Can you loan me enough change to make a call from the lobby pay phone?"

Scott shook his head. "Sorry, they're holding all my personal items, my wallet included. You should know that; I'm sure they took your purse."

"I didn't bring it. If I could get out of here, I've got bank accounts that have money—"

"Wow, you really are naïve," Scott said, looking at me sadly. "Don't you realize that once a judge grants your spouse custody of your kid, he'll close every single bank account that you're listed on?"

I stared at him in horror; this possibility had not occurred to me. But, of course, he was right. Peter would have closed off access to any avenue that would have helped me defend myself against him. The depth of my plight was now really beginning to sink in. All I could think to do was to run from the loud chatter of crazy patients that milled around me in the hallway, as if running from the idea that I may never get my child back.

If I couldn't raise a dime to make a phone call from a pay phone, how would I ever raise the money for a family law attorney to help me with my custody case? Tearing down the hall as fast as I could, I yearned for the quiet and dark of my bleak hospital room, wanting only to dive under the blankets and stay there forever.

"Mrs. Larkins!" someone called after me from down the hall. I stopped long enough to see who wanted me. It was the secretary from Dr. Ventura's office. "There's been a cancellation."

A few minutes later, I was sitting in the doctor's office.

"I've been in here long enough," I said firmly to Dr. Ventura, shifting uncomfortably in his office chair but feeling hopeful that I finally had an opportunity to state my case. He peered at me skeptically from across his large oak desk, waiting to hear yet another unreasonable patient's demand.

"I need you to discharge me," I said, stating what appeared to be my obvious reason for the appointment.

Looking at my medical file, Dr. Ventura read aloud from a long list of my husband's complaints, as though suddenly Peter himself had the power to decide my fate with my son and with this infernal sanitarium.

"Your husband reports that you've been seeing images and hearing voices that no one else sees and hears; that you've shattered windows in your home; that you've bounced checks to ghost-busters; that you're not sleeping well, and you report suffering from long-term nightmares; that you—"

"I have broken no laws, and have otherwise conducted myself in an orderly fashion," I responded sharply, as if addressing the Grand Inquisitor. "He broke the window, not me. Look, it's not against the law to have visions in the middle of the night! I need to be at my son's custody hearing in exactly three weeks. If I don't show up, I lose my child. Do you understand the position that I'm in?" I asked Dr. Ventura, who didn't seem the least bit sympathetic.

"It's way too early to determine your mental status. Your team has not yet administered a Rorschach test nor an MMPI.

Then, there's an individual assessment that needs to happen, and, last but not least, during this whole process I regularly meet with my colleagues to review your case."

"Oh, and with your business office as well?" I asked flatly.

"I don't know what you're implying, but I *do* know that patients do not dictate the depth and scope of their treatment here."

"I should be able to leave if I want to."

"You're welcome to leave. But if you do, your file will be notated that you've done so AMA; that is, 'Against Medical Advice.' A report that states that I will *not* vouch for your capability as a parent nor the effectiveness of your emotional functioning will go to the family law judge presiding over your son."

Leaning forward on his desk for emphasis, he removed his glasses, as though irritated at having to explain it to me.

"If you have an underlying mental disorder, you will need medication and *long-term psychiatric supervision.*" He took a long breath. "The safety and welfare of your child is of utmost concern to all of us . . . especially the family law judge. He's awaiting my findings. Nothing happens without my approval."

Dr. Ventura stopped talking and looked directly at me as though daring me to respond.

And the truth was, I couldn't. I was in shock, unable to breathe or even comment on any of his tidy little rules. My brain was searching and spinning, trying to find a way out of these deplorable circumstances.

Seeing my resolve slip away, the doctor summarized his position, clearly wanting to quash any further rebellion on my part and dash any hope I had of extricating myself. "As soon as you complete your intake evaluation, the team will decide upon the best course of action with respect to an appropriate medication suitable for your . . . delusions. In the meantime, I suggest that you find a way to relax. I can prescribe you something for that right now," he said, scribbling on a prescription pad.

Dr. Ventura then stood up, handed me the prescription, and escorted me to the door. "You should be starting your evaluation process in the morning. It's going to take a month or so. In the meantime, your attendance is mandatory at all group meetings. I'll see you there first thing in the morning."

I guess I had been excused from the after-lunch group meeting. That was good; I didn't think I could stand it right now.

As soon as I was out the door, Dr. Ventura picked up my medical file from his desk and walked down the hallway. I grabbed a nearby cleaning cart and pushed it after him. The doctor entered a roomful of other psychiatrists who had convened around a large conference table.

Purposely spilling something on the floor, I began cleaning it up so as to overhear their proceedings. The door was wide open, and I could hear everything that was said. The cart blocked me from view, so passersby could not tell what I was up to.

"Okay, let's begin case review on Lisette Larkins," Dr. Ventura said. "This is a thirty-three-year-old mother of a three-year-old son, whose custody has been temporarily awarded to the father, pending a formal hearing in three weeks. The mother—and her husband corroborates this fact—reports having delusions and faulty perceptions that no one else is able to see or hear. Her husband has encouraged her to submit to a full evaluation here, which is about to begin."

"Where are her family members?" one of the psychiatrists asked.

"I don't know. There's no report that they've come during visiting hours. In this case, she's probably estranged from them."

"Well, I think we can agree that her evaluation process should get underway immediately, since it will take several months to complete. At that time, we'll submit a diagnosis to the court along with her treatment recommendations, which, as we all know, will most likely be ongoing. I feel that a Rorschach test will be helpful in this case, especially in light of the fact that she appears reluctant to openly describe her thinking processes. Like everything else about her, *that's* a red flag."

I hurried back to my room, trying to suppress the urge to vomit in protest on their clean linoleum floors.

Chapter Thirteen

IT HAD BEEN ALMOST three weeks since my fateful private appointment with Dr. Ventura. Since then, I'd come full circle and was now attending to the business of being a well-behaved patient. There had been ink blots to interpret and questionnaires to fill out; there were group meetings and individual sessions in which to participate.

My hospital room was quiet while I brushed my teeth and got ready for bed. I was retiring early, exhausted from the several weeks of lengthy psychiatric interviews and testing. Then I heard a knock at the door. I wasn't surprised; it was no doubt an orderly announcing where I should report the next morning for yet another round of tests.

Already dressed in my pajamas and slippers, I answered the door. "Yes, may I help you?" I asked. It was the Hispanic maid, and I wondered why she was working so late.

"I brought you another blanket," she said kindly, in a thick Hispanic accent. "I heard you tell the orderly that you're cold at night," she explained, smiling.

"I didn't want to bother anybody," I replied, surprising myself at just how disempowered I had become. I was numb and vacant; after weeks of indoctrination, I had surrendered to my plight there.

"In the future, if you need anything, just ask *me*," she said kindly. "You've been in here too long to go without enough blankets."

"Thanks," I said smiling, accepting the thick blanket from her. Closing the door, I could only wonder at how quickly the time had gone by. I had almost given up, reluctantly realizing that perhaps my son might be better off without me. If I were indeed suffering from a full-blown mental disorder, I didn't want him to be raised by me. I loved him and wanted what was best for *him*.

Figuring that if I were a model patient, I might have a better chance with my visiting rights, I hunkered down, morphing into the dutiful, well-behaved in-patient and hoping that a good report from Dr. Ventura might eventually earn me a better standing with the family law judge.

Besides, though I was loathe to admit it to them, the psychiatrists had raised a good point: We had to see what results the testing provided. My son's welfare *was* the most important thing to consider. In the meantime, I was quiet and meek. I showed up on time to all my sessions; I spoke when I was asked questions. All in all, I had surrendered to this new life and seriously considered that my light-show experiences were nothing more than evidence of an untreated mental disorder.

After spreading out the new blanket on my bed, I turned off the bedside lamp and nestled under the covers. It was truly amazing that just as soon as I had been removed from the stress of my marriage to Peter, the bright lights and humming vibrations had completely disappeared. How ironic indeed, I thought, that Peter himself had unwittingly provided my own best cure: to remove me from our house and our marital turmoil.

No sooner had that thought entered my mind, when a loud blast of wind rushed past my face. From where I lay on my back in bed, I was blinded by a stream of light that poured from the ceiling. "Not again!" I cried out loud. "What is happening to me?"

At that moment, my body began to slowly lift off the bed! I tried to move, but I could not budge in the slightest. My entire form was rising from the bed, higher and higher, until I had risen to the height of the room's small, barred windows.

This cannot be happening, my logical mind screamed inside my head. I wanted to yell, but nothing came out. My entire body was frozen, with the exception of my eyes and my eyelids, but soon even my eyelids slowly shut against my will. I could still feel the sensation of moving through the air, and all I could think was that I was dying and had not been able to say goodbye to my beloved son.

Enveloping me as I moved through the air was a strong pulse of energy, and the zapping sensation felt like I was once again being electrocuted from the inside out. My stomach did somersaults—the same internal flip that you get when going over the edge in a steep rollercoaster. Where was I going? I wondered. Would I again meet the wise elders from my previous experience? Perhaps this time I will have truly died and could get on with the business of ending this ridiculously mysterious life of mine.

Without warning, my eyes slowly began to open; I had no control over whether they opened or closed. As they fluttered open more fully and adjusted to the dim light, I tried to move other parts of my body but could not. I seemed to see myself floating through the air, but my mind objected to this impossibility. I was inside some type of enclosure; beyond me,

I could see a panel of lights, similar to an airliner's cockpit. Was I on an airplane? I wondered.

Of its own volition, my body began to descend feet first through a narrow portal-like opening, as though I were moving through a submarine hatch. Nothing appeared to be supporting me. It was as though something or someone invisible to me was directing my body to float through the air!

As I passed through the small circular opening and came out the other side, I looked above me and realized that I had emerged from some sort of large, round craft. From what I could tell, it appeared that my body was being transferred to a large, dark area below me. My body, having cleared the ship's portal and now fully upright, slowly floated toward the ground until I came to rest, fully stationary.

Still unable to move, I gawked at what lay in front of me and blanched in complete shock. There, in living color, as though I had entered a pleasant animated Disney movie, were four small, gray extraterrestrial beings. They looked calmly at me, as if this were a friendly invitation to meet for a nighttime snack.

The beings had large, inverted-pear-shaped heads with equally large, wrap-around black eyes. I remembered those eyes from my previous vision when the alien being had appeared at the foot of my bed. How was it that he was here again but this time accompanied by others of its kind? He had brought reinforcements!

As I beheld an impossible scene, I could hear my heart beating loudly in my chest, and I wondered if I would hold up through the ordeal. I recognized within me strange sensations: My body's autonomic response mechanisms reacted with raw fear; my heart pounded; and all the saliva in my mouth disappeared. I knew that my brain was on real and potentially threatening overload. Then there was another part of me, perhaps the *real* part of me, that had always suspected that there must be more to life than just managing a household, growing old, then dying.

This was extraordinary. No, *they* were extraordinary, and I looked at them in awe, trying to gather myself. It seemed like a long time before one of them spoke to me; as he did, I noticed that his mouth was not moving at all. Inconceivably, I could hear him, although I didn't know how nor did I care. Then I realized that I was hearing *all* of them communicate directly with me. The four little gray beings spoke in a singular voice directly into my consciousness telepathically.

Listening intently, hoping their wisdom might unravel the mystery of my life's present grief, I felt my face break into an enormous smile as tears of joy streamed down my cheeks. What I was hearing was so clear, so palpable, so blessed, that I feared I would burst. Their message did indeed bring a much-needed quiver of hope to my pitiful circumstances. Thankfully they had come!

Staring at them in joy and gratitude, I finally understood the nature of my predicament. Right then and there, I knew exactly what it was I had to do. Blinking my eyes flooded with a stream of salty tears, I caught my breath, not wanting to miss one single tidbit of incoming communication.

Then, inexplicably, just as I was counting my blessings at the important message being relayed to me, my alien hosts were gone! I was dropping through the air, down toward my bed; my still, limp body thumped hard onto the mattress.

I couldn't believe it was morning already. I immediately searched the drawer of my bedside table and was thrilled to find a small pad and a pen. I excitedly began scribbling words that the ETs had communicated. It was all so utterly glorious!

There on my bed, now propped up on my pillow, I wrote as fast and as furiously as I could.

When finished, I jumped out of bed and ran out the door. I rushed down the hallway past patients in wheelchairs and orderlies calling my name. I ignored them all and raced into the large room where "group" session was in full swing. As I burst in on them, a sea of shocked faces gawked at seeing me still in my pajamas.

"There you are!" Dr. Ventura called to me. "I was beginning to wonder if we'd lost you," he said in a scolding tone, implying that he would speak to me later about my tardiness.

Scott motioned for me to sit in the empty chair next to him, and I happily obliged, proudly glancing at my notes as though I were about to present an award-winning speech.

Returning his attention to Lenny, Dr. Ventura said, "Okay, where were we? Lenny, please continue."

Noticing my Cheshire cat grin, Lenny pounced on me. "What's wrong with *you*?" he jeered in a challenging voice.

"I figured it out!" I said with a flourish of my notepad. "*I remember them*," I said, beaming like a small child. "I was little when it happened the first time, but then I forgot, until I saw them again just now. But they're back . . . they're my *friends*!" I said excitedly.

"Would you mind explaining what you are talking about?" Dr. Ventura said in a loud voice, interrupting my moment.

"The loud vibrations, the blinding lights! It's *them* . . . what I mean is, it's *theirs* . . . they have a completely different—"

"Who?" Dr. Ventura bellowed, losing patience with my rambling speech and holding a hand in the air to quiet the other patients' comments and snickers.

"Extraterrestrials," I said loudly, with no apology. "I was a child when they first made contact. Until now, all I remembered was that once, long ago, a shadow had passed over me while playing outside on the lawn. But even then, I knew that *someone or something* was trying to break through to me."

The chattering and comments stopped short as the room fell silent.

"They don't look like us, but they *do speak* . . . but not with their mouths," I said, relieved to finally explain the unexplainable. Waving my notepad in the air as though it was sufficient proof of my claims, I continued. "I can hear them, and they can hear me, too. It's so extraordinary!" I said, as tears of joy and relief welled up in my eyes. Now it all made perfect sense.

Next thing I knew, I began to cry in earnest and doubled over in my chair, allowing a steady stream of sobs to flow out of my very being—my years of struggle had now delivered a comprehensible truth. I now had a context for everything that had happened, and all I could think about was how much I missed my little boy. Maybe, just maybe, I was an excellent mother after all.

While I was deeply lost in my thoughts, and without speaking, Dr. Ventura had moved to my side and now gently led me out of the room. Five minutes later, I was again sitting across from him as he sat at his large oak desk holding my opened medical file.

Clearly humoring me, he leaned back in his chair and asked, "What did they say to you?"

Not realizing the consequences of my confession—or perhaps no longer caring what the good doctor thought about me and my psychiatric status—I gazed out the window and almost dreamily repeated the message that had been given to me by my late-night hosts.

"They said that we're here on Earth to grow spiritually and to learn by being exposed to wrongdoing, and they can help us."

"How's that?" he asked, feigning interest but writing furiously in my medical chart.

"How we respond to wrongdoing is the single most important way that our progress is measured. Most of us fail that part of the test."

"You're being tested?" he asked me, as though he were interested to hear that I had submitted to an evaluation, otherworldly or not, that he had not approved.

"We *all* are. And how we respond to wrongdoing *is* the test. But also, our council observes our choices, decisions, and actions to see if they align with our truest ideals and values. If we abandon them—if our ideals and values become submerged because of fear or the need to control others—well, then we've abandoned the very goals of our soul; we've abandoned *ourselves*. And that makes our heart weep. Get it?"

"Not exactly," the doctor said, writing more notes in my file. "Sounds like quite an undertaking, coming face to face with a . . . ?" He looked directly at me, inviting me to finish the sentence and prove my case for him.

"Spiritual teacher," I replied unapologetically.

"And they look like . . . ?" the psychiatrist asked me, bemused by my conclusion.

"I know what you're thinking," I said. "It's strange, I agree, but isn't it a prejudice to generalize about someone's character based solely on skin color and appearance?"

"Look, we're hardly prejudicial . . . our purpose here is to help you combat these delusions and to become a functioning member of society."

"I'm functioning just fine," I retorted, staring at him intently.

Noticing his cynical, scowling expression, I realized that I was wasting my time. I jumped up from my chair and headed for the door.

As I left the office, Dr. Ventura called out to me, "I know you must be confused and upset. Let's take a well-needed break, and I'll see you in session immediately following lunch."

Eating lunch alone in the cafeteria, I contemplated my next move, wondering how I could ever again forget or discount the beings who had made themselves known to me. It was an extraordinarily delicate bugaboo, I realized, to have one foot in the normal, everyday world and one foot in a mystical realm. Straddling them took more nerve than I could have ever imagined. Certainly it was not for the squeamish, and I wondered what consequences were in store for other human beings who had seen and experienced what I had.

I was startled out of my thoughts by a psychiatrist whom I had never seen. To my surprise, he leaned close to me and quickly whispered, "I'm Dr. Gray. I could get fired or worse for what I'm about to tell you. I've read your file. You're not crazy. Just get the hell out of here, any way that you can."

I stared at him, confounded by his words. As I opened my mouth to respond, he held up his hand to silence me. Turning on his heel, he rushed out of the cafeteria, down the hall, and out of sight.

Dropping my fork on the tray, I followed after him. Then he rounded a corner and disappeared. Rushing to the lobby,

I approached the counter where the administrative secretary was sitting at her typewriter.

"Excuse me?" I asked the secretary, who looked up at me and nodded. "Can you tell me where I can find Dr. Gray? I'd like to make an appointment with him."

"There's no doctor by that name on staff," she said.

"Okay, thank you," I replied, frowning and wondering what had just transpired. How was it possible that a doctor could speak to me in the cafeteria then disappear into thin air five minutes later? Slowly turning away from the secretary, I was deep in thought as to the identity of the strange visitor when I bumped into Scott.

Playfully grabbing hold of my arm, he tugged at me to follow him. "Come on, you're gonna be late for 'group,'" he said, herding me down the hall. "I think you're already in enough of a pickle. Let's not add absenteeism to the list."

Again seated in the large room where the group sessions were conducted, I could feel Dr. Ventura's eyes on me. I'm sure he couldn't help but notice that I was now quiet and detached, staring out the window.

"Lisette, why don't you tell us how you're feeling right now," the doctor ordered, attempting to bring my attention back to the business at hand.

Looking around the room at the blank, empty faces, I felt a sudden sadness and pity for these poor rudderless patients, realizing how unlikely it was that any of them would ever recover their sense of self-empowerment. I felt an inexplicable degree of compassion for them all, wishing that I could say or do something that would really, truly help them. But I knew that there was little I could do to make any difference in the way that their lives played out. At best, I could offer a smile and continue to find a way to rescue myself and find my own truth, which, at the end of the day, might encourage one or two others to find their own paths, too.

"I remember reading somewhere that scientists have determined that there are over a hundred million galaxies in the universe," I said gently to my fellow patients. "That's a lot of places to live. Who can say what's out there? Who can say *who* is out there?"

Lenny spoke up, excited to have a debate on his hand. "Are you talking about aliens?" he asked with a snicker, elbowing Diane next to him, whose mouth had dropped open. The patients burst into laughter, then their laughter was followed by applause, Lenny leading the fray.

Looking at the clapping patients, I smiled, suddenly hopeful that I had broken through their denial after all. Now they, too, had discerned that paranormal phenomena could be linked to any number of wise and helpful otherworldly visitors. The universe was much grander than what was "allowed" and approved of by psychiatry.

"Settle down everyone," Dr. Ventura instructed, attempting to bring the room back to order.

Enormously relieved at their hint of empathy for my plight and the opportunity to connect with them, I smiled broadly at the other patients, allowing the warm sense of inclusion to fill me up for a change. Feeling suddenly understood, I brightened, now beaming, until Lenny winked at me knowingly and summarized his point.

"Psychotropic drugs . . . good stuff, eh?"

As if a cold waterfall had suddenly washed over me, I caught my breath and looked around the room at the laughing faces, realizing that they did not understand me at all. They didn't want to know that a glorious universe awaited us just outside our window. Like the doctor who had evaluated and indoctrinated them, they had become followers of a false cultural belief. They didn't want their imaginations to run free nor were they capable of having a meaningful connection. They were just making fun of me.

Jumping out of my chair, I ran to my room, plopping into my bed and pulling the covers up over me. I stayed there for the rest of the day, not even leaving to eat dinner.

I fell asleep early that night, exhausted. Not long after I had started to dream, the paranormal firestorm came visiting again, and I awoke with a start. I had expected to again fall back into a dreamy, seemingly induced amnesia. To my delight, this time I was able to immediately open my eyes. Moving my arms and legs, I was intrigued to discover that I was curious, not fearful, that the electromagnetic surge no longer immobilized me. I had full use of my body.

As my eyes became accustomed to the bright lights, I saw the same four extraterrestrial beings that I had seen the previous night. They were positioned at the foot of the bed. Again without moving their mouths, a telepathic communication began in earnest.

"I hear you . . ." I whispered to them with the utmost glee as I cocked my head slightly, feeling their words penetrate deep into my core. "Gotta write this down," I said out loud, and again grabbed the notepad from the bedside table.

As I scribbled down their message, I read out loud what I was writing: "Learn and grow from beholding wrongdoing. It is the single most important way that your progress can be measured."

Looking up from my notepad, I addressed them with a puzzled expression. "But why? Why do you keep saying that?"

Now again writing furiously, I listened intently as each new word was relayed to me, and again I spoke out loud as

I wrote: "Because this is the conundrum of all your relation-ships: the manner in which you react to real or imagined wrongdoing. How you respond demonstrates your level of mastery—or lack of it. It's the basis for all your difficult rela-tionships; for all atrocities and world wars."

Just then, I heard the sound of my room door opening. To my dismay, the small gray beings completely vanished. Despite the fact that I had heard the door open, I was capti-vated by my experiences, and I was still somewhat under the effect of the vibrations that still permeated me. All I could do was to lie back on the bed, tingling with emotion and excite-ment, contemplating the importance of the message that I had just been given:

We are here to be tested on our ability to find solutions to dilemmas with courage and grace. In fact, we can gauge our true level of spiritual attainment by the difficulty of those problems that have been solved and overcome with dignity and compas-sion. Naturally, each opportunity for training involves risk, and of course many are not chosen, because of our fear of failure.

I was dreamy yet mesmerized as the reality of my new-found comprehension settled upon me. I was so distracted by the beings' presence just moments before that I continued to stare into space as a male orderly approached me on the bed.

Apparently mistaking me for a doped-up, despondent patient, the orderly sat down on the bed next to me and felt under the covers for my exposed skin. As he touched me, I jumped, my reverie breaking. I looked at him in horror, won-dering what he was doing.

"Relax, I won't hurt you," the orderly said. "You'll enjoy this, too, if you just lie back and remain calm."

Shocked at his gall, I snatched his arm, holding it in a firm vice grip, angry at his attempt to molest me. No doubt startled that he had chosen a patient who was *not* drugged and dopey, he blanched in alarm, recognizing his mistake.

Reading his name badge, I said his name out loud, startling him further. "Magdy, what do you think you're doing?" I asked, angry and annoyed, mostly because he had interrupted my reflective session with the benevolent beings.

Magdy tried to retrieve his arm, but was unable to, because I wasn't releasing him—not just yet.

Furious at the thought that the orderly was accustomed to groping unsuspecting, mentally disturbed, and vulnerable patients, I glared at him. Facing him down, just inches away, I stared intensely into his eyes, trying to find his humanity. Feeling only raw anger at first, my anger slowly turned to pity, then pity to understanding as a major revelation dawned on me.

I released his arm, and he ran from my room, just as the old Hispanic housekeeper walked quietly inside.

"Everything okay, señora?" the housekeeper asked me, looking at me curiously as I lay there on my bed, again utterly immersed in my brewing thoughts. I smiled at her without speaking, completely engrossed in the enormity of what had just infused my mind.

"I saw that bad man—Magdy is his name," the maid said to me, not waiting for any response. "He was in here. I saw him run out, scared that someone may have seen him. I wanted to check on you, make sure that he didn't hurt you," the maid said gently to me.

But I was deep in thought, images of the aliens and their message to me pushing and prodding against all the learned assumptions of a lifetime. They had challenged me in more ways than one, and I couldn't forget them. I couldn't respond and be diverted from my current mission of pondering their message, their very existence and the implication of their visit.

Images of Dr. Gray approaching me in the cafeteria were superimposed over images of Magdy groping me under the blankets; these in turn were superimposed over images of the alien being from before, who had shape-shifted into the wise elder. What did the three events have in common? I wondered, as the phrase "shape shifting" kept forming on my lips. There was an inexplicable connection between all of them and the aliens' message, somehow pointing to my life and my long-lost little son.

The housekeeper tidied up the room, speaking to me as though I were a little child—or a patient who had been over-medicated.

I whispered the phrase "shape shifter" over and over to myself.

I was vaguely aware of the maid sadly looking at me, probably assuming that I was incoherent, when the truth of it was that I was on the verge of one of the grandest discoveries of my life—a discovery that would change the course of my life and that of my child's.

"Don't worry, be happy," she said in a sing-song voice, reaching up to turn on a television set that was mounted to the wall.

"This will make you feel better," she said, adjusting the volume, wrongly assuming that I was upset and forlorn. "I always watch a little television to help me get to sleep," she said kindly. And with that, she picked up her cleaning bucket and mop and quietly headed for the door. "I hope you feel better soon," she said, closing the door behind her.

No more than three minutes elapsed after she had left the room when I fell into a deep state of reverie, the words "shape shifter" still repeating softly on my lips. Soon, my meditation rolled into a long, deep sleep.

Neither Dr. Ventura nor I had any way of knowing that as I slept the deep sleep of the spiritually initiated, I was in the process at that moment of internalizing and comprehending how the magnificent forces of the universe had masterminded my own lovely escape.

The next morning, I was awakened to the drone of a local newscaster announcing the morning news. The blare of the anchorwoman's voice filled up the room. I was surprised that the television was on, but then remembered the old maid's nighttime visit to my room. I propped up on one elbow when I heard the anchorwoman say the name "Dr. Gerry Helman."

Startled, I looked hard at the television screen.

"I'm here in front of the main courthouse in Los Angeles, where a ruling was just handed down regarding Dr. Helman's criminal case. Found guilty of 150 counts of insurance fraud, he's been sentenced to eleven years in prison, along with his office manager Elaine Hammer. Former billing supervisor Lisette Larkins, who originally brought the case to the attention of the Department of Insurance Fraud two years ago, has been awarded an unspecified amount for damages relating to her illegal termination and for her bravery in stepping forward."

I jumped from my bed and raced out of the room and down the hallway past mumbling psychiatric patients and orderlies who bellowed at me to slow down. Ignoring them, I rushed into Dr. Ventura's office, startling him. After attempting to eject me from the room, his secretary asked him, "Shall I call security?"

"No," he said, closing the door on her. "I'll handle this myself."

"You need to make an appointment like every other patient, Lisette," Dr. Ventura said sternly, taking a few steps toward me, as if trying to intimidate me into leaving on my own.

"I'm *not* like every other patient, for many reasons," I said. "Besides, last night one of your male orderlies fondled me when he thought I was asleep, and I have a witness."

Dr. Ventura went back to his desk, sat down, and pulled out and opened my medical file. "I'm making a record of your unfounded paranoia," he said, scribbling in my chart. "Now, Lisette, it's well known that you've been seeing and hearing things that others don't, so this sounds like one more example of—"

"This isn't the first time this kind of thing has happened in here, and you know it. The Hispanic housekeeper referred to Magdy as a 'bad man,' and I will press charges. So, consider me discharged with full medical approval."

"I'm sorry, that won't be possible. Your diagnosis is still pending, and frankly this unfounded accusation only confirms—"

"Three weeks in this place is long enough. You're signing me out, as I requested, or this place will be crawling with investigative reporters. If you've heard the news this morning, Dr. Helman was convicted of insurance fraud, and I was the government's chief witness."

"That was you? You're that 'Larkins?'" Dr. Ventura asked, blanching.

Standing up from his chair, he started to pace in the room, coming to a stop at the far window, where he gazed outside as though considering my threat.

With his back turned away, I eyed a small stack of blank forms piled on the edge of his desk; I grabbed one and looked at it carefully. The heading on the form read "Termination of Treatment."

Walking over to a table underneath the window where he stood, I slapped the form down hard in front of him; he jumped, surprised by the force of my hand.

"Sign it. *Now*," I said with a quiet strength that I knew he could *feel*. "Seems I've got talent as a whistleblower. Besides, I'm late for court."

For a moment, we stood there silently looking at each other, and slowly I picked up a pen and placed it in his hand. Taking a deep breath, he bent over the table and signed his name to the form.

"And I need a dollar in change to call my family and my attorney." He shook his head in disbelief but handed me the change in his pocket. I hurried out of his office and over to the pay phones to call my mother.

Thirty minutes later, now dressed in my street clothes, I called my attorney from the pay phone in the lobby. He was upset that he hadn't been able to reach me for the last three weeks. I asked him about the amount of the award, and his answer delighted me. I knew immediately what I would do with it.

I next stopped at the administrative counter and addressed the secretary, who was at her desk typing.

"Please buzz me out," I instructed her, motioning to the large security doors that were blocking my safe passage.

"I'll need to see your signed termination please," she said, accepting the paper from me. After looking it over, she handed it back to me, and pressed a button under her desk. There was a loud "buzz," after which the doors automatically swung open. I walked briskly outside and squinted in the bright morning sunlight, practically running headfirst into my frantic family, who were rushing up the steps to the hospital.

"Lisette! What are you doing here?" my mother asked, joined by two of my sisters and my young niece.

After hugging one another, and despite my mother's dazed expression, I motioned to her parked car, saying only, "I need a ride to my attorney's office, then you need to get me to the Los Angeles Superior Court, Family Law Division. I'll explain on the way."

An hour later, I bolted up the concrete steps to the front door of the courthouse. I rushed inside. In the distance, I spotted Peter's unmistakable form and my own darling boy who stood nearby. They were apparently waiting outside the courtroom for their case to be called by the bailiff.

Seeing me running down the hall toward him, my son rushed into my arms. Shocked to see me there, Peter bellowed, "Who approved your discharge?"

With my son still in my arms, I smiled at Peter despite his disapproving scowl. "Drop the custody case, and the thirty-seven thousand dollar award is yours, no questions asked."

"Your settlement's half mine anyway. California's a community property state, remember?" Peter retorted.

"You'll only get half," I responded, pelting my son with kisses. "But if you want the whole thing, go inside and take our case off the docket."

He stared at me for a long moment. "Do you have the check?"

I held it up; he reached for it, but I pulled it away. "After you cancel the hearing and sign this award-of-custody agreement that my attorney just wrote up."

I handed it to him. He read it over and nodded his head, then turned around and headed for the clerk's office.

Chapter Fourteen

KENT AND JEANNETTE'S MALIBU estate was filled with amenities, and their Jacuzzi was one of my favorites. I sank down into the bubbles; the hot water felt wonderful on my aching back muscles, and I could see that Jeannette was also enjoying its therapeutic heat. It had been more than two years since I'd started in this caregiver position, and while it had had its challenges, I felt close to Jeannette; her welfare had become my number one priority.

After a few more minutes of soaking, Jeannette gave me a hand signal that she was too hot and wanted to get out. The pink rays of the rising sun were just peeking over the mountains to the east, and I reluctantly helped her out of the Jacuzzi and wiped her down with a fluffy white towel. She smiled and I smiled back, but mine was tinged with a touch of sadness; I knew that today might be our most difficult day yet.

Jeannette groaned and made another hand gesture, so I helped her into her terrycloth robe, pulling the belt tight and knotting it. While she had lost the ability to speak, I was still able to understand her. In fact, Jeannette was so expressive with her grunts and moans, in addition to her flailing arms and hand signals, that I had no trouble discerning exactly what she wanted. Today was no exception.

How could I tell her that this special Jacuzzi bath would be her last? I wondered. Having almost lost the ability to swallow food or drink liquid, she was now painfully thin. I had woken her early, and she may have assumed that the reason was a sunrise dip in the Jacuzzi. But that was the treat that would be followed by an early morning drive to the hospital for an outpatient procedure that would be difficult for her to accept.

I could see Kent watching Jeannette from the kitchen window, his contemplation of his wife tinged as always with both love and sadness. He now motioned to me, pointing to his watch. The time had come to get Jeannette dressed and loaded in the car for the ride into town.

A half hour later, now cozy inside the warm coupe, the three of us sped down Pacific Coast Highway, enjoying the light morning traffic. In the backseat, Jeannette groaned and frowned, pointing out the window as if to say, "Where the hell are we going?"

"Into Santa Monica," I replied, as Kent and I exchanged nervous glances. We'd had many private conversations about this procedure and how best to explain it to Jeannette in a way that she could understand well enough to appreciate its necessity.

Turning around in his seat to begin the difficult explanation, Kent said, "You're having a procedure at the hospital; it won't take long, and we're going home afterward. The procedure will help you get the nutritional calories you need to stay healthy."

In the rearview mirror, I watched Jeannette smile and nod, clearly having no idea whatsoever what Kent was saying. She probably figured that we were going out to get milkshakes, her favorite treat. As we pulled up to the valet at Santa Monica Hospital, Kent and I stepped out, and each took one of Jeannette's arms to help her out of the backseat. She swatted both of us away, grabbing the tilted front seat headrest and pulling herself out.

Two hours later, the gastroenterologist stepped into the waiting room and motioned for us to join him in the recovery room. Walking in quietly, we each took up a sentry post on either side of Jeannette's hospital bed, waiting for the doctor's post-operative instructions.

"She should wake up any minute now," he said, pulling up Jeannette's hospital gown so that we could see what he had done, exposing the G-tube now in her abdomen. "The G-tube was inserted surgically via a small incision made in the abdomen, clear through to the stomach. The tube has a disc connected to it that sits on the inside of the stomach wall to hold it in place and stop it from being pulled out."

Kent and I exchanged worried glances, hoping that it was indeed secure, because Jeannette would certainly try to pull it out.

"And if she starts to yank on it?" Kent asked.

"It'll irritate the stomach lining and cause severe cramps that should dissuade her."

We again exchanged glances. Just how well did the doctor really know Jeannette?

"Now you can feed her with approved liquid nutrition," the doctor explained, showing us the length of the tube, how to open the end cap, and, using a sterile syringe, how to pour liquid inside. After giving us cleaning instructions, the doctor applied a light bandage to the surgical site, then pulled Jeannette's gown back over it.

"It's a very minor incision," the doctor said. "She won't need pain killers, just an aspirin. It's actually a very simple procedure."

"Okay, we understand how to feed her and how to clean the tube, right, Lisette?" Kent asked, searching my face to be sure that I understood exactly what to do.

I nodded confidently, smiling at both of them but knowing that this was the least of our problems.

Looking from Kent to me, the doctor started to shake his head, and his expression became somber. "I don't think that either of you fully realize just what lies ahead," he said. "Jeannette's condition is worsening, and not just mentally. Her body is now on a downhill trajectory along with her mind, but as both fail in unison . . . well, this is a terrible recipe for caregiver burnout."

Just then, Jeannette started to stir, groaning and pulling on the IV line inserted at her wrist.

"Amy," the doctor called over his shoulder to a nurse, "get the soft restraints please. She's waking up."

Returning to his lecture, the doctor picked up where he had left off. "Look, caring for an Alzheimer's patient who's entering the final stages of the disease . . . well that's a significant challenge for *any* professional nursing team—which doesn't fit either of you."

The nurse began to attach restraints from Jeannette's arms and legs to the guardrail, just as Jeannette attempted to roll over onto her stomach. It took all four of us to hold her down. Jeannette's eyes were still closed, but detecting the leather restraints, she began to kick and scream, wailing loudly in protest.

"Let's get her sedated," the doctor ordered the nurse, who immediately injected a solution into her IV.

Almost shouting now to be heard over Jeannette's protests, the doctor motioned for us to move away from the bed so that Jeannette could not hear his dire appeal.

"I implore you to begin thinking about placing Jeannette in an environment where she can get around-the-clock care. There are excellent facilities in Los Angeles that are staffed with nurses and doctors experienced in dealing with end-stage Alzheimer's patients."

Suddenly, a female patient in the bed next to Jeannette's groaned loudly, also waking up from her post-op anesthesia. A male orderly rushed to the pretty girl's side, and, strangely, he looked over at us self-consciously, as if afraid we were monitoring him.

Memories of my psychiatric hospital stay and the orderly who had groped me flashed before my eyes. As I looked at the male orderly who was tending to the female patient next to us, I wondered if this was a sign or a warning. Jeannette, who was writhing uncomfortably under the arm and leg restraints, drew my attention back to her.

"No, we can do this," Kent and I said in unison. Turning to the doctor, I said, "At those kinds of group treatment centers, the patients are usually overmedicated due to the lack of one-on-one care; they become blank and empty, and you can see it in their faces. Loved ones don't *really* know what's happening with respect to the patients' care," I said.

I stepped over to Jeannette's side and stroked her head as she moaned angrily, still quite groggy. "No, we couldn't do that to Jeannette. *I* couldn't do that to Jeannette. She'd feel betrayed, and no one should have to feel the depth of being abandoned by her family. If I have to, I'll move into the house and sleep on a cot next to her at night."

"We'll do whatever it takes. I agree wholeheartedly with Lisette," Kent said emphatically. "Jeannette is staying home with us. We're not putting her in any facility. That's final."

"The choice is yours," the doctor replied. "I've seen this scenario a thousand times. It's going to exhaust you. It's going to suck every last drop of your patience and energy right out of you."

Or we can all grow from the experience, I thought, but I didn't say it out loud. Perhaps Jeannette's illness, like my own previous struggles, was somehow predestined to create an inner shift for her, as well as for us.

Jeannette now woke up, tried to sit up in bed, and groaned loudly in protest at the sight of her hospital gown, her restrained position, and the IV in her arm.

"If you're up for it, more power to both of you," the doctor said, looking at us as though having trouble comprehending our reasoning, especially in light of Kent's ability to afford the very best care. "But you'll need to child-proof your house, if you haven't already done so."

After writing out an antibiotic prescription for Jeannette, the doctor handed me some papers and a bag of supplies for the G-tube. "This is no cakewalk. Call me if you need me."

Chapter Fifteen

ANOTHER SIX MONTHS HAD gone by. On a sunny morning in Malibu, Jeannette and I were slowly walking around a small shopping center when I noticed that Jeannette's leg was dragging behind her more than usual. Because this created a constant tripping hazard, I kept a close eye on the sidewalk; whenever it was uneven or when a rock or a twig lay on our path, I took hold of her arm. When I offered such assistance, she often frowned and grunted, pushing me away with flailing arms. She didn't like help walking, especially in public.

After exiting a gift store, Jeannette pointed across the street to a juice bar where she liked to drink fruit smoothies. With the help of a straw, she was still able to sip and to swallow just a few drops, and although most of the drink was thrown away, simply holding the cup satisfied her sense of normalcy. The G-tube still handled Jeannette's primary nutritional needs.

To cross the street, I had to first help her off the curb. As she stepped down, despite my best effort at holding her arm, Jeannette tripped and fell into the gutter. I retrieved her purse from where it had skidded away, but she snatched it angrily from me, afraid that I might be trying to keep it.

Jeannette was tall and had wide shoulders; no matter how much I tried, I could not pull her up to her feet. I looked around for another shopper or a pedestrian, but there was no one, and as Jeannette gathered herself into a sitting position, she looked at me pleadingly, as if to say, just pull me up!

First I tried pulling on her hands to heave her up, but that didn't work. Then I tried grabbing on to her forearms, then under her arms for leverage, but her body kept going limp—she didn't remember how to assist me by leaning forward to help herself up. She kept slipping back down onto the street. It was awful. I couldn't help her. Tears of frustration rolled down my cheeks; exhausted from the effort, I finally sat down on the curb next to her.

After a long while, a car drove by, and the driver looked at us curiously sitting on the side of the road; I motioned for him to stop. He slowed down and pulled over to help us. Jumping out of his car, he rushed over to assist me, and we eventually got Jeannette up to a standing position. After thanking him profusely, we walked across the street to the juice bar for her smoothie, then headed back to the car. At that point, I made a decision.

We drove to a shopping center in Santa Monica, but there was no parking near the medical supply store, and I had to park across the street in another lot. We got out of the car; Jeannette took her large purse and I my even larger satchel. It took forever to maneuver her across the street and the near side lot, but at last we arrived at the small store.

Holding open the front door, I helped guide her slowly through the entrance to the shop. Now visibly dragging her sluggish leg, Jeannette took a small awkward step, then slid the offending leg forward, repeating this motion to move along inch by inch. She swatted away my attempts to help her, instead grabbing hold of a store shelf, then a water dispenser, neither of which could properly support her weight. I rushed to steady her despite her protests.

Distracted by the array of medical supplies on the shelves, Jeannette took a step forward, and her toe caught the edge of the carpet. She plunged to the floor. Dropping my satchel, I rushed to her side, relieved to see that she wasn't hurt. As I tried to help her up, the store clerk hurried over and assisted me, then picked up my satchel and handed it to me.

"Thanks," I said to him. Now somewhat mobile again, Jeannette grabbed hold of a wobbly store display, and I shook my head in exasperation, taking hold of her arm. Furious, she swatted me away again, grunting in protest, too proud to be helped with such a simple act as walking.

"May I help you find something?" the friendly clerk asked, following along behind us and looking worriedly at Jeannette, who was now unsteadily shuffling down the aisle.

"I need to buy a wheelchair before she becomes too restless in here," I said, thankful that Jeannette was now busy gawking at another display in the cluttered shop. The packed shelves were lined with adult diapers and syringes, bandages and hot packs—anything and everything that might be needed to care for ill or elderly patients.

"Yes, I understand your predicament," the clerk responded. "The wheelchairs are over here."

The front of the store had large, floor-to-ceiling plate-glass windows, providing a sunny unobstructed view of the hectic boulevard outside. Placed against the window was a row of wheelchairs of every conceivable size, shape, and color. It was my mission to select one for Jeannette and help her make the seemingly impossible emotional transition from being semi-mobile to almost totally wheelchair bound. There was nothing pleasant about watching someone lose the use of their body. But Jeannette had taken so many falls and had become so bruised and banged up from tripping that this was an inevitable next step in her care.

"I hope you realize that if Jeannette should fall and break a leg, arm, or hip, we're cooked!" Kent had reminded me at dinner recently. "It'll be impossible to keep her in bed during such a long recovery," Kent had warned, preparing me for the difficult task of buying a wheelchair, then getting her to actually use it. "After you get the wheelchair, then you've got to figure out how to bathe her. She hasn't let us near her with a bar of soap in more than three days."

Today Kent was needed in the courtroom, so after this morning's debacle in the gutter, I had decided that this was the day to figure out the solution to both.

As I surveyed the huge selection of wheelchairs, I knew that it was this, or Jeannette would have to be moved to a full-time care facility. If she fell and broke her hip, her recovery would be exacerbated by her inability to understand her own care. That was an explosive combination that both Kent and I wanted to avoid. Tantrum or not, I was not leaving that store without wheeling her out the door.

The sales clerk showed me a few floor samples, and I called Jeannette over to join me. "These are too large," I told him, pointing instead to a small sporty model that appeared to be sufficiently compact. I would need to be able to easily maneuver Jeannette within the confines of the house, from the kitchen to the bathroom and into her bedroom.

As I surveyed the smaller wheelchairs, Jeannette started to moan and to point to the door, indicating that she wanted to leave. "Look, Jeannette," I said, immediately withdrawing her coloring book and a small box of crayons from my satchel. She eagerly placed it on the counter near the cashier's register and began to happily color a page, buying me a few more minutes to complete my transaction.

As I toyed with the levers of the wheelchair, becoming familiar with how it could be folded in half for transport, I hoped that it would prevent another tripping fiasco. Then it occurred to me that should Jeannette lose the ability to stand and to support her own weight, how on earth was I going to transfer her limp body from the wheelchair to the toilet or, for that matter, into bed?

What else could I do to prepare myself for her deteriorating condition? I wondered what the limits of my physical abilities were. At that very moment, one of the many wise messages that I had clairvoyantly received over the years arose in my memory—an uncanny prescription for the very difficulty that I was pondering at that moment: "Prepare for any physical contingency," I repeated out loud, running my fingers over the handles of the wheelchair. "Prepare your body for life's many demands." At that moment, I vowed to begin a vigorous workout regimen and stick to it. Jeannette's house had an upstairs gym, and there was no reason that I couldn't find a few minutes every day to lift weights and do a little cardio. Besides, my job duties practically demanded that I stay physically fit in order to properly care for Jeannette.

"Do you like that one?" the clerk asked.

Breaking out of my thoughtful reverie, I nodded and pointed to the portable model.

"Good choice," said the clerk, pulling the small sporty blue wheelchair out of the lineup. "It easily folds up and will fit in most car trunks."

"Is it waterproof?" I asked.

The clerk grinned at me in surprise. "No," he said. "If it gets wet, it will take a few days to dry out."

"Okay, then I'll take two of them," I said, turning to my patient who was still engrossed with her crayons. "Jeannette, which color do you like best—the red or the blue one?"

After looking at the wheelchairs, she grunted in annoyance, shaking her head vigorously. Placing her hands firmly on her hips, she grimaced disapprovingly as if to say, "Don't even think about it." She sidled up to the wheelchair and gave it a good kick.

It was amazing to me how, in some cases, Jeannette had difficulty understanding what was transpiring, yet in this instance, she was keenly aware of the situation, refusing to participate in a purchase that would limit her precious freedom.

Undeterred, I sat down in the blue wheelchair, motioning for the clerk to wheel me up and down the aisle in front of Jeannette. "I like this blue one. How about you?" I asked her, smiling broadly, as though I were purchasing a chair for the living room.

Perhaps because she wanted to exert some degree of choice, Jeannette pointed instead to the red wheelchair. "The red one it is," I said to the clerk, who smiled weakly when I handed him my credit card, glancing nervously at Jeannette's frowning face. He must have guessed that the hardest part of the transaction was yet to come, no doubt wondering how I would ever get this stubborn woman into the contraption.

"You're going to need a few different-sized ramps to get in and out of the house," the clerk said, motioning to a stack of stainless steel ramps that folded in half for easy transport. "Place them over the stairs or any door's threshold. You can wheel this right up and over it," he said, as I nodded in agreement.

I told him the approximate height of the front steps, and he pointed out the appropriate ramp, plus the adjustable

step-ramps for inside the house. "Can you have those delivered this morning?" I asked.

"Yeah, sure thing," he said helpfully. "I can ask the driver
to set it up at your front door, so that by the time you arrive
home, you'll be able to wheel her right into the house."

"That would be fantastic," I said, glancing nervously at
Jeannette, who had returned to her coloring book. After I
signed the credit card slip and wrote down our address, the
clerk removed the price tag from the wheelchair. "Let me help
you get that to your car," he offered helpfully, folding it up
and hoping to preempt my mission to wheel Jeannette out of
there. I know he wanted to avoid the inevitable showdown
with such a recalcitrant customer in the middle of his store,
but I could not agree.

"Thanks, but no," I responded firmly, pointing through
the glass window at our car that was parked not only clear
across a busy street but even farther away at the far end of the
large parking lot. "See that tiny speck of a silver Mercedes way
down there?" I asked dramatically. "It was a safari-like venture to get Jeannette here from that distance, not to mention
her two falls just this morning. No, we're not going back the
same way we came in." Speaking firmly to my charge, I said,
"Jeannette, come on; I'm going to push you across the street
in this. Hop in."

Miraculously, she sat in it, handing me her coloring book
and box of crayons, which I stuffed back into my satchel.
Beaming at the clerk, I was overjoyed at the thought of safely
shepherding my charge through the busy intersection, avoiding yet another possible spill onto the hard asphalt.

"I'll get the door for you," the clerk said, rushing to open the
wide double doors as I pushed Jeannette over the threshold and
out into the noonday sun. Our excursion was going smoothly

as we approached the intersection, and I pushed the button on the pole for the pedestrian "walk" signal. When the light turned green, I maneuvered the wheelchair down the cement corner ramp, thankful for civil codes that had turned an ordinary cement curb into one that was wheelchair accessible.

Halfway through the intersection, for some reason, Jeannette decided to stand up.

"No, Jeannette, you've got to stay seated!" I said firmly, pushing her back down into the seat. "I'm wheeling you; please stay seated. We're in the middle of the road."

Jeannette didn't listen and stood up, leaning heavily on one side of the wheelchair; it threatened to overturn with her still in it. Grabbing the chair before they both tipped into the street, I just barely steadied it in time. I felt a sudden, painful twinge in my back muscles, and I knew I had pulled something and would pay with soreness later.

Yelling at a driver who had the gall to impatiently pass close by our mishap without stopping, I pushed Jeannette back down in her seat, yelling loudly at her to stay in place. Just then another car startled us by honking because his light had turned green.

Just then, I caught sight of the store clerk, who was watching us in horror from the shop window. To my surprise, he raced out the door toward us carrying a curious wooden tray and wheeling the second wheelchair, which I had forgotten. By this time, Jeannette had stood up again. He motioned to some dangling straps that hung from the side of the wheelchair, and I recognized my mistake.

Nudging the chair closer to Jeannette, I then pushed her down into it, and before she could object, I buckled the seat belts snugly around her hips. She squealed in protest, kicking wildly and narrowly missing me as I tried to adjust the footrests.

Then, grabbing the wooden tray from the clerk, I undid its Velcro straps and secured it in place just above Jeannette's lap.

Then, withdrawing her coloring book and box of crayons from my satchel, I placed them on the tray. This distracted her long enough for me to push her to the car. Bringing up the rear was the second wheelchair, which I pulled behind me with my other hand. Finally, we were headed home.

I spent a long, trying day helping Jeannette acclimate to her wheelchair. By the early evening, she was yawning and rubbing her eyes. It was time to get her to bed, but not before she bathed.

I wheeled her into her bathroom, turned on the shower, and adjusted the water temperature. Then I helped Jeannette into her swimsuit and switched her into the second wheelchair that was next to the shower. I buckled her safely into it. After putting on my own swimsuit, I readied myself for what might be the fight of my life.

After taking a deep breath, and with as much finesse as I could muster, I firmly wheeled Jeannette in her wheelchair up the ramp and into the shower stall, closing the door behind us.

Hollering and screeching like a wild tigress, Jeannette kicked and fought at the sensation of warm water cascading down on us. As calmly as I could, I explained what we were doing, while I gently washed her hair and soaped her armpits, ducking the occasional left hook. She would not be consoled.

After rinsing her off and rolling her out of the shower stall, I dried her, put her into her pajamas, and got her into bed; she fought me off the entire time. Once I had her tucked under the sheets, I breathed deeply, wondering if the doctor was right. No matter her reaction, perhaps it was time to bring in reinforcements.

When Kent arrived home from work later that evening, I sat down to have a serious talk with him. "I think we need a Navy SEAL to watch over your wife," I said sadly.

"Sorry to hear that your day was so difficult. I think it's time to bring in outside help."

"Yes," I reluctantly agreed. "Today she almost broke my finger when I tried to feed her through the G-tube and when I gave her a shower," I said, showing him my bruised hand. "Yesterday, she locked herself in the bathroom for two hours. I wish I could handle it on my own."

"No need to feel that you've failed," Kent responded. "Let's find an expert, someone just right; someone whom we can trust to do the right thing."

Nodding enthusiastically, my thoughts returned to many years before, when, as a young mother, I had also sought out an expert, someone whom I could trust to do the right thing. Seeking validation and an outside opinion, I had finally found that someone.

Chapter Sixteen

AFTER MY DIVORCE FROM Peter, and having regained primary custody of my son, I realized that it was time to find a psychologist whom I could trust to objectively evaluate me. I was ready to know if my mind was fully intact or not.

My son and I had moved back to my childhood home in the Malibu hills. I'd left the psychiatric hospital with no assets other than my son, and my mother was more than delighted to welcome home her daughter and grandson.

Now that Walter was living with me full time, Peter was eligible to take him every other weekend, but he was often out of town on business, so we tried our best to get father and son together as often as possible.

I enrolled Walter in grade school and went about the business of acclimating to the life of a single, working mom. By day, I was an assistant to a real estate broker. By night, I was an extraterrestrial encounter experiencer.

Despite the fact that I had adjusted to the reality of my mysterious nightlife and had accepted the extraterrestrials' gentle mentoring, the protective mother in me wanted to be certain that my son wasn't being raised by a woman with a psychological disorder; this is why I felt it was time to revisit the subject of my mental health. However, this time, I wanted a thorough clinical assessment by an objective, brilliant clinician—one who was not limited by outdated psychiatric assumptions or motivated to find pathology due to the strategies employed by his business office. I began to search for an excellent, unbiased psychotherapist.

At my son's annual physical, Walter's pediatrician greeted us warmly and had Walter climb up on the exam table. The doctor proceeded with the checkup, and Walter was soon given a clean bill of health.

Afterward, Dr. Jones asked me, "How are those nightmares? I trust that they've stopped by now?"

I pondered how to answer his question without creating too much intrigue. "I'm doing great!" I responded, nodding happily. "I still have unusual dreams, but they're hardly nightmares anymore."

"Well, seems like you've acclimated to motherhood, which is healthy," the doctor responded.

"But I do have some lingering concerns," I added, and he nodded his head. "So can you please refer me to an excellent therapist?"

"Yes, I know a marriage and family therapist who's very well respected. I think you'll like him. My secretary can give you his contact information."

The following week, I was sitting outside the large corner office of Alan Ludington, MFT, whose private practice was located in nearby Westlake Village. I had received rave reviews about him from just about everyone I had asked, and it wasn't easy to get an appointment to see him. As I sat in his waiting area, I admired the beautifully decorated room and the plethora of framed certificates that lined the wall.

He was the founder of his own clinical practice, lectured at California Lutheran University, and consulted widely with corporations and universities. I hoped that he had the expertise to evaluate my unusual experiences and was someone who had stayed abreast of cutting-edge therapeutic techniques.

"What can I do for you?" Alan Ludington asked warmly,
as he extended his hand, then walked me into his office.

"Dr. Ludington, thanks for seeing me on such short
notice," I said, handing him my intake questionnaire.

"Please, just call me Al," he said. "I'm a therapist not a
psychiatrist."

I nodded my head. "I understand."

"Dr. Jones said you were having 'unusual' dreams, and
that piqued my interest."

"Well, it's a little more involved than that and kind of
hard to explain," I said. "I just want to know for certain that
my mind is, well, *intact*."

"Please, have a seat," he responded, sitting down opposite
me. He took a few minutes to read through my questionnaire,
stopping periodically to look up at me. "What makes you
think that your mind's *not* intact?" he finally asked.

"The truth is, I feel good about myself—at least I do
now—although that wasn't always the case. But not everyone
shares my confidence. I've grown to accept that my experiences and 'abilities' may not be that . . . common," I said.

"What type of 'abilities' are you referring to?"

"I'm seeing and hearing . . . mysterious phenomena and
. . . visitors." Al raised his eyebrows curiously. "But does that
necessarily mean that I'm crazy?" I asked him, leaning forward in the chair.

"Excellent question," Al responded with a nod. "But am I
to assume that someone else *does* think you're crazy?"

"I think it's fair to say that the majority of the population, with a few minor exceptions, would indeed consider that anyone claiming to have seen and heard what *I'm* experiencing *cannot* be playing with a full deck."

Chuckling, Al raised his eyebrows, asking, "Is that so?"

"Yes, I think that's a fair assumption," I replied directly, feeling that I did not have the luxury of equivocating on this one point.

"Exactly what are we talking about?" Al asked me unabashedly. "Just what is it that you've seen and heard?"

"I'm told that you're the best in this area, so I've come here with full confidence in your objectivity and expertise."

"Thank you," Al responded patiently, but clearly noting that I had not answered his question.

"And I can assure you that I would no more place myself in a position of vulnerability—diagnostically speaking—than I'd voluntarily give up my own son. *But* I'm a mother, and my son's welfare comes first. So what I propose is that you do what you do best, which is to analyze, assess, and ultimately decide what diagnosis, if any, best denotes my mental status, given certain variables."

"Such as?"

"I want to know if my mind's . . . normal," I said, trying to suppress a well of emotion, realizing that I would have to make a claim about the aliens to a degree that I had not yet revealed.

"Why would that be one of your concerns?"

"I've been talking to extraterrestrials."

"I see," Al said, with no overt reaction, and I had to wonder what he was thinking. I sat there looking at him, not needing to say anything. Al responded in kind, staring back and considering me, too, in silence.

Finally, he spoke, "I am in practice as a licensed marriage and family therapist, *not* as an expert who specializes in paranormal features. But I have degrees in religion and philosophy and a doctorate in theology, so these types of mystical experiences interest me. That being said, my colleagues and I would evaluate you simply on the basis of observing and assessing you in various clinical settings, possibly over a period of many years."

"Many *years*?" I asked incredulously. "Why so long?"

"I don't know much about you as of yet; however, it says here on your admittance forms that you were in a very difficult marriage; that your husband feared for your sanity, and you endured a psychiatric hospital stay; and that you have endured a great deal of stress as a result of your emotional response to, shall we say, apparent extraordinary events."

Nodding, I sighed deeply, agreeing that perhaps it would take longer than I had assumed to unravel the events of the last few years.

"It just takes time to really get to know someone," Al said. "Especially if they are anxious about revealing their innermost thoughts and experiences for fear of ridicule."

"I admit that I'm nervous about telling you everything, that you might certainly think I'm nuts," I explained.

"I can appreciate your concerns," Al said. "Carrying around all those secrets, for all these years, must be causing you severe stress. Your mind may be perfectly sound, but the weight of concealing your inner experiences—which are a huge part of your life and are ongoing—well, it can't be helping your adjustment. The only sane option is to give yourself the freedom to come in here, every week, month after month, and tell me exactly what has happened to you. Then, as I see fit, at certain intervals, we'll do some testing and also start you in 'group' therapy."

"So you agree to take me on?" I asked hopefully.

"If you agree to submit to evaluation," he stated. "If you really, truly want to get to the bottom of what's upsetting you, then it requires your utmost honesty and courage."

"I agree," I responded. "I'm ready to get to the bottom of it."

"Great," Al replied. "There are several modalities we use here, and, I might add, the most important one is a team approach to analysis. What that means is that we have a group of highly dedicated, educated, and experienced clinicians who together assess and cross-check our findings. It's not as though one person spontaneously comes up with an armchair diagnosis based on personal bias."

"That's exactly what I've been looking for."

"We've been around for a long time and have gained an excellent reputation, because we look deeply and carefully into all aspects of the mental health of our clients. There are no quick diagnoses, and there are no quick fixes. This is a thoughtful yet thorough approach."

"I'm very relieved to hear that," I replied, smiling and appreciating the fact that a team approach would temper any one clinician's negative opinion from getting in the way of sound, therapeutic conclusions. "I want to know that just because I *sound* weird doesn't necessarily prove that I am," I explained.

"I can understand your concerns," Al replied. "It would be simple for anyone in my profession to immediately dismiss you as unsound rather than evaluate you objectively, while still considering your remarkable claims. However, I must warn you: If you are impaired and disordered—that is, if you *do* have a psychological disorder—it *will* inevitably surface. If there's a crack, I'll find it. But if it *is* there, at that point we can discuss what to do about it. It's not the end of the world. In that case, there are viable and effective treatment options."

"That's reassuring," I said.

"My goal here is to consider whether or not you could be diagnosed with any significant disorder, while taking into consideration variable diagnostic information. Throughout your treatment here, there are several different types of pathological disorders and acute diagnoses that I will have to 'rule out' or consider. Then, as part of my routine case management, I will be presenting your case to my team of clinicians.

"We have twenty-six professionals, including psychologists, psychiatrists, and marriage and family therapists. I will be holding case review sessions once a week, at which time your case will be discussed."

"Do you have any precedent here with respect to my types of experiences?" I asked. "What I mean is, have you treated other patients who've made claims such as mine?"

"During the past twenty-five years, I've counseled other clients who were clairvoyant or who have reported unusual paranormal experiences—and they were *not* disordered or psychotic. Just because a person sees and hears things that others don't, does not alone suggest mental pathology."

"Okay, then, I'm ready to start," I said, confidently. "How about if I start at the beginning?"

"Yes, I agree; at the beginning."

It took me almost two years of individual therapy to recount to my therapist all that had happened to me since the nightly light show first erupted in my bedroom, including snippets of memories from experiences as a child. Then, one day as we began our session, Al asked me to follow him in to a large conference room at the rear of the building. Here Al introduced me to nine of his clients who were already seated and asked me to join this interactive group.

"Thanks, everybody, for being here on time. As you know, this is a group consisting of nine sophisticated professionals, who have each had a few years of individual therapy with me or with one of my colleagues. The goal in group therapy is to observe and evaluate each of you over a period of an additional four years.

"During that time, if any of you are impaired or disordered, your psychopathology will become very evident in intensive group therapy such as this," Al explained. "But there's nothing to be afraid of or to guard against. You're here because you want to feel better; to live the fullest life of which you are capable."

All of us nodded in agreement, after which Al introduced two clinicians who would assist him in conducting the ongoing weekly sessions. Al looked around the room at each of us. "We've received signed waivers from each of you, agreeing to be videotaped during these weekly sessions. We use these for training purposes as well as for evaluation."

Al stopped to point out the camera and invited us to become comfortable with its constant presence in the room. "What happens here is confidential, but this allows for an excellent training opportunity; also effective team assessment. You can always opt out if it feels too uncomfortable."

We all nodded our understanding.

"It's possible for a person with a significant personality disorder to 'hold' one personality with me throughout the duration of *individual* therapy. But if any of you are really impaired and placed in the midst of this extremely confrontational group, over the next four years something will have to give. This is the beauty of group therapy. It's extremely effective over a long-term period, because we can truly observe the way that your mind functions and operates within a group setting."

We all nodded again, curiously looking at one another and wondering how each of us had arrived here for such an intense process of group therapy.

"You all have your different reasons for being here," Al said. "I applaud your courage and your discipline in advance for participating in a process that will be very enlightening for you. Your team of clinicians here with you today and throughout these sessions will be looking to see how you react. Your clinician, who will have consistent existential and clinical experience with you—over the long term—will be able to determine if there are personality switches or indicators that point to pathology. Even if there are, as I keep telling you, solutions are available, so there's nothing to be fearful of or to try to avoid.

"We're here to help you live a full and satisfying life. Whatever challenge brought you here today, consider it a great gift, because you have enrolled in a constructive program to ensure that the quality of your life and your future experiences meet with your satisfaction."

As incredible as the possibility seemed to me at the time, four years of group therapy passed quickly. There were certainly some bumps in the road; not everybody could accept the reality of my ET experiences, but eventually we all settled into the dynamics of the group process and allowed it to unfold.

This was totally different from the few group therapy sessions I'd had years earlier at the psychiatric institute. Now group therapy with expert clinicians and other sophisticated, highly functioning adults was a completely different experience from what went on in the psychiatric hospital. The sessions were downright empowering and invigorating, and I knew that I would heal.

Then, after an unbelievable span—after completing a grand total of six years of intensive therapy—Alan Ludington invited me into his private office once again. Having reserved Thursday mornings for therapy all these years, my "time in the chair" with Al, as well as my group therapy sessions, had slowly unraveled the long story of my lifelong experiences. Somewhere along the line, I stopped censoring and simply allowed myself the freedom to clearly articulate all that I had seen and heard, without fearing the result.

Now Al smiled, thumbing through a stack of papers on his desk and my personal file. "You've been here six years," he said, grinning, as though congratulating me for my commitment to therapy. "During that time, you've done testing, including a second MMPI, six years after your first test. Interestingly enough, the results bear out what is evident to you and to your assessment team: You have made peace with your unusual experiences and have gained profound spiritual meaning from them, the very same experiences that had once turned your life upside down."

Al looked through some papers, then back at me. "But despite the clinical testing, it's limiting to attempt to derive conclusions simply from contrived psychological testing. Such tests are designed by my profession against culturally standardized norms. Any result outside that norm is then referred to as a deviation, and it is given one type or another of adverse label. This is why your long therapy here has included many years of both individual *and* group therapy—to assess you along a spectrum of experience.

"I can say with confidence that emotionally and mentally impaired and disordered clients do not present themselves as you do. Clients presenting a plethora of emotional and mental diagnoses, including drug and alcohol addiction, or thought disorders do not conduct the details of their lives as you do. Despite your extraordinary experiences, no pathological diagnosis fits you."

"So does that mean I've graduated?" I asked, smiling broadly.

"It has only been about one hundred years since Freud developed the discipline of psychotherapy. From the perspective of a historical timeline, the professional psychotherapist is virtually brand-new. Conversely, the 'field' of spirituality preceded the formal study of psychotherapy by more than *six thousand years*. Surely, there is more to humankind's spiritual experiences and potential than what clinical professionals have *approved of and categorized* during the past hundred years."

"Exactly!" I said, hoping that Al might contribute his opinions to a professional journal.

"History has provided us with many people whose lives have been marked by experiences that many of us could not replicate. Some of those experiences have been so unusual that to attempt to define them within the framework of any of our present-day psychological testing would show marked psychopathology."

I nodded, understanding his point.

"Your claims of visions and mystical experiences, like many others throughout history, have had a sudden and dramatic impact on your life. Are you crazy? No. Are you outside the norm with respect to your surprising experiences? Yes. After thoroughly evaluating you for these past six years, my team and I conclude that your mind is as solid as a rock."

Six years ago, I probably would have cried with relief at that glorious validation, but now I had grown so comfortable with "second sight"—clairvoyance, clairaudience, etc.—that I had very little reaction. I had come to know in my own heart that I was mentally healthy—even *gifted*. "So, do I get a mental health diploma to hang on my wall?"

Al laughed. "No, but I'm publishing your case history in a professional journal, and I'll give you a copy."

"Fantastic! Al, how can I ever thank you enough?" I asked, jumping up to shake his hand. "I'm looking forward to reading it."

Chapter Seventeen

As Alan Ludington escorted me out to the lobby of his counseling center, he handed me a brightly wrapped gift.

"A little token of our appreciation," he said.

"How thoughtful, thank you," I replied, smiling broadly, unwrapping what appeared to be a blank aluminum automobile license plate.

"Turn it over, silly," Al instructed, flipping it over for me to reveal the three bright images that made up a humorous message.

"It's from the entire team here," Al said, chuckling at the colorful pictures emblazoned on the plate. "It's in appreciation of your courage and discipline throughout these six years."

Ceremoniously holding it out in front of me, I read it aloud, "I Love Aliens"—a red heart represented "love," and a bright-green alien face, complete with large black eyes, for "aliens."

"I love it!" I said, embracing Al in a big bear hug. "I'm going to find just the right *vehicle* for this." I winked mischievously.

"I get the feeling that you're not talking about which *automobile* to place it on. What do you have in mind?"

"I've got an idea brewing," I said, turning to walk out into the bright midday sunshine.

"I have a feeling that this won't be the last of you. Keep in touch!"

"I will. I promise," I responded, walking away from the family practice center as a confident and secure woman, due in no small part to my years of therapy there.

"So now that you're not crazy," Al called to me from the doorway, almost as though he were intuiting my new resolve, "what new worlds are left for you to conquer?"

Waving the "alien" license plate in the air as if it held a hint as to my next mission, I smiled, yelling back at him, "I think it's time to give voice to this whole idea!"

As I drove home that day, I wondered if I were to write a book, would I be breaking some kind of cosmic secret?

That evening, after saying goodnight to my son, he complained that he couldn't sleep. Reclining on the lounge chair next to his bed, I watched him play with his kitten, and we chatted about our day.

Suddenly, I heard and felt the unmistakable sound of the electromagnetic pulsing. Looking in alarm at my son and the kitten, I was amazed to see them instantly fall asleep as the phenomena enveloped me alone without seeming to touch them at all.

What had previously felt like a full-blown paranormal firestorm now felt less intense, because I had acclimated to the different energies, and my own energy field had become "conditioned." For the last six years, I had been receiving ET messages and seeing visions and otherworldly visitors, all in the privacy of my own house. But now, as I lay still on the lounge chair, my body began to rise and my eyes automatically closed. While floating through space, I was overcome by excitement, exhilaration, but also I could hear and feel my nervous heart thumping wildly. By the time my eyes reopened, my body was approaching a small opening in a craft. Amazed that I was awake and conscious of what I was observing, I was nonetheless unable to move at all. The only exception were my eyes, which moved back and forth to take in my surroundings with both excitement and anxiety. Where was I? I asked myself.

As if directed by a mysterious force, my body floated through the small portal and came to rest on the "ground" of a dark, expansive area. Before me, were several gray extraterrestrial beings, the same ones who had greeted me so many years ago. Except for the sounds of my loudly beating heart and my short gasps of breath, it was dead silent as we stared at one another. I was anxious yet excited; then, moments later, I was in awe yet again as the extraterrestrial beings began to speak to me. It was the same telepathic communication, and its message was as clear and succinct as any exchange of language.

"Welcome, once again," they said.

I got a distinct feeling of absolute joy and celebration.

Suddenly, I looked beyond the gathering of ETs to discover hundreds of inert cattle and sheep suspended by cords of light. As though discerning my concern, the aliens floated my body over to a small canoe-like vehicle that was moving across a wide expanse of utter darkness toward a distant location. Two extraterrestrial beings sat directly behind me in the vehicle.

Slowly gliding through the darkness, we approached a dimly lit area where I could see a kind of nursery: There were hundreds of fetuses in varying stages of development—they appeared as half-human/half-ET hybrids—suspended in clear liquid inside glass-like jars. At first I was alarmed. Was I about to become a full-grown specimen?

Magically, the "team" of extraterrestrials again appeared before me, and they told me about a grand ecological plan underway between themselves and certain humans that had been initiated long ago in case of Earth's planetary annihilation, enabling the survival of our species' genetic line.

I had a million questions: "How did these fetuses come into being? Does this mean that our planet is destined to be destroyed?"

As if reading my mind, I heard, "Of course not." It was a calm, almost joyous, telepathic response that infused my mind and expanded my understanding.

"Certain of you have previously agreed to participate in a joining of your DNA with ours, which produces these young beings."

My immediate follow-up question was answered before I had even fully formed it in my head.

"No, there is no need to create offspring in the traditional way that your species procreates," I understood them to say. "The sexual act that produces offspring is relegated to species who have not yet evolved beyond the need to procreate by the conjoining of body parts."

"So how does it happen, then?" I asked, looking incredulously at the numerous hybrids at varying stages of development.

"It's a joining of DNA between certain of your species and our own. But this in no way suggests that your species is doomed. This is only one of many ways in which beings of universal heritage co-create. But even so, each soul who participates does so as part of their own soul's agreement."

"Most people would say that such activities victimize humans," I said.

"Divinity, the divine source who sponsors all that is, cannot make mistakes. Human participants, when beholding that which is not understood, erroneously believe that a violation has occurred that must be rectified. Instead, imagine if every single event and every single apparent 'accident' is part of a greater Divine orchestration resulting in the progression of all souls toward a perfect outcome."

"It doesn't feel that way when I've made mistakes."

"The potential for faulty choices is built into your training program, which produce growth opportunities that ultimately continue to serve the development of your soul. From this perspective, mistakes can be recognized as misunderstood determinism that also allows free will."

"Those are contradictory concepts."

"The reconciling of apparent opposites is what spiritual maturity is all about. You are making constant choices, in the context of an ultimately perfect training program and a known outcome. Difficult obstacles and challenges are presented along the way until they can be appropriately solved with courage and confidence. A 'failed' test simply elicits another opportunity to try solving it once again, but in a new and different way, and presented in a slightly different package."

"But many people feel that they're failures. Look at addicts and criminals."

"One must consider a single lifetime's reckoning in respect to the sum of all of one's lives, and view the larger picture of one's progress toward self-fulfillment, not to mention that the grand purpose is that these so-called 'failures' serve you and those around you. And later, you may repay that service with your own so-called failures. Earth is a training ground for the incarnating soul. Over the long term, each soul moves toward the development of its potential—although some do move more quickly than others."

"As joy denotes success, emotional or physical pain *does* feel like failure," I said.

"Happiness or dissatisfaction, success or tragedy in life *do not* reflect blessings or punishment by God."

"That goes against what most people believe to be true."

"You are the master of your own destiny if your actions in the face of adversity demonstrate mastery, which means you are finally able to move on to a higher lesson; or, if not, this sets up a karmic debt to others or to society, which must be balanced over the span of your lives. The wealthy man who hordes his money and uses his wealth to exert power over others, could return as a beggar; this is not punishment, but an opportunity to balance out extremes in behavior, which helps the soul to gain compassion for others, thus the soul grows wiser and wiser. When facing the pain of adversity, it only means that something of importance is unfolding," they responded.

"Even in my case, with the intense emotional pain of my younger years?"

"*Especially* during intense upheavals. Everyone has helpers. But like any wise parent, we don't manage too closely or too often. We do not interfere with your natural unfolding. You must learn to bring all your experience to bear on the solution of each new problem. The advanced soul radiates composure, kindness, and understanding toward others, and does not limit their help to blood relatives. We inspire and encourage, but we, like all spiritual guides, cannot do the hard work for you."

"Then why come at all? What do extraterrestrials want with humans in the first place? Why all the secrecy?"

"The spirit world presents itself in all sorts of physical disguises. No one or no species is without a mentor. Also, some souls are driven more than others to expand and achieve their potential. Souls who want more vigorous training assignments will face more strenuous problems. The more diverse and complex the problem to be solved, the greater motivation a soul brings to their training program that is often a characteristic of a mature soul."

"I don't want any more major upheavals in my life."

"That's your human *mind* talking. Your soul's intentions are frequently quite lofty and courageous, and you will continue to be provided with personal spiritual helpers along the way."

"Well, I've seen some weird apparitions, involving human discarnate spirits and otherworldly beings; am I to assume that you can also shape-shift? Can you appear as humans and move among us?"

"*Evolved* spiritual beings have special abilities. Even though we, too, are housed in physical bodies—no matter our appearance at the moment—we display a universal coherence with one another that is so absolute, it's incomprehensible to your understanding."

"It sounds as though human/ET contact serves a divine but glorious purpose, even if we don't understand it."

"The young child does not always discern the rhyme and reason for divinely inspired, seemingly complex interrelationships between all that is."

"When people are sad or angry, it's because they feel that something's gone terribly wrong," I said. "It's hard to believe that painful outcomes are perfect, especially when we seem to be making hard choices to avoid the everyday problems of our lives."

"Choosing and being chosen—all at the same time—is another idea that may be difficult to comprehend."

"Those are opposites and make no sense."

"Beholding the application of an apparent contradiction requires great wisdom. Ultimately, you are each trending toward an expected perfection, no matter the *apparent* detours and obstacles that seem to arise from so-called 'faulty' choices. All experience serves a greater good," they said.

"That's hard to believe, especially when unpredictable disasters occur."

"Each life is a miracle. Even the attributes of miracles would have to be miraculous. As your spiritual perspective matures, you will be able to comprehend the astounding arrangements and agreements that were made prior to such 'unpredictable' occurrences and the way and manner that you or your loved ones have agreed to participate. You will all see your loved ones again, of this you can be certain. No matter how upsetting the death, you will each arrive back at your spiritual home and joyously reunite with them again, ready to begin the coordination and preparation for another round together on Earth, or elsewhere."

At that moment, my eyes closed, and I felt overwhelmingly sleepy, despite the fact that there were so many more questions to ask. Another query was just forming on my lips, then I opened my eyes and found myself on the lounge chair as the sun was rising over the mountains.

Leaping out of the chair, I rushed into my room and over to my desk, opened my computer and started to type furiously, until my son came in before leaving for school.

Grinning mischievously, he kissed me on the cheek and said, "While you were distracted, I had ice cream for breakfast." I could only laugh out loud.

～

Over the next many months, I stayed up late to write after ensuring that Walter was asleep. The writing flew out of me, fast and fluid. Then, after several hours of writing, I would retire, quickly fall into a deep asleep, only to wake up in the early morning hours to start up again. Before long, I had written an entire manuscript.

One morning, a large stack of paper sat next to me at the kitchen table.

"What are you doing with all that?" my son asked as we ate breakfast. "That's a lot of pages," he said, touching the stack.

I gathered it up, placed a large rubber band around it, and, tucking it under my arm, headed out the door with Walter to drop him off at school. I planned to make a copy of my manuscript for safe keeping.

"As soon as I mail this manuscript to a publisher, I'm officially out of the closet," I told my son, as I tightly held the stack of pages so that it wouldn't be buffeted by the brisk Santa Ana winds. Whipping my hair around my face, the wind blew hot and strong, and we ran from the house to the parking garage to avoid the windstorm.

Once in the covered garage, I turned to Walter and asked him an important question: "If I get this manuscript published, shall I use a made-up name?"

"Why?" he asked curiously, unaware of the consequences of his mother writing a book about aliens floating her through the ceiling of their house to a waiting spaceship.

"To save you from embarrassment," I replied. "I can use a different name so that your friends won't know what your mother's writing about."

"Most of my friends won't read books anyway," he joked. I had to laugh at his cavalier attitude. My son was all right. Taking my hand, he led me to the car and opened the door, gesturing for me to climb in. After buckling my seat belt, he smiled, saying, "We'll be just fine."

Delighted by his sweet disposition and his generous out-
look, I drove the few miles to his school, noticing the trees
being bent and whipped about by the Santa Ana winds. As
we passed the local fire station, I saw a large red banner hanging from their front entrance. It exclaimed that, due to high
winds, today was an "extreme fire danger" day. Given that it
lies on the fringe of an extensive chaparral wilderness area,
Malibu's dry brush and steep clay slopes make it prone to
fires, floods, and mudslides. When the hot winds blow, emergency personnel are on constant lookout for any small spark
or brush fire—anything that could potentially turn into a
full-blown wildfire.

"I'll see you later sweetheart," I said, kissing Walter on the
cheek and chuckling at how he jumped from the car to join
a sea of rambunctious kids, all rushing headlong toward the
school to avoid the whip of the hot winds.

En route to the local photocopy store, I noticed a curl of
black smoke in the distance, and I pulled over as two behe-
moth fire trucks zoomed past me on the highway. I had no
way of knowing that at that very moment, thirty-five thousand acres—and my own house—had just ignited and would,
ultimately, burn to the ground. The infamous Malibu wildfires had struck again.

Later that week, when a local TV news crew wanted to
interview a young family who had been affected by the wildfire, my son and I stood among the ashes of my childhood
home. While Walter poked among the ruins, the reporter
said, "You must be devastated. I understand that this house,
where you were living, is also the home where you grew up.
What a horrible tragedy to have to endure."

"We'll be okay," I responded hopefully. The ETs had
helped me to understand that apparent "accidents" are not

actually "accidental." Their words from my earlier encounter replayed in my head, and I wondered how the reporter would respond if I shared what the extraterrestrials had told me: "Divinity, the divine source who sponsors all that is, cannot make mistakes. Human participants, when beholding that which is not understood or which is upsetting, erroneously believe that a violation has occurred that must be rectified."

But I didn't tell her all that. I just summed it up as best as I could. "Actually, my son and I are the lucky ones. We had a place to live, and tonight we'll stay with friends. We'll always have a roof over our heads. But right now, somewhere in the world, maybe even in this very city, people are suffering in silence, because they don't understand the way of the world."

"And what way is that?" the reporter asked, now curious. "What do you mean by the 'way of the world'?"

"All experience serves a greater good," I said, "although I know it may not feel like that at the moment. We may not understand it at the time, but imagine if every single event, all suffering, and even every single apparent 'accident' are all part of a greater Divine orchestration resulting in the progression of all souls toward a perfect outcome."

"And what, pray tell, is your perfect outcome following this disaster?" the reporter asked skeptically as the camera panned the expanse of gray ashes. The only thing standing was the fireplace chimney.

"Like others, I'm learning how to solve difficult problems, and I'm getting better and better at it," I replied, smiling. "And another outcome of the fire, is that I now have the courage to leave my home because I was offered a position out of state. Prior to the fire, I was reluctant to leave my home town of Malibu."

"You mean that you're going to move out of state as a result of losing your house?"

"Well, when you learn a lesson in one job or place, the universe gives you a nudge to move on. You never know how one thing leads to another," I explained. "I've now decided to accept the position. The fire burning down my house is my official divine boot."

Chapter Eighteen

LATER THAT MONTH, my son and I moved to Oregon, where I was hired as personal assistant to *New York Times* bestselling author Neale Donald Walsch, the author of the *Conversations with God* books. In addition, I served as the administrative director of Walsch Books, Neale's small publishing company imprint. In this capacity, I met his editor and publisher, Josh Roberts, the president of Hampton Roads Publishing Company. Following a wonderful period of employment with Neale, Josh offered me a position as the sales director for his company, so Walter and I packed up and moved to Charlottesville, Virginia.

It was both an exhilarating and a frustrating time for me; I loved the subject matter and our authors, but it was an uphill battle against mainstream publishing's skepticism of these cutting-edge topics, and many reviewers considered them pseudoscience. Although I had written a manuscript about my extraterrestrial encounter experiences, I had held back at presenting it to a publisher, because I didn't have any proof that extraterrestrials actually existed. It was time to take matters into my own hands.

"Be careful with that," I instructed my teenage son, taking the video camera from him and placing it back on its tripod. Now settled into our new home in Charlottesville, I was still having ET contacts and figured that I would try to capture some evidence of the encounters on videotape.

Angling the camera so that the lens was facing my bed, I turned it on and looked through the viewfinder. Satisfied that it was operational, I clicked it off.

On my bedside table were a Polaroid camera and a brand-new tape recorder loaded with a cassette. Like most teenage boys his age, Walter was curious about electronics and came over to check out the camera and recorder.

"What are you doing with all this?" he asked me earnestly, picking up the Polaroid and taking a picture of me as I struck a pose.

"Do you remember when you were a child, and you used to have those dreams about the aliens?" I asked him thoughtfully.

"Yeah, vaguely, but I don't dream about that anymore," he replied, now fiddling with the tape recorder and recording his own voice.

"I know," I said, looking over at him. "But I do." Noting that he had no reaction, I continued. "Well, sometimes, those dreams seem so real, it feels like I can reach out and touch them," I said, studying his face. "I thought it would be fun if I could record them."

"Tonight?" he asked, gesturing at the equipment but not seeming to fully comprehend the nuances of my endeavor.

"Yes, tonight," I said, smiling broadly, relieved that he was satisfied with my oblique answers. It was a relief that he didn't completely understand my situation. My therapist had told me, "When children and teens are emotionally *ready* to know the answers to delicate questions, they'll ask." Until then, I was content to avoid discussing paranormal phenomena too thoroughly.

"But suppose they don't come?" he asked.

"No harm done," I said. "But I'll be ready when or if they do."

"You gonna show it to everyone?" he asked innocently, removing the cassette from the player and inspecting it. Chuckling at the idea, I could imagine his father's reaction if I included a videotape of such an "encounter" in Walter's suitcase on his next holiday visit.

"Not to everyone," I said. "At work, we have these sales meetings about the books we publish. Some of the books are about aliens."

"So you're gonna show it at work?" Walter asked, brightening.

"You got it!" I replied, laughing. "You've met my boss, Josh Roberts. Well, because he's a publisher, he wants proof of stuff that seems mysterious and strange."

"You mean like ghosts and aliens and things?"

"Right. So I'm curious to see if I can get proof."

It was an amazing idea that I might actually be able to capture some portion of these phenomena on any of my recording equipment. Since I was receptive to the light show my alien friends continued to display, the least they could do was to wave their magical paranormal wand and allow me to get evidence that they really existed.

"Can I sleep in here tonight?" Walter asked, pointing to the sofa in the corner of my room. "It would be really cool to see them."

"I don't think so, honey. If they come to *you*, in your dreams or in your imagination, or in any other way, then that's fine," I said, realizing that perhaps I was breaking new ground for appropriate parenting by coaching a young teenager about visiting aliens. "But if they come to *me*, in my room, then it probably means that it's for me and not you. Okay?" Since he was still a minor, I didn't want to frighten him, and so any video recordings of otherworldly life would be shown only to my adult friends and colleagues.

"Well, I wish they'd come into my room," Walter said, looking through the viewfinder of the Polaroid camera.

"Everything in good time," I responded, content to wait until he was older before expanding our discussion.

A little later that evening, after ensuring that Walter was asleep, I returned to my room and rechecked my equipment. Setting the "play" button on the tape recorder and video camera, I settled into bed with a good book. Soon after, I turned off the lights and fell into a deep sleep.

No sooner had I begun to dream when a pulsing electromagnetic surge awakened me with a start. Glancing at the red "on" lights on the video and tape recorders, I grinned, knowing that the brilliant light show and its loud zapping noise were being captured on two recording devices.

At that moment, a small extraterrestrial being appeared in front of me, positioned precisely between me and the video camera as though helping to stage the perfect home movie. Since I was no longer immobilized during the visits, I grabbed the camera next to me, aimed it at the ET, and clicked off a stream of photos. Delighted that the small alien hadn't disappeared, I was surprised to hear a telepathic communication begin in earnest, and I put down the camera and picked up a pad and pen.

"Learn the goals of your soul. What did you come here to do? How will you be of help to others and to society?"

Pondering his words, I wondered why it was so important to drive home this ongoing message. But they were, after all, good questions; concepts that I wasn't so sure that I had fully actualized myself. What *did* I come here to do? How *can* I be of help to others and to society?"

As I considered his message, I kept my eye on the recording equipment, ensuring that the red lights remained illu-
minated. Then, without any warning, the small gray being
disappeared.

I checked the Polaroid pictures, which were slowly devel-
oping and seemed to have captured an image. Jumping up to
turn off the recording equipment, I suddenly felt exhausted
and fell back into bed, looking forward to the morning when
I would proudly exhibit my "proof."

The next morning, I woke up late and had to hurry out
the door, with my pictures hastily stuffed into the camera case,
to get Walter to school on time. At work, I called a marketing meeting and bustled around the conference room, erecting
the white projection screen for my surprise demonstration. I
popped the videotape into the projector just as the door swung
open and the sales and marketing team entered the room.

Josh asked, "What's happening here?"

"Everyone please take a seat," I instructed the group, grinning at Josh and pointing to his chair at the head of the table.
"I've got a surprise presentation."

Sitting down reluctantly, Josh glanced at his watch. "Mike
Newman's just pulling up in the parking lot," he said. "What
are you up to?"

"It'll just take a minute," I replied, motioning to the art
director to close the door. All heads turned to me for some
explanation.

Standing up ceremoniously, I pointed to the array of
equipment. "Josh keeps griping about the scarcity of our
authors' *proof*," I said, smiling. "The problem is, paranormal
phenomena are elusive and hard to get a fix on. I know, since
I've had my own share of such experiences."

I picked up several Polaroid photos and passed them around. "I took these last night, and you can see *something*, even if it's just a white blur," I explained, moving to the video camera.

"Naturally," said Josh, taking the photos from me. "As you said, it's *illusive*. It evades analysis. That's precisely why all of us are in such a quandary."

"I know," I replied, "but last night at my house, this video camera was pointed straight at the . . . phenomenon. I'm sure of it."

"What are you talking about?" Josh asked.

"Let me show you what I mean." I turned off the lights, then clicked on the video projector. Bright flashes of white streaks were displayed prominently on the screen, and for one long, beautiful moment, the proof that I so desperately wanted appeared to be emerging on full display. But no sooner had the unmistakable zapping sound filled the room, when the videotape went dark and the screen went black.

"What happened?" Josh asked me, rising from his chair and turning the lights back on.

"Well, the phenomenon did its *illusive* trick again, but this was two seconds of what was a much longer paranormal display," I replied haltingly, embarrassed by my meager evidence.

At that moment, the door opened and in walked Mike Newman. "Josh? You got your marketing team ready?"

"Yes, of course, Mike; please come in," Josh replied, rushing over to shake his hand. "We were just finishing up." Josh pulled out a chair for the author.

"We're lucky to have Mike Newman join us this morning," Josh said, addressing the room. "When our authors are in town, we always appreciate their input as to how we can best promote their books. Mike is a well-known expert on

UFO phenomena and, particularly, UFO abduction theory . . . Mike?"We all clapped our hands, and Mike stood up, smoothing his hair and buttoning his jacket. He moved to a lectern in the corner, then cleared his throat and smiled winningly, as if he were about to address an adoring public.

"Most of you know me, and if you don't . . . well, you've never read anything about the alien agenda," he said, winking at us mischievously. Taking a more somber tone, he continued, "Look, the job of sales and marketing is to transform my moniker and my book title into a household name. Anne, let's see the new cover."

Our art director propped a large poster board on the easel. Gasping in surprise, we gawked at the mock-up: a portrait of a mean, grimacing alien. Above the portrait was the title: *The Evil Alien Agenda*. Beaming proudly, Mike nodded approvingly at Anne.

"My extensive research indicates that the evil alien perpetrators use unsuspecting human guinea pigs to further their own secret agenda," he said. "What I've learned from brave abductees, and hundreds of them can attest to it, is that—"

"Excuse me," I said, raising my hand. "Have you, *yourself,* ever been contacted by extraterrestrials?"

Before Mike could respond, and as though apologizing for the interruption, Josh added, "Lisette is our sales director."

"My subjects are *terrified!*" Mike responded, glaring at me and completely avoiding my question. "These unfortunate victims are abducted against their will. Their memories have been erased. I help them fill in the missing pieces," Mike said, turning to the group with a dramatic flourish.

"But *how* do you accomplish that?" I asked him. "By filling their minds with the idea that they're *victims?*"

"They *are* victims!" Mike retorted. "Most of them are traumatized."

"But suppose that there's no intent on the ETs' part to harm anybody?" I asked. "Suppose that many of these beings are here to help us, like mentors? But first, we need to get beyond our cultural assumptions—and *that's* what's causing the trauma!"

The whole room was dead silent, listening to this exchange.

"Sounds like you've been brainwashed by the same aliens who are abducting my subjects," Mike said. "These aliens have ruined people's lives. Come to one of our group meetings and hear it for yourself."

"I might just do that," I said, nodding my head and letting him proceed with his "indoctrination."

～

Later that week, I walked into Mike Newman's local support group, which was being held in an annex room off the community's main library. At the back of the room, a long table offered his many books and tapes for sale. Many of the participants held his most recent book in their laps, highlighting pages as different attendees took turns sharing their insights and ghastly—as they perceived them—experiences.

Mike's frequent comments helped to facilitate the conversation whenever attendees broke down into tears or were overcome with emotion. Offering friendly encouragement, Mike coaxed the participants to use the forum as a safe venue at which to vent.

"Let's now go around the room in turn," Mike instructed, "and, in a sentence or two, summarize the main thrust of our feelings about the abductions."

The members nodded their heads, and a few sat at attention, as though readying themselves for their turn.

Looking at his watch, Mike said, "We won't be able to get to everyone's story in depth, but this forum will help you to start the healing process. You can't heal if you're in denial. John, you want to begin?"

Collecting himself and looking at a few note cards, John said, "It's an insidious evil agenda, and I resent the aliens' intrusion into my life. I haven't gotten a decent night's sleep in many months, and it's upsetting everyone around me."

Mike nodded approvingly, gesturing to the person sitting next to John.

"My name is Karen," the young woman said. "It's terrifying when you don't know what's happening to you." Removing tissue from her purse and dabbing her eyes, she tried her best to regain her composure before continuing. "There's missing time, headaches; my husband thinks I've lost it." The rest of the group nodded with understanding.

"But I read something in the local paper that sounds like you're doing something healthy to take back your power and to express your outrage. Isn't that right, Karen?" Mike asked, as all eyes turned back to Karen.

Sniffling, Karen sat up straighter in her chair, as though proud of her recent accomplishment. "Yes, I sent a story to the local paper, and the editor published it. It's about my alien abduction and the trouble that it's caused me. It's a small paper. I don't know how many people read it, but it feels good to vent."

"Well, I for one would like to congratulate you on your courage," Mike said. "We should all take note of how important it is to get in touch with our vulnerability and to express anger in appropriate ways."

"I mentioned our support group in the article," Karen said. "We may be getting more members."

"That's great, Karen. Thank you for your thoughtful efforts in reaching out to others who still suffer."

Another young woman was next. After coughing a few times, she regained her composure and said, "The worst part is not being able to remember everything, as though the little buggers have purposely erased my memory. I've been journaling my frustrations and anger, but that's about all that I can recall. It's infuriating."

Nodding in agreement, an older man at the back of the room stood up suddenly and said, "I've been keeping silent for a decade, and like Karen did, that stops here and now!" The entire room applauded with shouts and affirmations, and someone whistled enthusiastically, as though at a football game. "The truth is, Mike is right," he continued. "And so is Karen. It's time we spoke up and fought back against these ongoing alien abductions. The aliens burst into our rooms late at night, scare us half to death with their evil intentions, and—"

"Are you sure about that?" I yelled out, before I could stop myself. As surprised at myself as everyone else was, I noticed that every person in the room had turned to look at me. Mike started to stand up, but it was too late for me to quash my own insight. I, too, stood up to address the group.

"'Abduction' implies kidnapping, right?" I asked the group earnestly, most of whom nodded in agreement, waiting me out.

"But what if they're just *neighbors*, actually introducing themselves, trying to be helpful?" I was dismayed to see that most of the attendees shifted in their chairs and glanced nervously at Mike for his reaction.

"It's just my opinion, but I'm offering another perspective," I said, noticing that Mike did not look pleased. "It can be terrifying, I agree—and I have had contact myself—but my experience has been totally different. And *why*? If you really break it down and look carefully at the part that is the most upsetting, it's not what the *aliens* are doing. It's what *we're* doing—we're making up our own *faulty* assumptions."

"Excuse me, Ms. Larkins," Mike said, moving to the center of the room. "I can appreciate that you've had your own experience, but my book is about . . . *their* experiences, and that's what your publishing company needs to promote."

"And we will, but I'm not here in my role as sales director," I said firmly. Mike looked questioningly at me.

"I'm here as a concerned contactee. I don't know how it serves us to assume wrongdoing by aliens or, for that matter, anyone else," I said. "A *victim*, by its very definition, is a person who's disempowered. Is that really who we are? Does the label 'abductee' really help us?"

Addressing the group, Mike pointed to me, explaining in his best authoritative voice, "This is very instructive for this entire support group to hear firsthand, the way that denial *sounds*. Listen up. She exemplifies the classic response of a victim who is stuck in denial."

"I don't think so," I said to the group. "Denial is disempowering. This is different. Maybe we're terrified not because the aliens are hurting us but because we don't know what's happening. When you think about it, maybe the *real* cause for upset is others'—and our own—*faulty reactions* to the aliens.

"When our friends, family, and society think we're nuts, and we doubt ourselves, that's what's mostly upsetting us, *not the aliens*. The emotional pain comes from our *own* thinking and *not* from the aliens themselves. We're just meeting our extraterrestrial neighbors. What's so bad about that?"

I looked around the room, trying to make meaningful eye contact, wondering if any of what I said was making any sense to anyone.

Karen raised her hand somewhat timidly, and Mike quickly responded, nodding for her to interrupt me. "Are you saying that every alien out there has good intentions?" she asked.

"No." I replied. "The universe is a big place. And like this planet's population, it's just as diverse and reflects varying levels of spiritual maturity. Here, we have Saddam Hussein and Bernie Madoff at one end of the spectrum, and Gandhi and Mother Teresa at the other. Most of us are somewhere in between. The same can be said for all populations everywhere. The key is to become aware of who we are attracting to ourselves, then take some responsibility for who shows up in our experiences."

"But a victim should not be held accountable for being a victim," Karen responded.

"If I'm a fearful and angry person, I'm far more likely to attract those same kinds of experiences to myself," I explained. "And I'm not likely to see any connection between the two."

"Are you saying that like attracts like?"

"There are *two* mechanisms at work that inform the creation of all experiences. And this is what is missing from every discussion pertaining to UFO abduction theory. First, the Law of Attraction applies to everyone throughout the entire cosmos. All that means is that not every single alien or human is evil, *and* not every one of them is sufficiently evolved to be of pure intent. We have to take responsibility for who and what *we* are, and who and what *we* are attracting to ourselves. And, if we perpetuate wrongdoings ourselves, we can expect to later experience the pain that we ourselves have inflicted on others and society to balance our karmic debt. To pretend that this does not occur is merely being ignorant of spiritual principles."

I paused and looked at Karen to see if she understood, and she nodded at me while scribbling a few notes. Mike, however, was frowning.

"You're taking this discussion in a direction that is beyond the scope of our mission here," Mike stated loudly. "We're a support group! Not the Theosophical Society!"

The others turned to look at me, wondering what my next response would be.

"Just bear with me another minute," I replied, turning to Karen, and the rest of the group. "There's a second mechanism that undergirds all experience, and it's *perfectly relevant* to this discussion." Mike glared at me. "Just let me explain it, and then I'll go."

I cleared my throat and started again. "What is also playing out is that all incarnate souls must *learn and grow* from being *exposed* to the circumstances and wrongdoings that challenge us."

"I can't agree with that," Karen responded. "Others' wrongdoings are not serving any higher purpose. I'm not responsible for the evil in my life."

"Oh, but you are, to some degree or another," I replied. "Some part of you sets this up: because the very act of confronting wrongdoing is a spiritual opportunity to train the soul."

"You make it sound like we should be thankful for the bad people or bad aliens in our lives," Karen retorted.

"The adventure of life is all about us trying to overcome our human limitations while confronting and overcoming these issues. This can be a tremendous challenge because it's the *soul* that brings in the characteristics of ethics and kindness to evolve our selfish animalistic instincts."

"Are you saying that each one of was bad when we were incarnated?" Karen asked.

"No. We all come in to learn, each at our own level, and that's all that's going on with any kind of experience that you don't like: some of us are inconsiderate beginners and some of us are further along. It's an opportunity to find creative, alternative solutions to problems, but feeling victimized by this process is a characteristic of an immature soul and will significantly delay your development."

"Well you might have a point there," an older man said thoughtfully. "I was having a lot of depression and anger in my marriage and also at work long before I ever began to be abducted by aliens. Now that I stop to think about it, that's why I hate the aliens. I'm blaming them for all of my problems, but nothing changed before or after their arrival. Maybe the way to stop this from happening is to figure out what I can learn from my wife instead of divorcing her, and to improve my attitude." He chuckled to himself.

"It does take great courage to look in the mirror and to reflect on the signals that we're sending out," I replied gently. "And to recognize difficulties as previously arranged training opportunities. The universe is a magnet. We get more of who we are, whether or not we like it. If you want to talk about denial, *this* is denial: *taking no responsibility* for the types of experiences that we are attracting to ourselves."

"I see what you mean," another woman said, nodding her head. "Our predominant fearful attitude attracts more experiences that leave us justifying our fearful attitude."

"Exactly," I said.

"I too was depressed," she continued. "I hated my job. Then, one day at work, my coworker found a drawing I had made of the aliens, and she showed it to my boss. Next thing I know, I'm unemployed and feeling more depressed than ever. And I blamed the aliens, because now I've got a whole lot more to be depressed about. I do need someone to talk to about all this, but who?"

"Well, you can find a skilled therapist, but choose one who doesn't unwittingly support your *victim identity*," I added for emphasis, looking directly at Mike Newman.

Another attendee stood up. "It's hard enough dealing with difficult people and challenges right here on Earth. Then when you add in the aliens, with all the different agendas; wow, it's really confusing and stressful."

"I agree," I responded. "But that's the key: to break the cycle, once and for all. We must move out of depression, anger, and fear so that we don't keep repeating those cycles by unwittingly attracting more of those same experiences to ourselves."

Mike moved closer to me and, placing a hand on my shoulder, said, "Thank you for sharing. That will be enough for now." Motioning to my chair, he looked at me with intensity, and I sat down quietly.

Mike addressed the group. "Most of us have worked long and hard to come to terms with the insidious consequences of alien abduction. The first step in this healthy, therapeutic process—no matter how difficult it is to confront and no matter how long it takes us to get there—is to *face the reality* of these difficult abductions. Denial is not a river in Africa." The room burst into laughter, applauding. "Denial is our worst enemy; that is, after the alien agenda."

As the meeting ended, I rushed to my car, realizing that perhaps I had spoken out of turn and had no right to crash Mike's group. I had not intended to cause problems, but upon hearing the sadness and fear of many of these attendees, it triggered memories of my former hopelessness. From my perspective, I couldn't see how it would help anyone to believe that they were disempowered pawns caught up in an inescapable nightmare.

Despite the fact that I didn't have definitive proof of my alien visitations, neither did Mike Newman or, for that matter, any of the other authors or writers who were providing well-meaning but misguided and disempowering advice to "abductees."

The day had come to give my manuscript to Josh. I had something valuable to offer, I realized. Proof or not, my viewpoint was just as viable as anyone else's.

The next day at work, Josh called me into his office. I had been just about to turn in my manuscript, so I carried it along with me in a book bag.

"Have a seat," Josh said, turning away from his computer and looking at me with a serious expression. "Last night, Mike Newman called me," he said. "He claims that you threw a monkey wrench into decades of his clinical studies by suggesting, and this is a quote, 'that the real cause for our upset is our own negative emotions and reactions and not the alien's agenda.' He says some of his abductees are now questioning his theories about the evil nature of aliens."

"His theory *should* be questioned," I retorted. "Josh, *you have always* agreed that extraterrestrials may be misunderstood. And besides, even if someone has been contacted by an alien with unknown intentions, there's something that can be done about it. We are each tested on our ability to find solutions, and not to become powerless victims. We've got to look at how our own anger and fear attract more of those same experiences to ourselves—worldly *or* otherworldly."

"Be that as it may, I'm a publisher. You're a sales director. We've already agreed to publish his new book. It's going to print. It's not your job to question our authors' theories in public. If you don't agree with him, write your own damn book."

"Well, actually, that's what I've been meaning to talk with you about."

Josh shook his head. "Lisette, I need you to focus on promoting our entire line of books and their authors, even if you don't agree with their theories."

"I know, but Mike Newman isn't the only person with a theory. I mean, he's never even had any contact himself. And he doesn't have a clue as to how the Law of Attraction applies to so-called alien abduction, or for that matter, the reason why we are confronted with challenges in the first place. Souls are here to train under many different circumstances and in many different settings, even within a paranormal context! Mike is just a guy writing about other peoples' experiences, drawing naive conclusions, then convincing everyone that aliens are evil because *fear sells*. Evil aliens sell better than friendly ones."

Josh leaned in to respond. "Well, that may be true, but until you've got your own book, your job is to market *his*. Got it?"

"I *will* market his book," I said, then pulled my manuscript out of the bag and handed it to him. "But I'd like to add one more theory to the list. And my theory is fully empowering, not disempowering."

"What's this?" Josh asked.

"My manuscript. Publish it for me."

Reading aloud, Josh said, "*Talking to Extraterrestrials: Transforming Our World with the Help of Enlightened Beings.*" Surprised, he removed his glasses and stared at me. "You've been holding out on me, Lisette."

"It's taken me a long time to sort it out."

"Let me take a look at it," Josh said, thumbing through the pages. "I can't promise you anything, and I can't do you any favors. The quality of the work has to stand on its own. In the meantime, get back to your desk and promote the hell out of Mike Newman's book. Got it?"

"Yes, sir," I replied, standing up to leave. "And thanks for considering it. I believe there are lots of people out there who've had similar experiences to mine but don't want to buck the evil alien trend. It's another thing entirely to announce that you've met your friendly neighbors who've stopped by to help. Now that's a paradigm shifter."

Josh smiled. "It's called a 'counterpoint' position, a very viable approach."

As I walked out, he set the manuscript on his desk and began to read it.

Chapter Nineteen

THE MONTHS LEADING UP to my book's publication went quickly. Despite my responsibilities as sales director, I was excited to soon be wearing the hat of "author." As with any proposed new book, my own manuscript went through a long series of departmental reviews: editorial—Josh had even gone so far as to ask the ETs some of his own questions to include in the book—art, production, sales and marketing, and publicity.

Once we'd had everybody's input, production began. Long months later, it would end with the final completed file being sent to the printer, which printed the book, then shipped it to the publisher, wholesalers, and bookstores across the country; it was even translated for foreign markets.

As the ship-date approached, I routinely glanced through my office's second-story window to the parking lot below, searching for any sign of a large semi-trailer.

Next door to the Hampton Roads building was the company's huge warehouse. It was where the trucks would arrive from various printers to deliver freshly printed books stacked high on pallets. I loved to walk down the aisles, gaping at the rows and rows of wonderful books, shimmering with bright covers and interesting titles, stacked high overhead. It was better than visiting any bookstore, I thought, as I wandered around the warehouse.

On the target date, I didn't want to go out for lunch, afraid I would miss the delivery of my book. Josh had placated me by ordering Chinese takeout so that we could stay on hand for the big event. Walking into my office with two small boxes of food, Josh gazed out the window, then set up the picnic on my side table.

"Any sign of the truck?" Josh asked, sitting down with his chopsticks and selecting a morsel from his small box. "I realize that this is pretty exciting for you, but these truck deliveries are no big deal."

"It is for the author," I said, scanning the parking lot, just as a huge semi rolled slowly into view. "There it is!" I squealed, jumping out of my chair and pointing out the window.

Josh didn't even look up, responding dryly, "You can't be certain that it's delivering *your* books." Josh was more interested in his takeout than the hulking eighteen-wheeler coming to a stop outside. "We're scheduled for several deliveries today from three different printers."

Inspecting the rig more closely, I was amazed to read the company's logo on the side panel. "No, I think you'll find that this truck's mine," I said, laughing at Josh's surprised expression as he stood up and gawked at the truck: "Gray-Line Trucking Company."

"What the heck?" Josh said, swallowing hard.

"That's no coincidence," I yelled over my shoulder, as I rushed out the door.

I trundled down the stairs. Josh followed after me, mumbling to himself, "That's weird; of all the trucking companies, you get this one."

"Wouldn't expect anything else," I replied, chuckling, as we burst out the front doors into the sunny parking lot. The semi was slowly backing up to the rear of the warehouse. Giving me one of his looks, Josh said, "What are you saying?"

"When I was in the psychiatric hospital, a mysterious doctor came up to me in the cafeteria and told me I wasn't crazy. His name tag read, 'Dr. Gray.' Turns out, there was no such doctor on staff."

"I don't get it," Josh said.

"They're just having fun," I replied. "You might not expect otherworldly beings to have senses of humor, but they do," I laughed. "Consider it a greeting card: 'Surprise! We're watching out for you.'"

"Well, why don't the little gray people just 'arrange' to land on the White House lawn if they have something to say?"

"They're careful about interfering in our natural unfolding, but they can inspire people like me to . . . spread the word."

Pointing to the pallet of books that was sitting on the forklift's tines, Josh said, "Come on, let's open up a case and get your precious book in your hot little hands." He opened the case and withdrew the brand-new paperback; he held it up for me to see. "*Talking to Extraterrestrials*," Josh said, smiling and reading the title.

"You better know what they're talking about," a voice said. Janet strolled into the warehouse with a flourish. "Cuz guess what show I just booked you on?" she asked. Janet was the company's publicist, and Josh and I turned to see her huge grin. "It's only one of the most listened-to late-night radio talk shows on Planet Earth."

"Are you kidding?" I asked nervously, not realizing that the radio interviews would start so soon. Janet had sent out galleys of the book to the media months earlier.

"Yep, *Coast to Coast* with George Noory," Janet said proudly. "Several million interested listeners will be tuning in to hear what you have to say."

"Well, I guess I better use these next few weeks to prepare," I replied, thankful that I would have time to calm my churning stomach.

"You don't have weeks; you've got *one week*. You're on next Friday, midnight until two a.m. You've got the whole two-hour slot."

I glanced at Josh worriedly, as if to say that I'd just as soon pack up my books and send them back to the printer.

"You'll do just fine," Josh said.

"Well, I hope so," I said nervously.

Janet raised an eyebrow. "Their producer assumes I'm submitting a real pro. Are you sure you can handle this?"

"How hard can it be? He asks questions; I answer them. I didn't have a problem speaking my mind to Mike's alien support group," I said.

Janet nodded her head, seeming reassured. "Okay, here's the call-in number." She handed me a contact sheet. "Call five minutes before the hour. The producer will patch you in *live*. Good luck."

~

A week later, Josh and I ate dinner at his house, staying up late for my midnight interview. Preparing for the long show, I got a full glass of water and sat down, looking at the clock. As I got in position on the couch, Josh relaxed in his easy chair with a newspaper.

"Put your book in front of you," he said, "and just remember, you're the author and the authority."

I grabbed my book and placed it on the coffee table next to me. At precisely five minutes before midnight, I dialed the number, and it was immediately answered, "*Coast to Coast;* Ms. Larkins? Please hold for George Noory. You'll be live in three minutes."

Soon after, I was patched in to the live on-air show and listened to the last few minutes of commercials before my interview began. Then, after the theme music played, the broadcast began with George Noory introducing me.

"Tonight we have a new guest joining us for the first time. Her name is Lisette Larkins, and she's written a book, *Talking to Extraterrestrials*. Welcome, Lisette, it's a pleasure to have you on the show."

"Thank you for having me," I said, clearing my throat and noticing that it had already become dry. I reached for my glass of water and took a few gulps.

"As my audience knows all too well," Noory said, "we cover everything on this show: exciting stories ranging from UFO sightings and encounters to other strange occurrences, such as near-death experiences, psychic powers, and other unexplained phenomena. We like to say that we're overnight talk radio with daytime ratings—North America's premier late-night radio talk show. Now, Lisette, tell our listeners how this all began for you."

"Well, I . . . when I was a young mother, I started to see strange explosions of light burst from the ceiling of my bedroom at night, and at first I didn't know what was happening. It got a lot more intense and continued for a long time."

"Did you wonder if you were losing your mind?" Noory asked.

"Yes, as a matter of fact, I did. I tried to figure it out, but my husband became concerned that I was acting strangely. Of course, anything out of the ordinary was strange to him, but I guess my nerves got frayed by this nightly fireworks show."

"Yes, of course they would," George replied. "But it says here in your book that you did time in a psychiatric hospital. Can you tell us how long they locked you up for?"

"Well, uh, my husband, he felt that I should get checked out, but I didn't realize that it was a psychiatric hospital until it was too late. But, after I left three weeks later, I went into therapy for years and got a sound diagnosis."

"Let's skip ahead, shall we?" George said. "Fast forward to the aliens themselves. You say that you were taken on board a craft. Isn't that so?"

"Yes."

"Please tell us exactly how you got there. I mean, did they pick you up on your front stoop, or did they beam you up like Captain Kirk on *Star Trek*?"

"It's very hard to explain and not at all like what's been portrayed."

"Well, try," he insisted.

"Yes, well, I was asleep on my bed, and my son was also asleep on his bed. The explosion of light descended on me, and also this incredibly strong electromagnetic vibration stung my skin. It was actually kind of painful, at least at first. Then I would feel my body rise off the bed, then my eyes closed on their own; and the next thing I was on one craft, then I was taken to another craft where I saw these small gray extraterrestrials."

"Please describe the interior of the craft for us in greater detail."

"Oh, well, mainly the background was washed out, but let's see. Um, I do remember a lot of bright lights flickering on some kind of control panel, and—"

"That's not very specific."

"Well, no, it's not, but I don't really remember because I was so startled. I mean, my body was floating through the air, and my heart was pounding, and I was terrified at first—"

"And did you actually *see* aliens?"

"Yes. They greeted me. They were very friendly."

"Were these the classic 'grays' with the large heads?"

"Uh, well, I guess you could say that; I mean, they were indeed gray, but their skin was like that of a dolphin's."

"How many fingers did they have?"

"Gosh, I'm trying to remember, but you know, I wasn't really paying attention to their fingers, because I was so *stunned* . . . and I was focused on the fact that I could understand them talking to me."

"We're going to take a commercial break, and we'll be right back. This is George Noory on *Coast to Coast AM*. Don't go away. When we come back, author Lisette Larkins is going to tell us how many fingers the Grays have and where they come from."

Placing the phone down on the table during the commercial break, I got up to stretch my legs.

"You're doing great!" Josh said sleepily, looking at his watch.

Yawning, I looked back at him, "You know as well as I do that this show's not going so great."

"Just do the best you can. That's all anyone can ask of you."

"He's not asking me about anything that I find of interest—like their *message* for example. It's all about the hardware, the phenomena . . . Who cares about that."

"Apparently, his listeners do. Don't worry; it's your first radio interview. You're just warming up." Pointing to the phone, Josh said, "You better get back on before the commercial break ends."

Settling myself on the couch with the phone tucked under my ear, I took a deep breath, wondering why I had agreed to be put in a position where I had to defend myself. At that moment, George Noory's voice boomed through the phone.

"And we're back, *live* with Lisette Larkins, who was just describing her incredible alien abduction. Lisette? Tell us again, how many fingers do they have?"

"As I was saying, I don't remember. I think it was four, or maybe it was three. The point is, they were *amazing*, standing there in front of me, speaking to me telepathically. It's incredible how—"

"Can you please tell our listeners exactly where these aliens are from?"

"I'm not sure," I responded tentatively.

"How can you not know where they're from?" Noory asked me. Josh shifted uncomfortably in his seat.

"I don't know. The science of it all—I don't understand it."

"Did the aliens attempt to explain where they're from, this galaxy or further afield? I mean, it does say here in your book that you're their ambassador, right? You would think that, at the very least, you'd be able to get a fix on how far away they come from in order to abduct you."

"Well, you see, that's the thing. I don't really feel that I've been *abducted* because that word, it means that a kidnapping has taken place."

"But you were *taken*?"

"I had an experience, one that I agreed to at some level. It wasn't a kidnapping."

"Is it possible that the aliens have brainwashed you, Lisette? Let's face it, there are hundreds of abductees who've been through scary abductions; but in your case, you sound as though you don't hold it against them. It says right here in your book that you saw hybrid beings in test tubes, which can only mean one thing. Frankly, these monsters are having their way with you and you're brainwashed."

"No, it's not like that at all."

"Are they corporeal?"

"Pardon me?"

"Are they *corporeal?*"

"Uh, I'm not sure exactly what you mean."

"If you don't know the answer, just say, '*I . . . don't . . . know,*'" he said, somewhat patronizingly.

"I don't know."

"Well, all right then. The call-in phone lines are lighting up. Let's turn now to the topic of where they are from before we take some caller questions."

"Uh, I thought I already covered that. I don't understand where they came from."

"Okay, but, Lisette, I'm sure I'm not the only one who wants to know the answer to this question. I've got three million listeners out there, and I feel pretty confident that they share my burning desire to know why the aliens picked, or *abducted you,* out of millions of other people."

"It wasn't an abduction, as I've said. And I'm someone who's gotten beyond such fear-based assumptions. Maybe that's why they picked me and I picked them, because I could see them as enlightened beings."

"Enlightened aliens? That's a new one. And how can you know that for sure? But before we explore the answer to that question, let's take another commercial break. When we come back for the next segment, our new author, Lisette Larkins, will describe why she was abducted by the aliens. And we'll be giving out her website info so you'll know just how to find her."

Placing the phone on the table, I threw myself down on the couch and buried my face in the cushions.

"I hate this!" I said, turning to look up at Josh, who had rushed to my side with a fresh glass of iced water.

"You're doing okay," Josh said. "It's not easy holding a counterpoint position, but you're doing fine. Just hang in there. It's almost over."

I looked at Josh and shook my head. If I had only known that this talk-show host's response was just the beginning, I might've packed my bags at the outset; but I went on to write two more books and conduct many more radio interviews, never knowing what kind of reception I would receive.

Chapter Twenty

Two years later, the Barnes & Noble bookstore near my house in Charlottesville, Virginia, prominently displayed my books on a long table in the center of the store, where I had been signing them for nearly an hour. A few customers waited patiently for their turn while the rest of the line wrapped around a mounted placard displaying my name and pictures of all my book covers. Josh had published a total of three of my books.

"I love your books," the next woman in line said to me, as I signed my name on the inside page. "They're filled with such beautiful life lessons. Thanks so much for writing them. I recommend them to everyone on my Facebook page."

"Thanks for coming," I said, nodding my head in appreciation and handing her the book. "I appreciate your support."

A young couple approached me next, smiling happily, the woman holding out her hand for me to shake.

"Thank you," I said, a little surprised at their display of enthusiasm.

"We heard that you were signing books today, and we wanted to come here and say, 'well done.' We know telling your story took a lot of courage, but it's made a huge impact on us. Your books have opened our eyes to a broader spirituality."

"That's very kind of you to say," I said, continuing to sign books. "It's not something that everybody gets, and I really appreciate your comments."

Occasionally new customers entered the store and, upon seeing the crowd gathered around, would walk up to see what was happening. One woman in her mid-fifties stopped by my table, picked up the book from the stack and read the back cover copy. Apparently disgusted, she slapped it down on the table.

"The occult is Satan's domain!" the woman called out loudly, startling me and those standing in line. Looking up at her in alarm, I watched as she turned to address the crowd, now holding up my book and continuing her sermon. "This is Satan's influence! It invites demonic attacks and pollutes the soul! This book is an abomination!"

Sighing deeply, I looked around the store in search of staff members who might come to my rescue.

"The bodies of believers are earthly temples! We must keep them pure, clean, and free of desecration! We must guard our mind, body, and soul from evil satanic worshipers! She's a witch, practicing *witchcraft!*"

In a fury, she swiped the stack of books off the table with her arm; they crashed to the floor and scattered.

Several bookstore employees and a security guard rushed over as the rest of the customers stepped back. Just as the woman was being escorted away, Josh walked into the store, and seeing the disarray of books, he rushed over to gather them and stack them back on the table. He put aside two books whose covers had been damaged.

"What happened?" he asked, looking back over his shoulder at the woman.

"A witch hunt," I replied sadly, watching some customers hanging back, unsure if they could again step forward. Josh waved them over.

Seeing my dejected expression, Josh continued to help tidy up the area and gave me an encouraging smile.

"Your website got over *667,000 views* and thousands of emails after your second radio show on *Coast to Coast AM*. Your books' popularity continues to grow."

"How much of that was hate email?" I asked, grinning.

Josh shook his head, then stepped back to allow the next customer to come forward and have their book signed. Fifteen minutes later, the book signing was over, and Josh and I gathered up the few unsold books and put them in a large book bag to carry away.

"Come on, now, cheer up," Josh said. "You sold an entire case. That's a lot for one of these events."

"The witchcraft claims are really disturbing. I mean, it's centuries later. Is it ever going to let up?"

"There will always be those who take safe refuge behind religious condemnations. You need tougher skin, Lisette."

"Charbroiled, if she had her way."

"There'll be more sophisticated people at the party," Josh said, taking my arm and escorting me toward the double glass doors. "Let's go; we're running late."

"Josh, I really don't feel like getting all dressed up for a cocktail party tonight. Why don't you go without me? I mean, it's not a book event."

"You're not cancelling. You're still relatively new to Charlottesville, and it will do you good to make new friends. Don't worry; it's just a normal party with normal people—except that our hostess is one of the wealthiest heiresses in the country."

After he convinced me to accompany him and following a quick stop to change clothes, Josh and I arrived at a beautiful gated entrance surrounded by hundreds of acres of vineyards. Located just down the road from Thomas Jefferson's Monticello estate museum, the large home was notorious for its twenty-three thousand square-foot size and its forty-five rooms. We passed through the open gate and drove up the long driveway toward the sparkling mansion on top of the hill.

A butler dressed in a black tuxedo greeted us at the front door, opening it with a flourish. "Please come in," he said, gesturing toward the living room where the party was in full swing.

After accepting glasses of sparkling water from a roving waiter, Josh and I walked around the room and mingled with the guests, eventually joining a small group of people admiring the collection of fine art spread along the back wall.

Turning at one point to survey the room full of guests, I was surprised to see the familiar face of a young woman entering the room, her husband at her side. This was none other than the baleful young contactee I'd met at Mike Newman's support group years earlier. I remembered that her name was Karen. She was dressed in a conservative black dress.

We all turned to greet the couple as her husband gave her a sweet kiss on the cheek. They both stepped out onto the veranda to admire the view as a guest next to Josh made a sudden announcement.

"I thought you all might like to know that we're graced here tonight by an actual victim of an alien abduction," he said, slurring his words, a bit tipsy. "She submitted an article a while back, and the local paper actually printed that nonsense, if you can believe it."

Surprised by his outburst, the guests stopped talking and turned to look at him, wondering to whom he was referring.

Startled, and believing that he was about to point me out, Josh and I exchanged worried glances. After taking another long swig of his drink, he turned to face the veranda, pointing directly at Karen.

"If you want her autograph, you better hurry before she gets whisked away by a flying saucer," he slurred. In unison, all the guests in the room turned to look outside at the young couple.

An elderly woman wearing a diamond tiara started the gossiping. "I read her article. Can you believe such a nice young man is married to that nut?"

"I can't imagine what her family's going through," another guest concurred.

"There are actually many otherwise *normal* people who claim to have had some kind of extraterrestrial contact," Josh added. "It's not just the domain of kooks."

Glaring at Josh, I shook my head to communicate that I was in no mood to take on an entire party of scoffers.

"There's no cause here for debate," bellowed a stern voice from the back of the room. "As a noted author and nuclear physicist, I have little tolerance for claims that violate the laws of physics. I continue to speak out publicly against such ignorant claims as hers," he said, stepping forward to take center stage. "Such experiences are simply *not possible*."

"But they are," I said, before I could stop myself, noticing that all the guests had now turned to gawk at me. At that moment, I noticed that Karen and her husband had stepped back into the living room and were listening intently.

"Extraterrestrials are here," I said emphatically. "Don't believe what you read in the *National Enquirer*. The ones I'm in contact with are spiritual teachers." Looking as though she were about to faint, Karen shuffled over to the couch and sat down, her husband hastening to bring her a glass of water.

"Young lady, just saying the word *extraterrestrial* is unacceptable to me," he said, looking at me intently as though daring me to respond. "I cannot abide the ignorant suggestion that laws of physics could be violated in order to allow *extraterrestrials* to traverse the vast distances of intergalactic space in order to land here."

Many of the guests nodded in agreement, quick to defer to the physicist in the room. Encouraged by their support, he drove his point home. "Yours is a cockamamie suggestion that disputes sound scientific fact. Frankly, the idea is absurd. Even if aliens exist, they could *not* travel to Earth. I mean, Alpha Centauri, the closest star system to ours, is four point three light years away. You *cannot* simply overturn Einsteinian physics merely on a whim."

Frozen by his barb, I was utterly speechless. I could sense Josh ready to counter his position, but I took his arm and led us out of the room. I just wanted to get away from this close-minded scientist who demanded that I recant the truth of my own experiences simply because it was beyond his education and his comprehension. How could I respond? What could I say to such a person?

Driving back in the car, Josh and I were quiet as I looked out the window, a burning cauldron simmering in the pit of my stomach. "I'm not doing any more radio. In fact, I'm not doing any more speaking or book signings," I said, trying to stanch my overflowing emotions.

"Let's not overreact," Josh said. "You've been at this for a couple years now, and you've been holding your own. You've done well over 150 radio shows and had numerous book signings across the country. You can't allow one arrogant idiot to make you give up your life's work."

Tears of humiliation were now streaming down my cheeks. The thought of standing there in the middle of that room of "sophisticated" partygoers having my life's experiences trashed made me sick. "I've decided that it's *not* my life's work, not anymore. I've had my say, and now it's time to move on."

"But you're just starting to break new ground," Josh insisted. "Remember your radio show in New Jersey?" he said, chuckling. "The producers were shocked when the ETs shut down their live show for thirty seconds after they challenged you to provide proof of the aliens' presence."

"That was classic," I agreed, nodding. At the time, the show had simply disappeared from the airwaves for no apparent reason, shocking the producers and the show's listeners. "That'll teach them to have a little more respect for an evolved species," I said. "But even though that was fun, I still think I need to take a break from my role as alien spokeswoman."

"But what are you going to say to your readers?" Josh asked. "What are you going to say to the ETs?"

Looking at Josh and suddenly feeling relieved, I rolled down my window and leaned outside, yelling into the night sky, "Hasta la vista, baby!"

Little did I know that this catchphrase, made famous by Arnold Schwarzenegger, literally means "until the (next) sighting" in Spanish, which was an appropriate parting salvo given that I would soon return to California, where it had all started, to apply what I had learned during these many years.

Chapter Twenty-One

CARING FOR JEANNETTE HAD become an all-consuming job. An Alzheimer's patient in the late stages of the disease was not easy to handle. Despite the difficulties, I never did hire a Navy SEAL to help me, although occasionally a part-timer helper would come in for a day or two. Now living with Jeannette and Kent in their Malibu home, I was caring for her day and night on an almost twenty-four/seven schedule. Kent had become concerned that the long hours and unrelenting responsibilities would result in me burning out.

Stress was merely a result of wrong thinking, I told him, no longer agreeing with his conclusions. I had learned this fact from many wise elders, both otherworldly and human, and I often reiterated this idea for Kent's consideration; I thought that we should practice this concept with more certainty.

Feeling that I needed to manage not only Jeannette's care but our caregiving routine, I practiced and preached that we should take frequent time-outs in our own minds—to stop and breathe deeply to rein in fearful thinking and thereby reduce our stress. I felt that we could overcome all obstacles if we closely adhered to conscious spiritual practices.

There were stories of other caregivers who had survived their sick patients' long ordeals, who had not succumbed to emotional and physical exhaustion, but there were not many of them. Caregiver burnout is legendary and is reflected in the little-known fact that a high percentage of family caregivers die within three years of their patients' deaths.

Clearly, if Kent and I were to avoid becoming untimely statistics, we would need to be bolstered by the latest and greatest Alzheimer's playbook. While Kent's appointment to the prestigious board of directors of the Alzheimer's Association provided reams of the latest research, I concluded that, as her caregivers, we would need to continually reinvent ourselves.

Kent even appeared on the front cover of the *Los Angeles Times*, from an article that discussed his, and the Alzheimer's Association's, goal to find a cure for the dreaded disease. Personally, I felt certain that many diseases of the body just might begin with the cells' declining ability to remain "charged," electromagnetically speaking. Obviously while not a physician, I had nonetheless personally experienced strong electromagnetic body charges over time, and I couldn't help but wonder if those charges could improve the failing performance of unhealthy cells and provide effective pain relief.

All body cells, I would imagine, required homeostasis or a balanced state to do their assigned job. If the cell's performance declines, organs begin to malfunction. What would happen to a cell if it received a constant, steady flow of directed electromagnetic energy? Kent and I often discussed this topic, especially in regard to my caretaking abilities with Jeannette that seemed extraordinary to him. Was my hands-on care enhanced over many years by an ongoing stream of electromagnetic current from my extraterrestrial encounters?

Interestingly enough, there were plenty of peer reviewed studies in prestigious medical journals touting the results of pulsed electromagnetic field therapy (PEMF) with certain devices. But as our debate continued, Jeannette's doctors' use of certain drug therapies sadly did not slow her precipitous decline, and we never got a chance to use PEMF therapy on her condition.

In the meantime, Kent and I debated on whether we should hire an additional full-time caregiver to help me. Because Jeannette didn't respond well to strangers in the house, I did not agree that an additional employee would best serve our needs or hers. Feeling that my role as caregiver might offer a rare opportunity for my own deepening spiritual practice, I insisted that I could single-handedly manage whatever challenges arose. I believed that difficulties could provide opportunities for higher learning, spiritually speaking. Moment-to-moment issues, I reckoned, could prove to be the fast track on which to demonstrate my own empowered way of living.

Over time, however, the cold reality of my situation was that the sicker and more disabled Jeannette became, the harder it was on me. One hurdle after another presented itself, almost on an hourly basis. Once Jeannette became completely confined to her wheelchair, her fury at being incapacitated intensified even more. She was increasingly distraught that her limbs no longer worked.

Helping to maneuver her limp body from the wheelchair to the toilet or bed and back again was not merely a physical task requiring bodily strength. I soon realized that if I were to effectively shepherd Jeannette through the final stage of her disease, I would need to become infused with tangible, *practical enlightenment*, and hopefully some of this "energy" would infuse her as well. I firmly believe that dying is a transition from the physical to the spiritual plane, and part of my caregiving was preparing Jeannette for her ultimate transition.

Although I felt that I had moved along the evolutionary scale, spiritually speaking, the reality of my challenges with Jeannette told me that there was still something else to learn, still some resistance left in me, still some lack of total acceptance, and the learning of those lessons might change everything.

As many new difficulties presented themselves each day, I realized that I needed to *better* apply the wise teachings that I had learned from the ETs. There was no shortage of books, newspaper articles, research papers, emails from friends and family, greeting cards, and "keep up the good work" pep talks from everyone who crossed my path with regard to my monumental task. But I realized that sound bites, no matter how well-meaning and no matter who was sending them to me, were incapable of quelling the tsunami that was broiling under my roof. *Application* was everything.

Merely *talking* about an enlightened way of living was not the same thing as *living* it. Who among us is able to *demonstrate* that they can surmount extraordinarily difficult conditions and do so with grace, courage, and tolerance? It would be one thing to steal away to an isolated mountain ashram to seek inner peace. But who can demonstrate spiritual mastery while remaining in the gutters and trenches of everyday living? Night after night, I lay in bed, tossing and turning, wondering if anything could be gained by another round of ET contact. After my parting salvo to the ETs years earlier, my nights had been quiet and devoid of any fireworks show. I had wanted to take a break from the aliens, and that's just what had occurred. But now, facing my deepening trials with Jeannette, I missed them and wanted their wisdom.

I had long grown weary of debunkers and skeptics and the constant negative energy their criticism generated, but I wondered if perhaps fielding this feedback might be a small price to pay after all. Besides, there was no longer any good reason to tell anyone about the contact. I had written my books, which were still in print, but I had withdrawn from discussing my experiences in public forums. So now I had two questions: If I decided to invite them, would the ETs return? Second, if they *did* return, why tell anyone about it?

In hindsight, publishing books about my ET contact had been unnecessarily problematic, inviting ridicule for no good reason. Skeptics and debunkers were not open to another opinion about the spiritual nature of extraterrestrial contact phenomena. I had come to realize that cynics often proudly displayed their cynicism and doubts, and in fact they considered cynicism as a characteristic of intelligence.

Late one night, after getting Jeannette to sleep and following through with my gym workout, I showered and dressed in warm clothes and put on my jacket. I walked quietly outside, so as not to wake Jeannette, and took a seat on a bench at the far end of the property. I gazed up into the still night sky and pondered my two questions. Was anyone or anything out there? I wondered.

Seeing nothing unusual, I realized that perhaps I'd closed the door on them for good. Perhaps the ETs were now jetting to some distant galaxy, having forgotten all about me. Buttoning my coat against the chilly evening air, the only thing I heard was the call of ordinary crickets and the lonesome hoot of an owl. I wondered, if the ETs were still around, what other brave human was now benefiting from their wisdom.

Alone with my sad thoughts, I scanned the night sky one last time; the thousands of twinkling stars offered me little solace. Finally, shrugging my shoulders, I surrendered to the lonely night, regretfully admitting that I was now on my own.

I looked out over the ocean. My position on the bluff offered a spectacular view of the dark Pacific below me. In the distance, circling the Santa Monica coastline, I could see a long line of bright dots in the sky—jetliners waiting their turn for a final approach. Los Angeles International Airport's lights and those of the city surrounding it sparkled like jewelry.

The ocean spread out before me, the calm light of a half-moon shining upon it. The faint scent of blossoming sage and *Ceanothus* flowers filled my nostrils. After a while, I picked myself up to head back to the house. Despite the beautiful setting, I needed to get a good night's sleep before Jeanette's restless stirring provided my early morning wake-up call.

Gingerly stepping through the darkness toward the back entrance of the house, I felt totally alone and my heart was heavy. My duties as caregiver for a difficult woman suffering from an even more difficult disease seemed overwhelming. Breathing deeply, I focused my attention on my breath, wondering what spiritual strategy could possibly save me from the rigors of my daily routine.

As I returned to the house, the ETs' words returned to me; words that had once suggested that I "become aware of what I had come here to do" and to "become aware of the 'goals of my soul.'"

What have I come here to do? I asked myself. What are the goals of my soul?

Maybe I had failed in my mission. Maybe the real goal was simply to find the inner grace to allow for my unusual experiences, then write a book about what I had learned, not allowing skeptics to *thwart* that mission. Did it really matter if I was the subject of ridicule? It was ironic, I realized, that while skeptics and debunkers were confidently accomplishing *their missions,* I had forsaken mine.

That idea had no sooner passed into my awareness when a beautiful, bright, aqua-blue flash of light burst in the air in front of me, lasting only a few seconds. It was as though a flashlight had been turned on, then off. Next, the unmistakable zapping pierced my entire body, and a small, almost transparent extraterrestrial being appeared in front of me on the path to the back door.

I wondered if I were dreaming, because I could hardly see him. Usually they appeared so solid. It was as though a thin film of cheesecloth stood between us. At the same time, appearing out of thin air, a sudden silver streak blazed noiselessly overhead, catching my eyes. Looking up, I was blinded by a stream of white lights.

I was unable to focus due to the glare of this strobe-like light. Then the beam suddenly moved beyond the house and shot off into the distance, just as I saw an enormous oblong craft race silently away from me and shoot out over the ocean.

It was as large as any cruise ship and had lights on its outward rim. Seconds later, it rocketed straight up into the night sky. Then, reversing its direction, it moved straight down toward the sea. I gaped as the disc quickly disappeared into the water, likely defying all laws governing aeronautical flight.

Returning my attention to the small being in front of me, I could feel the weight of my beating heart as it pounded loudly inside my chest. Could nervous excitement stop my heart? I recalled being frightened and how my heart had thumped wildly while beholding the alien hybrids. Now it was beating with the same jarring ferociousness, and I wondered if I would suffer a heart attack.

Then these words entered my consciousness, as though the ET were answering my query about my ever-pounding heart. "The electrical currents of the heart muscles produce one of the body's strongest magnetic fields, creating a 'bio-magnetic' field, as it were," I heard in my mind.

"The heart can do all that?"

"This biomagnetic field extends indefinitely into space and is what connects *us* and every living creature, no matter the distance that appears to separate all beings. These pulsations have long been used for healing. Even primitive peoples on Earth exposed sick people to electrical eels to heal them. The earliest recorded use of electricity for healing dates from 2750 BC. There has long been an intuitive understanding that life is indeed an electromagnetic event and that healing is accomplished by moving this energy."

"But how," I asked out loud, considering the pulsing organ that was bursting within me. Cupping my hand over my chest, I wondered how a small fleshy gadget the size of my fist could connect me with every living thing.

"Energy fields are unbounded, and each heart emits bio-magnetic waves that transmit far out into the cosmos. These waves merge with others, including those that rise up from the center of the Earth."

"Energy waves arise out of Earth?'"

"How else do you suppose that your neighbors from afar are able to be here?"

"I don't get it," I said.

"Life is an electromagnetic event. Electromagnetic waves *connect us*," said the ET. "We don't *travel* here; we *are* here. We're *already* connected by electromagnetic, or biomagnetic, impulses. No distance need be traversed."

"I don't understand."

"Every living being—planets, humans, animals, and otherworldly beings—are connected by invisible electromagnetic impulses. When those impulses *merge*, an immediate alignment takes place by frequency. Our ability to unite with one another occurs instantaneously, because we are part of the same electromagnetic field."

"But the planet is *solid*; the ground beneath us is mere dirt. It's not a living *being*."

"It's *alive*, as is *all* creation. We are all deeply connected by invisible waves that are part of our shared aliveness. We are not machines."

"But my heart's afraid of you," I admitted.

"No," the voice assured me. "Your heart is a broadcast station. It sends and receives strong, invisible impulses that other living beings intercept."

"You can feel my heartbeat?"

"It's precisely what *unites* us. We have the same frequency."

"But you said that the Earth has them, too."

"Earth emits the same kind of electromagnetic waves that you do."

"Can I feel them?" I asked.

"Ever heard of geothermal heat?"

"But Earth is a *rock*. The human heart is *flesh*. Earth is a *thing*. It doesn't have a heart."

"Earth is a living being and, like all other living beings, within her is a primary access point to the divine source. Its heart or inner core provides this access point," the voice explained.

"And this is what unites us?"

"Each living thing is connected to this same access point and cannot be separated by time, distance, physical appearance, or species."

Memories returned to me of the fireworks shows and electromagnetic pulsations that had regularly erupted in my bedroom and seemed to announce the ETs' presence. I recalled how powerful those lightshows could be, creating a seemingly mini-rocket launch in the middle of my bedroom. Suddenly it all made sense.

As if in response to my thoughts, the voice continued, "Your beating heart sends out an electromagnetic *surge* that merges with our own. Every living thing is connected this way."

"But I thought that my loud beating heart was a symptom of *fear*."

"*It's* not frightened, although your mind may be," the voice corrected me. "Your heart emits a *healing force* when powered by emotions of love and elation."

"So it's not my *mind* that's making things happen?"

"It's your *heart* that broadcasts carrier waves that co-create every outcome. In turn, the heart informs the mind."

Pondering this for a moment, I wondered at the miracle of how the ticker in my chest could produce emanations that traversed all barriers, connecting with others who share the same wave frequency.

"Do *you* have a heart?" I asked.

"All beings everywhere are hardwired for a compassionate response toward others who suffer," the voice said, as though explaining their presence in my life and those of others. "No matter our physical differences, we share many of the same genes. All beings everywhere emit electromagnetic frequencies that call out across apparent time and space."

"Well, there are humans, and aliens, and animals . . ." I retorted, not trying to sound snarky but questioning the way in which they consistently refuted scientific facts. "How can *all* physical beings share the same genes?"

"There are very deep connections between all beings in existence. Everything and everyone is connected everywhere, at all times, by electromagnetic pulsations that unite us as one," said the voice.

"But what does this all have to do with caring for Jeannette?" I asked, remembering the reason for my nighttime stroll. What does my struggle with *her* have to do with my heart's electromagnetic surge?

"You are looking for solutions. When you feel love and elation, your heart sends out a strong electromagnetic vibration to your mind that, in turn, affects everything in the cosmos. But it starts with the compassion that you feel in your heart."

"*This* is the solution? How can I feel elation when there is so much to be worried about?"

"Simply infuse with *elation* one small act of kindness after another, and the rest will take care of itself."

Chapter Twenty-Two

AFTER THAT NIGHT, THE *harder it* got, the *better I* got, because now I understood the solution: By simply performing one simple act of kindness after another, it would all take care of itself.

Long ago, the extraterrestrials had asked me three important questions:

"Do you care about others?"

"Are you engaged in service to others?"

"Do you feel compassion for others?"

When my actions showed that my answer was a resounding yes—without losing myself in the process—it all began to work out. The key was to feel a sense of elation, no matter the awful march of Jeannette's illness. I began to better understand the way that Jeannette's suffering could teach me rather than destroy me.

The ETs' earlier words rang truer than ever: "The most important indicator of your spiritual progress is the way you respond to actual or perceived wrongdoing."

Could Jeannette's disease, with all its ramifications, serve as my shaman to lead me to practice more effective surrendering to what *is*? Surrender is not the same as giving up, I discovered. Surrender is a state of *allowing what is.*

Simply allow life to show up as it is, in the form of people and situations. Once it does, respond with appropriate kindness while simultaneously working to create a beneficial outcome. Don't complain about it; don't tell endless stories about it to incite sympathy; don't argue against it. Simply *allow*, then act.

In the early days of our struggle together, Jeannette and I had done what most everyone else did. We reacted negatively to problems until the weight of our advancing mental suffering pushed us both onto a higher plateau of awareness out of the sheer necessity to survive.

Eventually, we surrendered, due in no small part to the accelerated pace of our mental suffering. Jeannette and I began to cease the chronic habit of trying to force a different outcome from what was happening, and miraculously life started to flow better.

Although I attained this realization as a result of conscious practice and its application, Jeannette grew too. Her fading mental clarity created a simultaneous softening of her strong ego. Her once-resistant thought patterns were eroded, which resulted in a quieter, less furious response to her disability. Slowly, over time, our mutual "emptiness" led us to more peaceful day-to-day experiences.

Each real-life lesson of spiritual instruction unfolded in myriad ways, in a practical sense, *because* of Jeannette's worsening condition. As she lost one faculty and ability after another, miraculously we both moved into a more complementary way of being with each other. When Jeannette totally lost her speech, I became more aware of *my* speech. Every word I uttered had an effect because I now understood that I was part of a deeply connected, universal energy field.

I asked myself frequent questions:

Attitudes are contagious, was mine worth catching?

When Jeannette lost the ability to vehemently react against that which she hated, was I also softening my own egoistic reactions?

Were my words and actions imbued with grace and courage?

Was I breaking the habit of complaining to others as an unconscious attempt to gain sympathy?

When Jeannette was no longer able to express herself verbally, I looked more closely at what *I* was attempting to express. When Jeannette could no longer take in anything by mouth, I looked more closely at what *I* was allowing to enter my *mind*.

Was I resistant, or was I in a state of grace?

As Jeannette declined further, could I use her physical deterioration as a springboard to recognize the nature of both of our immortal souls?

All the spiritual *theory* that I had learned from the extraterrestrials now showed up in reality to test me. Could I apply all that I had been taught but had not necessarily mastered?

Jeannette had become an extraordinary example of how one's painful life circumstances can obliterate peace of mind. Without a broader spiritual perspective in which to see disasters, accidents, and illnesses as part of the soul's training on Earth, there could be no relief for their suffering, emotionally and physically. Jeannette's disease prompted my inner searching, and, by observing her, I couldn't help but to reflect on my own past struggles with Peter and the upset that I had once allowed them to produce.

No matter the degree of Jeannette's emotional and physical resistance to the circumstances of her disease, her Alzheimer's symptoms worsened, and her and her family's opinions could not allay them. I learned about inner peace by closely observing the absence of it in those around her. Together, Kent and I began to discuss and explore how we could change the way we felt when upset, and, at his encouragement, I began to compile those teachings into a book.

I discovered that if one could peacefully behold an undesired outcome without resisting it, it would produce a gentle surrender to what *is*. But then it was necessary to look deeply within one's self, to discover what "training" was occurring as a result of dealing with the problem at hand. Without this concomitant shift, anyone dealing with a dying patient—or one's own suffering, for that matter—would deteriorate along with them. It takes great calm and awareness, I soon discovered, to prevent one's self from devolving to the patient's level of emotional upset in the process of trying to help them.

Jeannette's deteriorating condition practically forced me into a more peaceful state of surrender, because her anxiety about her condition was so complete and unrelenting that I could not allow myself to become as angry and sad as she was. Most friends and some family members, who spent any length of time around Jeannette, soon became caught up in her mental anguish, I observed. Unless they were shielded by their own resolve to look beneath the drama for Divinity's calm perfection, they, too, spiraled into upset. Applying spiritual wisdom was the only remedy; otherwise, the observer was pulled into the same histrionic mental state as that of the observed.

This is why caregiver burnout is so legendary, I realized. Most caregivers and family members do not have the appropriate *spiritual* training to comprehend the true nature of their task: to align with inner peace despite outer problems. Stress and spiritual equanimity are not reconcilable.

The ETs had told me that my heart, and everyone else's heart, was hardwired for a compassionate response that was capable of generating a strong healing force. But if I then allowed reactive mental states of worry and stress to overshadow my kind acts, then I was no longer effective as a healer.

Memories of past troubles now provided a deeper context. Others who had once upset me—Peter, Dr. Helman, the antagonistic physicist—were all part of my *perfect* past that now unfolded into a *perfect* present. This was my spiritual boot camp, training my soul by challenging me to solve difficult problems and bringing all my past experience to bear on them. Sometimes, the very best solution is recognizing that there is none, and finding inner peace despite that fact.

As Jeannette's condition worsened, I opened up my laptop during the wee hours of the night and began again to write about what I had learned. Although I had started writing when she was still in the middle stages of her disease, I now began again in earnest.

Soon, a brand-new manuscript, *Difficult People*, began to emerge, and I sent along a few chapters to my publisher, Josh Roberts. Delighted that I was writing a new book, Josh encouraged me to continue and offered to publish it. Like me, he was interested in observing how otherworldly phenomena could positively impact people, their problems, and the world in general. Even Kent was excited about my new book and offered to write the foreword to the book.

Because Alzheimer's disease causes memory loss, impairs judgment and orientation, and affects one's ability to understand and communicate effectively, I ran out of suitable activities that would appease Jeannette. Keeping her calm was an ongoing challenge.

One day, I followed a strange, mysterious intuition to leave the house and embark on a special quest. Although I was not sure why, aqua blue flashes of light led me to locate a certain yellow lab puppy who was in need of adoption that day only. Time was of the essence in order for me to locate her. I didn't know where it was, or why I was being encouraged to find it. After visiting several kennels where dogs were offered for adoption, I almost gave up because I could not find the right one.

It was much later in the day when I finally came across a particular puppy that I immediately recognized as the one that I was meant to bring home. She was surrounded by flashes of blue light.

Needless to say, Kent and Jeannette loved her, and I named her Kelly. Together, we trained her to canter alongside the golf cart that we regularly used to take out the trash, collect the mail, drive around to visit neighbors, or buzz down to the putting green. Kelly trotted along happily, getting lots of exercise, with her squeaky toy in her mouth. She became our mascot. We even trained her to surf on a large floatie in the swimming pool by getting a running start and then taking a flying leap onto it, as the floatie skidded across the water to the far end of the pool. Kelly's antics were hilarious and provided hours of entertainment for all of us. As it turned out, when Jeannette later transitioned, it was Kelly who provided Kent and me with an extraordinary amount of love and affection. She proved to be a strong healing force in the household.

As Jeannette slowed down even more, I rented a specially outfitted van that allowed me to strap her wheelchair into the passenger's side. We started to go on more frequent outings. Our van became our daytime home away from home as we peacefully traversed the Golden State's shoreline.

One sunny weekend, I decided to take Jeannette on the long drive to Ojai. Our frequent drives were at times the only possible solution to her restless periods of anguish. She sat up front next to me, strapped into her wheelchair, and I could not help but notice her further decline as she had trouble holding on to her crayons. She fiddled with her seat belt.

She soon tired of playing with the straps, so I adjusted the wood tray on her lap and handed her a small carton of clay. Still annoyed, she began to moan, indicating that she wanted to go home.

Remembering to respond with an act of kindness, and allowing myself to feel love and elation, I invited Jeannette to look out the window at the beauty of our surroundings. I remembered to make a mental adjustment, to perceive of Jeannette's upset as a test requiring my own proper response. I looked for a calm solution to the problem and found a way to distract Jeannette from her discomfort. As we drove north on Pacific Coast Highway toward Ojai, we could see a beautiful long v-line of pelicans that were heading to the Malibu lagoon for their afternoon rest.

After driving for another hour, we headed off the Ventura Freeway toward the foothills of Ojai, and, strangely, I could feel a deep sense of calm; I relaxed more fully. Pleased that Jeannette was now also quiet and contented, we continued on.

We made a left turn in Ojai onto the pass that would take us north into the mountains. Suddenly, a state of the d--- est, most sublime peace infused me. Jeannette, too, see unusually satisfied and attuned.

Soon, I became aware of a warm, lightheaded sens: that moved up and *through* me so thoroughly that I b to feel euphoric. We had crossed into new territory, both literally and metaphorically, as unmistakable electromagnetic vibrations filled the van. How could the same pulsations that accompanied my extraterrestrial visitations erupt in the van? Were we about to be lifted up into the heavens?

Then I remembered what the ETs had told me: "Earth is a living being, and, like all other living beings, there is a heart within her that is the primary access point to the divine source. All hearts emit electromagnetic pulsations. These pulsations unite all beings as one."

Were these vibrations a result of the Earth's heartbeat joining with my own? I looked at Jeannette to see if she could also feel them.

She had become downright peaceful. What had come over her? Amazed to see her sanguine expression, I thought that she must be feeling them. What else could have caused her sublime composure? As we wound through the mountain pass, the mysterious surge pulsated more strongly than ever, and Jeanette surprised me by sweetly taking hold of my hand.

Was her uncharacteristic demonstration of affection induced by joining her heart's current with that of the Earth's and of my own? The electromagnetic surge was palpable; Jeannette looked at me and smiled, squeezing my hand harder.

Breathing deeply and luxuriously, I felt the sun's rays streaming in through the open windows as we sped happily along the green mountain pass. No longer vigorously protesting her deteriorating condition, Jeannette seemed to experience the peace that permeates all that *is*, and I felt the same.

As we drove up another incline, bountiful trees full of avocadoes flanked us on both sides of the road. With tropical-like weather and warm summer days, Ojai is home to one of the most fertile avocado crops in America. Despite the beauty of our surroundings, it was the activity of our inner worlds that mostly grabbed my attention.

Miraculously, everything seemed utterly *perfect*. The colors around us became vibrant; it was as though I could *feel* them: the emerald-green avocado trees that flanked us; the fluffy-white cotton-ball clouds that dotted the distant sky; even the music we were listening to was *palpable,* as though I had suddenly merged *with* it instead of simply hearing it. I felt ecstatic and in utter acceptance of all that *is*. Had I died and gone to heaven? Or maybe I was dreaming and would soon awake.

As our favorite CD played, I joined in, singing the delightful melody of Hawaiian singer Israel Kamakawiwo'ole's remake of "Somewhere over the Rainbow." The perfect melody added to our joy. Jeannette swayed to the music.

Paradise. This moment had become paradise. This unusual feeling of bliss had seemingly emerged out of nowhere. All the struggles and challenges of my daily hurdles with Jeannette had melted away. The rigors of Jeannette's Alzheimer's and all the problems that arose in caring for her had, at times, felt overwhelming. But now I saw a patient reborn, as was I, too.

Jeanette was no longer moving toward death but instead moving to a new level of experience. I could see now that she was not really dying but was transitioning to another dimension altogether. Even though she could not walk, talk, nor swallow food or liquid, I knew that everything would be okay for her.

I pointed out several raptors that had appeared outside, and we both marveled at their beauty. High in the yonder blue sky, they floated gently aloft, not losing altitude; yet they did so without any movement of their wings. The branches on the trees were not moving either, and I noticed that this was a still, windless day. While we watched the raptors, the gentle electromagnetic pulses continued to envelope us. Jeannette just smiled, enjoying the experience as much as I was.

The beautiful birds remained suspended, as though they were heaven's Christmas tree ornaments on invisible strings. Any bird peacefully floating in the air without flapping its wings and without benefit of any wind would have to be riding an invisible current of energy, I imagined. Were they, in fact, riding the Earth's electromagnetic waves? If so, were these the same waves that connected with my own heart?

Perhaps somehow, and in some way, all living beings were indeed intrinsically connected by this invisible life force that emanates from the hearts of us all.

That which unites us, binds us for all eternity.

Chapter Twenty-Three

As Jeannette moved closer to physical death, I could see that she began to withdraw from the world around her. Because I was so attuned to her needs and allowed her condition to set the pace of our day, we lost interest in newspapers, television, movies, and the news of the world. In her final months, this detachment occurred with greater intensity. The drama of politics and world events seemed far away and immaterial. We both seemed to lose interest in all outside activities also, as our focus shifted to inner experience. She was dying, and I was shepherding her through the experience.

Previously sociable and the first person to enjoy a party, Jeannette began to withdraw from social visits, the neighbors, and even friends and family. I, too, could not help but notice the identical shift was happening to me as well. I just wanted to be home and quiet.

Although Jeannette's body was dying, it was impossible for me to imagine that the powerful essence of who she was could possibly end with her body's demise. As such, to me, even though her body was failing completely, in my eyes we were *both* experiencing something of a renewal.

For this reason, this period felt like a rebirth as we shifted from an outside focus to our inner world. In Jeannette's case, this happened slowly over the course of more than a decade, but the intense final phase occurred over the last six months of her life; particularly, in the last few weeks. I was aware that, in some ways, a part of me was dying right along with her.

A different frame of reference arose as Jeannette began to lose all sense of her surroundings; she didn't even seem to notice that we had placed her in a different bed. Both Jeannette and I had once been fully aligned with time-bound reality, but now that was shifting. Strangely, we didn't mind that we had no idea what day or hour it was.

We stayed in her room as her body struggled to handle basic functions. She was fully aligning with the realm of timelessness as her soul prepared to leave her body; as that happened, my inner world expanded as well. This timeless period felt strange but natural; the hustle and bustle of the world passed by with us hardly noticing it at all. At one point, as I lay close to her on her bed, Jeannette's breathing became slow and irregular, as if she were taking her last breaths.

The day before she died, Jeannette rallied for a moment and exhibited a sudden surge of energy, becoming lucid and aware of those she loved who were gathered at her bedside. I, too, became more active—in stark contrast to the stillness of my inner world. As a result, it felt as if my body were moving in slow motion, even though I was moving normally.

As Jeanette's last hour approached, we entered a period during which our orientation to the peaceful, timeless realm completed itself—a process in which Heaven above and Earth below merged within us. This is how we both came to wholeness. I wondered if this was how a new civilization would be born: as each person changed and grew, humanity would seamlessly evolve into an Age of Enlightenment.

Jeannette passed away peacefully at home, surrounded by me and her family and the dog. Moments before her last

breath, I kissed her hand, feeling a well of emotion. As I held
her hand in mine, I felt that we had both made our spiritual
transitions. I was also adjusting to the prospect of a new life
without our union being a major part of my day.

Understanding that our trials actually train our soul to
grow required an entirely different way of thinking and being
in the world. Responding to problems and acts of wrongdoing with daily acts of kindness, rather than anger and upset,
required tolerance and courage. It was as if Jeannette and I
were dying together. As her spirit began to withdraw from
life, my own *inner* wellspring of wisdom rose to the surface.
My "death" involved leaving behind my upset about the
world's opinion of me and claiming my own truth. Outside
the window, even the sky seemed to send its own tribute to
Jeannette, as stunning white cumulonimbus clouds raced out
of sight, disappearing beyond the mountains.

I got in the golf cart and quietly drove down the winding
driveway a few hours after Jeannette's transition. Kelly trotted
along next to me. The two bronze deer were still there as silent
sentries. One of them had toppled over again, no doubt having been struck by the same territorial buck.

Getting out of the golf cart to consider these guardians
of the property for a moment, I approached the fallen deer to
see if this time, now three years later, I was strong enough to
pull it to a standing position. Surprisingly, I did so easily. My
quiet reverie was suddenly interrupted by a large brown UPS
truck rumbling up the driveway and heading to the house. I
jumped back in the cart with Kelly and met the truck halfway.

I called out to the driver. "I'll take the package," I said,
gesturing to the back of the golf cart. Happy to oblige, he
stopped. After rummaging in the back, he emerged with a

large box. "It's heavy," he cautioned, placing it in the rear area of the golf cart. He waved goodbye and backed up his truck.

Using the golf cart's key, I broke the tape binding and opened the box. Inside was a stack of my books, fresh from the printer. I withdrew one and ran my hand over the glossy cover. The title read: *Difficult People: A Gateway to Enlightenment*. I opened the book to the foreword, which Kent had graciously offered to write, and I now read it again.

My book detailed my process of finding inner peace, even while in a difficult situation and being challenged by a difficult person. While caring for Jeannette, I had been able to practice a concept to which the ETs had long alluded: demonstrating that I could respond to "wrongdoing" and difficulties by acting with compassion and one small act of kindness after another; being of service and allowing love and elation to fill my heart, despite the difficult circumstances. Together, Jeannette and I, and my ex-husband Peter before her, had grappled with the synchronistic roles that had joined our destinies.

Now, beholding my new book—the end product of my three years with Jeannette, our journey through the maze of Alzheimer's, and all its attendant trials—its arrival on this day brought tears to my eyes. How is it possible, I asked myself, that these two events, even down to the morning of her passing, could have been arranged without us knowing it?

Divine timing and its mystery were too perfect even to fathom. No amount of human planning could have timed those two incidents: Just hours after she had passed away, a truck arrives from the printer to deliver books that chronicle her end-of-life transition. It was as though Jeannette's soul had conspired in the timing, her higher self remaining as silent witness to the completion of our joint spiritual project.

Although the ravages of Alzheimer's had eventually claimed her, Jeannette and my union had its own perfection. In the same way that my dismal marriage to Peter and my employment by Dr. Helman also were fraught with difficulties and upsets, ultimately these relationships had provided stellar growth opportunities. I had come to know that it was my responsibility to find the gold within those dynamics and learn why I had called those experiences to myself. My soul was indeed becoming trained.

Chapter Twenty-Four

It had been a year since Jeannette's passing, and I busied myself with a new venture: I had become a health coach, providing pulsed electromagnetic-field therapy to clients experiencing pain. Using an ultra-high-tech device that emits electromagnetic pulsations, I offered clients remarkable relief from aching muscles and other painful discomforts. I had come full-circle, now helping athletes and others benefit from the same strong electromagnetic pulsations that had replenished me.

After Jeannette's death, Kent had asked me to stay on and to continue managing the estate and assisting him. I was delighted to do so. Occasionally, I did radio interviews at my publisher's request and spoke at various public forums, so I continued my mission with the ETs—both as a speaker and with my new PEMF coaching endeavor.

It was a busy weekday morning, and the day that I was leaving on vacation. After loading my suitcase in the car, I double checked that my passport was in my purse. Before heading to the airport, there was a lot to be done.

First, I had visited a sick client at her home, followed by a fellow Crossfit athlete at his home, coaching both with my pulsed-energy replenisher. They claimed to feel immediate relief.

After finishing up with them, I carefully packed my equipment in the car and headed to Malibu Crossfit for a vigorous workout. Kent and I planned to meet up following my workout so he could say goodbye before I headed to the airport for my trip. He said that he had a going-away surprise for me and would meet me there.

At the end of the workout, we all tidied up the area, returning our bar bells and jump ropes, and then I quickly cleaned up and changed clothes. After waving goodbye to my friends, Kent pulled up in his car and parked next to mine. Kelly happily jumped out with her squeaky toy in her mouth. I threw it across the parking lot and she bounded after it.

"Okay, what's the big surprise?" I asked playfully, running out to meet him in the parking lot and petting Kelly, who dropped the toy at my feet. I looked in the backseat of his car for a wrapped present.

"My surprise is actually an amazing *idea*," Kent said, his eyes twinkling with mischief. "I just had to tell you before you left on your trip."

"Tell me what?" I asked.

"It's about your beloved magical contraption . . . your lightning zapper."

"You mean my PEMF device. It's a Tesla Coil, which was probably inspired by an ET experiencer if you ask me."

"Very funny," Kent said, grinning at me. "Which brings me to the subject of my idea. What if I could arrange for someone to *fund* a clinical trial, using an official double-blind study, but not with drugs. We'd use your PEMF technology on Alzheimer's patients. There's still no cure, and the Alzheimer's Association may never find one."

"Great idea! But they have to use *this* model," I said, pointing to my precious equipment in the back of my car.

"There are hundreds of PEMF devices, but *this* is the most effective. Who do you have in mind to fund it?"

"Nicola Tesla."

"You must be kidding! He died in 1943."

"True. But what if I approached his protégé?"

"He has a protégé?"

"Well, sort of. Someone like Elon Musk, the CEO of Tesla Motors and Space X. He's someone who loves Tesla's technologies, and the prospect of interstellar space travel. Your device has already been peer-reviewed in medical journals, and it shows real promise," Kent said.

"You're talking about my favorite subject. Energy medicine! I would *love* to be involved in that study," I replied excitedly.

"I've been reading about two areas of medical research that are being extensively investigated. The first area is the study of magnetic fields produced by living things, referred to as—"

"*Biomagnetism*," I replied smiling, interrupting Kent. "I already know about it from the ETs."

"Then you probably know about the second area of interest, which is called magnetobiology: the study of the effects of magnetic fields on living systems."

"Now you know why I've got my very own PEMF device!" I blurted out. "My own personal study is already well underway! I'm using it on myself regularly."

"Okay, but what if I could coordinate a major clinical trial on how your PEMF Tesla Coil replenishes the body's cells and, who knows, can possibly even help Alzheimer's patients."

I was so thrilled with his idea that I ran over and gave him a giant hug. "What an amazing idea!" I exclaimed. "When do we start?"

"Since we've already visited the factory where it's manufactured, now I need to talk with the owner, and a potential benefactor like Elon Musk. I need to find a medical researcher who's willing to go beyond the present medical model and try something new."

"Your surprise is wonderful and I absolutely love it!"

"I've got one other small gift."

"Two surprises?" I replied, genuinely intrigued.

"Because you're leaving today on your long overseas trip, I wanted to make your flight more comfortable." Kent removed an envelope from his shirt pocket and handed it to me.

"I called your travel agent—the one that I referred you to last year—and I upgraded your flight to first class: It's a small token of my appreciation."

"Wow, thanks so much!" I said, beaming, peeking inside the envelope. "What a surprise. You didn't have to do that."

"Well, I figured, by the time you stop over in New York, it's gonna be one long flight. Flying first class, well, at least you won't have to fight your neighbor for more room and you can sleep on the way there."

"It's very nice of you, really, and I'm very appreciative. Last time I flew coach on a long flight, the guy next to me snored on my shoulder the entire flight."

"To tell you the truth, I had an additional motive in upgrading your seat." Kent looked at his watch. "I know your son will be here any minute to take you to the airport, so I'll make this quick. I was actually checking to be certain that you'd purchased a *round trip* ticket. I want to be certain that you'll come home after you find the end of that rainbow."

"Of course I'm coming back, silly," I said emphatically. "I'm both PEMF health coach and an author. Iceland's just a vacation, with one lecture at a bookstore. I'm not bringing my device to Iceland."

"What I mean is, I hope that when you *do* come back that . . . you'll . . . well, I guess . . . teach *me*, like you did Jeannette."

Puzzled, I looked at him carefully, wondering if he was teasing me.

"You want *me* to teach *you?*" I asked, somewhat confused by his statement. "And exactly what do you want to *learn?*"

"A couple of times, I've thought I saw flashes of blue light, so who knows, maybe your bizarre paranormal stuff is contagious!"

Laughing, I nodded my head in understanding, knowing exactly what he was describing. "It sounds like you're being *initiated!*"

"What does that mean?" Kent asked cautiously.

"It means that you're opening to a broader spiritual awareness," I replied, impressed with his interest. "Does it frighten you?"

"Not at all," Kent replied. "You're always challenging yourself to grow and to find positive meaning in difficulties and challenges. I thought you could show me how to . . . get in touch with my inner self and to become even *more aware.*"

"You've got to be kidding?" I replied, grinning at Kent. "A contentious trial lawyer wants to learn inner peace and psychic awareness?"

"I was reading your book, *Difficult People*—I did write the foreword, if you recall—and it said that a person should open their heart; to allow their heart to *feel compassion* and *elation*; then to infuse that in all areas of life."

"That's right," I said, "especially when we're in situations that are uncomfortable or difficult. The idea is to try to refrain from putting up armor around the heart to protect it from pain. When we do that, it's hard to get in touch with how we feel."

"Okay, so I also want to get in better touch with how *I feel*. Surely, I'm not that much of a hard case," he added with a sly grin.

"I smiled, impressed by his desire to learn and to grow. He was a dyed-in-the-wool big-time lawyer, after all. Attorneys were legendary for their cynical and skeptical view of the world. I knew that his thinking couldn't help but be influenced by the common cultural mindset of negative skepticism and doubt.

"Okay, but there are a lot of *weird* ideas to consider," I said, deliberately teasing him. "There's a lot more going on behind the scenes of life than you might first imagine."

"So you keep saying. I've read your other books," Kent said mischievously.

"Really? I'm amazed to hear that," I responded with a sly smile. "That means that you know that my extraordinary experiences helped me to see beyond the veil; to look at and read other's energy and what is *really* occurring at a deeper, unspoken level."

"I don't really know what any of that means, but it's entertaining to hear about your wild ideas," Kent said, chuckling.

"Fair enough. Being entertained is a good first step. But it takes courage to be willing to consider that maybe there's a lot more going on behind the scenes than you'd care to admit. It takes courage to look *deeply*."

"So, it sounds as though you're trying to tell me that—"

"It takes a strong desire *to change and to grow*," I said firmly. "But first you have to have a *willing heart*."

"I think that, with your help and guidance, caring for Jeannette those last few years really started me looking at things in new and different ways."

"It sure was a wild ride," I said, nodding.

Kent looked at his watch. "Well, I should let you get to the airport. I'll come by later and pick up your car," he said. "Your son will be here any minute." He then handed me a couple of his business cards. "Here's my card for your wallet, just in case." He smiled, waved goodbye, then he and Kelly got into his car and headed back down the driveway, Kent still smiling at me mischievously.

I stood in the parking lot waving back at him as he drove away and I noticed that he was holding a colorful aluminum license plate out the car window—the one with the big red heart and the neon green alien face—and I laughed upon seeing it. It read, "I Love Aliens."

He sure does have a great sense of fun and humor, I thought, laughing at the way he poked fun at me.

At that moment, my son's car pulled into the parking lot and parked. Walter leapt out. "Hi, Mom!" He gave me a big bear hug and a kiss on the cheek. "Ready?" he asked. "Let's get you to the airport!"

Now a handsome, strapping young man, all of six foot five, he had no trouble heaving my heavy suitcase from my car into his trunk. After grabbing my coat and purse, I jumped in beside him and we headed down the highway and into town, en route to LAX.

When we arrived at the terminal, Walter pulled up to the curb and leaped out, unloaded my suitcase, then turned to embrace me. "I love you, Mom. When you get back, I want to introduce you to Rachel," he said, his brown eyes twinkling. "I just met her. She's a very special girl."

"I can hardly wait to meet her," I said, thrilled to hear his news. I tightly hugged him back and kissed him goodbye. I gathered up my things and waved to him as he pulled away from the curb.

Two hours later, I walked down the long gangway to board my international flight. Upon boarding the plane, a friendly flight attendant checked my ticket and gestured down the aisle. "First class is to the left," she directed me, smiling. "We'll be making a stop in New York and then we're off to Iceland," she said cheerily.

After settling into my seat next to the window, I relaxed and closed my eyes while the rest of the passengers stored their carry-on luggage overhead and got comfortable in their seats. A gentleman sat down next to me. I turned to greet him, only to have my smile freeze on my lips. I recognized that sour face. It was none other than the skeptical debunker and author from the lavish party in Virginia: the physicist! He was no doubt on one of his debunking tours, and I hoped that he wouldn't remember me.

"Oh, it's you again," he said dryly, fastening his seat belt without so much as a feigned smile. The reality of my predicament quickly became apparent. I would be sitting next to this guy for the next six hours, assuming that he got off in New York.

"Yes, it's me again," I said, leaning back in my seat, and sighing deeply. Maybe I could just plug in my earphones and listen to music the entire trip. Enduring another one of his public rebukes was not my idea of a pleasant plane ride.

"And what brings you to New York?" he asked, thumbing through his *New York Times*.

Was I really going to have this conversation? I thought, wondering how I could get it to end. "I'm going on to Iceland."

"Iceland? What's in Iceland?" he pressed, as though daring me to take the bait and start up where we had left off more than seven years earlier.

"I'm giving a talk at a bookstore. Besides, it's the land of fire and ice, of stark contrasts and stunning beauty; it has one hundred and thirty volcanic mountains, eighteen of which are active. I just have to see it . . . and *feel* it, if you must know."

After studying me for a moment, he said, "Let me guess. You believe that these volcanoes have something to do with your aliens?"

Rummaging through my seatback for the headphones, I placed them over my ears, taking a deep breath. This guy had some gall. Then, taking my headphones off, I volleyed my last comment, hoping that the conversation would be done.

"Geothermally speaking, Iceland is one of the hot spots of the planet," I said, sidestepping his question. "This geothermal energy, in my opinion, translates to high electromagnetic vibrations and an intense experience of nature. These pulsations replenish cells and are great for pain relief. I'm now a PEMF coach."

"Greenland is mostly ice, but Iceland is mostly green," he replied politely enough.

I sighed in relief, hoping that perhaps we could limit our chat to this kind of ordinary tourist talk and avoid the subject of aliens altogether.

"I hope you realize that geothermal heat has nothing whatsoever to do with electromagnetic vibrations," he continued, peering at me over his bifocals. "And, furthermore, there's no evidence to suggest that such pulsations do a thing for you."

Turning to look intently at him, I calmly and clearly set the record straight. "Did you know that only two months before the Wright brothers' historic flight, a famous scientist declared that the nonsensical idea of a flying machine violated the laws of physics?"

"Well, I don't see what that has to do with—"

"In fact, did you know that germ theory didn't become widely accepted until late in the nineteenth century but that the idea was first proposed in ancient Sanskrit texts, thousands of years before Western scientists validated it?"

"Look, there may be some—"

"And did you know that space travel was declared ridiculous in 1956 by a British astronomer who *proved* to his peers that it was impossible? It was just one year later—and it heralded my birth—that Sputnik was launched. That's why the entire world was so stunned, because *no one* thought it was possible. Another idea that 'violated the laws of physics.'"

"This proves nothing."

"What it proves is that whatever at one time may seem to be 'above and beyond' the realm of possibility or 'above and beyond belief,' is later often proven to be quite possible after all. And the so-called 'experts' are proven wrong. Do you know what else experts are wrong about? That extraterrestrial space flight violates the laws of physics. But the only violation is your limited assumption about what's possible, such as worm holes between galaxies or interdimensional travel, which are beyond the physics of three-dimensional space/time."

"Young lady, anyone who would claim to have actually met an alien from outer space is clearly confused."

"I'm not confused. I've been extraordinarily blessed by my experiences. My books explore the whys and the hows, and I believe that there are thousands of people, like me, who've met ETs but have been ridiculed and laughed at. One day, history will show that we were merely pioneers, discovering something that, eventually, everyone came to accept as normal."

"Excuse me," said a man from the seat directly in front of us. "I couldn't help but overhear your conversation," he said, peering at us over the back of his seat.

"Oh, sorry, was I speaking too loudly?" I asked, embarrassed that my voice had carried any farther than my own row. "I'm done anyway," I said, adjusting my headphones over my ears. "I'm just going to listen to music."

"Actually, it was quite interesting," he said, smiling at me. "Did you say that you'd written books about these aliens?"

Without commenting, I reached into my duffel and pulled out all four of my books, handing them to the man. I just wanted to be left alone. No more debates. The man reached over his seat to accept the stack of books and took a moment to read the descriptions on the back covers.

"Do you mind if I ask you a few questions?" the man asked me, and I couldn't help but notice the physicist lean closer so as not to miss a single word. I reluctantly nodded my head, removing my headphones again.

The man asked, "So, you've actually had meaningful encounters with extraterrestrials . . . but also . . . difficult people?"

"Yes," I said, clearly and calmly.

"Interesting. Let's take these one at a time. What have you learned from the alien contact?"

"Actually, it's like dealing with Zen masters or enlightened beings. They've helped me to become more *fully human*, interestingly enough. They prod me to be more compassionate, to be of service to others, even when it's difficult. They've also taught me about the therapeutic effects of electromagnetic pulsations."

Interrupting us, the physicist interjected, "Come on, now, what have you *really* gained from claiming that you've met aliens, besides the scorn of others?"

"Nothing in the worldly sense," I responded. "In fact, I've lost an awful lot in that area."

"There, you see?" the physicist said, gloating to the man in the next row. "Well, it's what benefits you in this world by scientifically explaining how things operate, now *that* is the only gauge of what's real and what's not."

"Would you like to know exactly what it is that I've *lost* as a result of my ET contact?"

"Yes," the physicist said. "But let me help you, shall I? Let's see, I would imagine that you've lost your good reputation, your family's respect, and your sense of self-worth. Does that cover it?"

"No," I corrected him. Then turning my attention to the man in the seat in front of me, I said, "What I've lost is my anger, anxiety, depression, insecurity, fear of old age, and fear of death . . . and *that's* what it means to be more *fully human*."

"That's quite an amazing transformation," the man said, grinning at me. "But what does your *Difficult People* book have to do with your extraterrestrial books? They don't seem to be related."

"Well, like many people, I was suffering as a result of difficult person in my life. I couldn't figure out how to stop suffering, because as soon as I got rid of one difficult person, another one showed up to take their place. So I was desperate for help. And the aliens—or ETs, as I refer to them—well, they showed up, offering to help."

"So they help us to grow?" asked the man.

"Yes. They help humanity, although on an individual basis, because they understand that we're struggling with our evolution. We're all trying to find a healthy way to feel better, to *become* better."

"But were you ready for the aliens?"

"My mind's initial reaction was fear. Ultimately, my heart's reaction prevailed. Like all of us, I had to grow up and mature, spiritually. When it came right down to it, most of my pain was created by my own faulty thinking. I felt like a victim."

"So the aliens . . . I mean the ETs . . . helped you with your difficult people?"

"Yes, because difficult people are common to all of us. That's the basis of any war. It starts with an individual conflict, then it goes global. We need help, training, to effectively deal with our difficult people . . . without blowing up our marriages, jobs, and our planet in the process. It's our insufficiencies that inspire evolved otherworldly beings to help us. Every living being is actually hardwired for a compassionate response. Because we share the same universal neighborhood, the better *we* do, the better *they* do."

"So our individual struggles with difficult people can be a training ground to learn how to handle all difficult groups on Earth. Is that what you're saying?" he asked.

"Exactly!" I said. "Most of us are quite inexperienced at beholding wrongdoing and responding appropriately. So are politicians, which is why there's so much global conflict."

"Balderdash," said the physicist.

I looked at him and smiled, and the stranger didn't lose a beat, adding, "I see what you mean. Difficult people stress us to the max. We're left humbled, pleading on our knees for the universe to help us."

"That's exactly how it all started for me. As a young woman, my first difficult person was my husband. Next was my employer. I was upset and wanted to learn how to fix these people, because as soon as I got rid of one, another showed up. The ETs said it would be better to learn what the problem was, once and for all."

"Which is . . . what exactly?" the man asked me.

"The problem was *me*. I had to fix myself first. My upset reactions, fear and anger in response to my difficult person, were the *real* problem. I learned that the single most important measure of my spiritual progress is the way that I react and respond to the wrongdoings or disapproval of others. Because we all are constantly dealing with others' wrongdoings or disapproval in one form or another, that's where the real work must begin," I said, beaming at the physicist, who was scowling so furiously at me that his brow was sweating.

Now smiling, the stranger said, "I'm a film producer. Sounds like a great story to adapt into a screenplay. Great idea for a movie. Do you have representation?"

"Of course," I replied, reaching into my purse and withdrawing Kent's business card. "Here's my attorney's information. He'll be happy to field any offers."

After shaking his hand, I turned to the physicist and shook his hand, too. "Thanks. Without your goading me, I would never have expressed myself and would've lost this fine opportunity."

Appalled by this suggestion, he erupted into a fit of coughing, and I calmly handed him a bottle of water. After adjusting my pillow, putting on my headphones, and leaning back in the seat, I closed my eyes and soon fell into a deep, restful sleep.

Chapter Twenty-Five

I LOOKED OUT MY tiny window as the plane descended into the Keflavik Airport in Iceland. The ground was visible from miles above in the land of the midnight sun. It was also *steaming*. Craning my neck to get a better view, I could see steam vents and hot springs dotting the lava landscape below me. Steamy swirls from these geothermal pools curled onto the lavascape as the plane passed over the famed Blue Lagoon. It attracted visitors from all over the world, and was apparently the most popular health spa on Earth. Apparently, I wasn't the only one who had noticed that geothermal energy and electromagnetic pulsations have remarkable, almost magically effective, healing properties.

Several hours later, I had checked in to my hotel and now readied myself for the adventure of a lifetime. The next day, rested and refreshed, I checked out of my hotel and headed out after breakfast, beginning my grand traverse of the island.

As evening fell, I stopped at a small, cozy inn to spend the night, continuing my exploration in the morning. Bound by no schedule and having no firm itinerary—except for the one local bookstore signing—my sole intent was to explore the beauty and grandeur of Iceland's steamy terrain and soak up its waves of naturally occurring electromagnetic and geothermal energy.

Each day brought a new surprise. There were black sand beaches, stunning waterfalls, and the largest sandurs on Earth. Sandurs are created by volcanic eruptions that often produce flooding, but when the water stops flowing, the ash and sand create outwash plains. Where beached icebergs melted into unusual shapes, I found a natural sculpted garden. Everywhere I looked, there was wild and stunning beauty.

The days flew by as I became enveloped in this energy, until, suddenly, it was time to go home. I had saved the best adventure for the end. On my last full day on the island, I was far from any sign of civilization. As my rental car sped along the road, I viewed the majesty of the Snæfellsjökull volcanic glacier as it beckoned me. This is one of the locations in Jules Verne's famous book, *Journey to the Center of the Earth,* a real classic of early science fiction. Now, there it was in the distance, extraordinary in its legend and beauty.

My attention was suddenly pulled away from the volcano; I became focused on my immediate environment as strong winds buffeted the car. The expansive lava fields were devoid of trees, allowing the blustery ocean winds off my left side to blow unimpeded across the plain. There was no doubt that I was just two hundred miles south of the Arctic Circle, located at 66 degrees north of Earth's equator.

I wondered if I would see any puffins—Iceland's adorable penguin-like bird that has a multicolored beak. They swim underwater and can catch many fish at one time. One can frequently see pictures of the birds with fish dangling from their colorful beaks. The puffin is a symbol of Iceland's unique beauty and contrasting colors.

I rolled up my windows to keep out the wind and carefully checked to see that the car door was snugly closed, as instructed by the counter clerk at the rental car agency. As she had handed me the car keys, she had rattled off some last minute advice, "Don't drive the car off-road in the interior of the island; watch out for small pieces of flying lava that can crack the windshield, and hold on to your door."

"What was that last one?" I asked.

The sweet young woman smiled cheerily. "It can get windy here. When you get out of your car, hold on to the door."

She was right about the wind. When I had first stepped outside the airport terminal when I arrived, my jacket had almost blown off my body.

Now, as I drove along with the wondrous volcano in my sights, Icelandic folk music was playing on the car radio. The music's varied melodies provided a soundtrack for the gorgeous scenery. A stunning carpet of lavender flowers blanketed both sides of the road. They waved in the summer wind and spread out around me in a great vista. Then, in the near distance, the carpet of flowers stopped, in its place, lava fields continued on as far as the eye could see. It looked like a moonscape.

Many hours' drive from the capital city of Reykjavik, dramatic volcanic cliffs rise up from a deep blue sea. Eyeing the view of an immense snow-capped volcano that lay ahead, I couldn't help but smile at what I imagined Jeannette's reaction would have been. "You would have loved this," I said out loud to my absent charge. Even though she wasn't physically there, she was very much so in spirit.

As the island's geothermal energies acted upon me, more intensely here than elsewhere, I could again feel the warm buzzing sensation of an electromagnetic pull. Like what Jeannette and I experienced in Ojai, there was an intense, sudden "frequency expansion." The telltale warmth of its strong magnetic charge permeated the inner energy field of my body. I had entered a new world. Truly this moment in time was paradise, despite its stark, bold, and bleak setting. I now understood Kent's unease about my not returning—very intuitive of him.

Like the terrain of Iceland, my roles as Jeannette's caregiver and as Peter's wife and my greater ET experiences themselves had been a tableau of stark contrasts and paradoxes. It was truly amazing when I stopped to consider that all of those outrageous experiences, that at the time produced so much emotional pain, were ultimately the tests that precipitated my greatest transformation.

Iceland's terrain of fire and ice, its volcanoes and glaciers, its lava fields and breathtaking waterfalls, is a landscape of stark opposites. So too were my adventures with Jeannette, Peter, and the extraterrestrials—all challenges that provided glorious growth opportunities. Those were the extremes of my personal experience. All the difficult stages of my life, with both the worldly and otherworldly characters, had produced intense reactions that, in turn, produced inner turmoil. That intensity forced me to adopt spiritual practices that led me, as it does others, into the ever-present perfection of the lovely stillness that undergirds all life.

The great gifts that I received were superhuman courage and an ability to feel lasting inner peace and joy. I believe that I had witnessed that shift within Jeannette, too. In her last days and hours, it seemed as if she had found great courage to face her own death, as well as an inner peace that replaced her deep fear. Ultimately, I know that each of us has the opportunity to return home once the body dies, because as immortal souls, we all have the gift of eternal life.

All of these difficult and challenging experiences had made this gift of awareness possible, and Iceland's terrain brought these memories and these last decades of struggle to an appropriate close.

Now, on the open, windy road of Iceland, at the foot of the Snæfellsjökull volcano, this adventure was the perfect corollary to my life's journey. On this stunning but cold island on the edge of the Arctic Circle, my visit to this amazing geothermal and electromagnetic hotspot was the perfect graduation ceremony befitting a spiritual initiate.

As I trundled around a sharp curve in the road, I brought the car to a sudden stop. There, happily curled up in the middle of the road, perhaps also enjoying the warm geothermal heat seeping up through the ground and warming the asphalt, were twin lambs. The ewe grazed peacefully in the distance, keeping a watchful eye on them. Since there were no other cars on the road, and we were far from the city or any sign of human life, there was nothing to interrupt this magical scene. I shut off the engine, and, sitting in my car, I merged into the harmony of this sundrenched moment. The wild rush of the wind across the lavascape was the only sound in the vast empty plain.

Leaning on the steering wheel, I gazed serenely at the lambs, allowing them to enjoy their nap, even though they were blocking my forward progress on the road. "It's okay, take your time," I said. "I'm in no hurry." The famous quote from Thoreau came to mind: "You must live in the present, launch yourself on every wave, find your eternity in each moment."

Never before had the perfection of the cycles of life seemed so palpable to me: The inflow and the outflow, birth and death, the ewe with her lambs, Jeannette gone, Peter and I long since divorced . . . and I now acutely aware that in another twenty-five or thirty years—who knew how much

longer I had—I, too, would follow Jeannette from this world
into another. None of us really have that long here, I thought.
Suddenly, life and death seemed to be two perfect sides to the
same exquisite journey.

There on the road with the lambs, I thought of everyone
I had known who had passed on before me and ventured into
the great beyond—and perhaps into a new life. They had gone
from my sight but continued nonetheless in my memory of
them. Their inner fire had merged with mine, and with the
Earth's. In this way, all of those whom we have loved and who
have passed on have left parts of themselves, like a branch lit
from a larger bonfire that goes on alone to ignite other worlds.

Suddenly, my heart began thumping inside my chest; I
smiled, because I knew that it was producing a strong bio-
magnetic field and that I had become healed. I knew that
my growing, compassionate heart had helped me to learn to
maintain my self-identity, despite others whose own fear had
caused them to belittle and devalue me. I knew that at one
time or another, all of us will have to experience the discomfort of being around others who do not fully understand us.

I knew that after all these last many years, my soul had
undergone an intense training. Important lessons had been
learned and internalized, and what I had gained would serve
me for all eternity: the ability to behold others' judgments
and wrongdoings with courage, dignity, and grace.

Other people's faulty behavior could no longer disturb
me, because I understood that their unkindness or insensitiv-
ity were merely characteristics of souls who had not yet begun
their own intense spiritual initiations. But they had taught me
well. Because of them, I knew that I could now demonstrate
that I would no longer allow adverse circumstances to impinge

on and derail my self-definition. I had accomplished this by consciously aligning with the immortal nature of my soul.

Indeed, this is the gift that all spiritual teachers and healers receive from their significant others, their employers or family members who chronically belittle and devalue them. Often, this type of belittling and devaluing occurs in a context of concealment and subterfuge, meaning that those who belittle and devalue others would vehemently deny doing so. Alas, self-deception may still be strongly in place and suggests a spiritual training that has not yet been mastered. Overcoming an irresistible tendency to exert an authoritarian power over others in myriad ways, is itself a potent test in life. As a result, each of us, no matter difficult circumstances, is learning and growing, always presented with opportunities to rise above imperfections.

I knew that to be in the midst of difficult people had been a very bold *choice*, not an accidental happenstance that created pitiful victimization or unplanned discomfort. It had been an *opportunity for growth*. Difficult people had provided me with the greatest training imaginable. This type of intense and painful soul training is unparalleled in its scope and effectiveness because it pushes the initiate to strengthen and to build significant inner spiritual fortitude.

How else could the student train to become a teacher and healer?

While there on the road with the lambs, immersed in Iceland's geothermal energy, I also knew that it was time for me to go home.

As if in perfect synchronicity, the ewe bleated to her lambs, which woke them, and they jumped readily to their feet.

Life is an electromagnetic event, and all the parts of the whole are perfectly synchronized to resonate with one another.

The lambs ran off the road to join the ewe in the pasture, then all turned to look back at me before scampering away.

The bright morning sun slanted through the windshield as I watched them trot into the distance. In the sunny silence, I could feel the pulsations of my own beating heart, an energetic call from somewhere far away.

Then I saw a flash of aqua-blue light.

Someone or something was calling my name.

About the Author

After her initial surprise at being contacted by extraterrestrials, for more than three decades of contact experiences, Lisette Larkins has been implementing her ET mentors' counsel and helping others find their way.

Look her up at *www.LisetteLarkins.com*.

To contact Lisette, please write to:
Lisette Larkins
P.O. Box 481
Malibu, CA 90265

Related Titles

If you enjoyed *Above and Beyond,* you may also enjoy other
Rainbow Ridge titles. Read more about them at
www.rainbowridgebooks.com.

The Divine Mother Speaks: The Healing of the Human Heart
by Rashmi Khilnani

The Buddha Speaks: To the Buddha Nature Within
by Rashmi Khilnani

The Cosmic Internet: Explanations from the Other Side
by Frank DeMarco

Conversations with Jesus: An Intimate Journey
by Alexis Eldridge

Dance of the Electric Hummingbird
by Patricia Walker

Coming Full Circle: Ancient Teachings for a Modern World
by Lynn Andrews

*Afterlife Conversations with Hemingway: A Dialogue on
His Life, His Work, and the Myth*
by Frank DeMarco

*Consciousness: Bridging the Gap Between Conventional Science
and the New Super Science of Quantum Mechanics*
by Eva Herr

Jesusgate: A History of Concealment Unraveled
by Ernie Bringas

Messiah's Handbook: Reminders for the Advanced Soul
by Richard Bach

Blue Sky, White Clouds
by Eliezer Sobel

Inner Vegas: Creating Miracles, Abundance, and Health
by Joe Gallenberger

Flames and Smoke Visible
by Danny Lliteras

Your Soul Remembers: Accessing
Your Past Lives through Soul Writing
by Joanne DiMaggio

When the Horses Whisper:
The Wisdom of Wise and Sentient Beings
by Rosalyn W. Berne, Ph.D.

Lessons in Courage
by Bonnie Glass-Coffin and don Oscar Miro-Quesada

Channeling Harrison
by David Young

Rainbow Ridge Books publishes spiritual, metaphysical, and self-help titles, and is distributed by Square One Publishers in Garden City Park, New York.

To contact authors and editors, peruse our titles, and see submission guidelines, please visit our website at *www.rainbowridgebooks.com*.

For orders and catalogs, please call toll-free: (877) 900-BOOK.